Think Like a CTO

Think Like a CTO

ALAN WILLIAMSON

MANNING
SHELTER ISLAND

For online information and ordering of this and other Manning books, please visit www.manning.com. The publisher offers discounts on this book when ordered in quantity. For more information, please contact

    Special Sales Department
    Manning Publications Co.
    20 Baldwin Road
    PO Box 761
    Shelter Island, NY 11964
    Email: orders@manning.com

 Manning Publications Co.
20 Baldwin Road
PO Box 761
Shelter Island, NY 11964

Development editor:	Dustin Archibald
Review editor:	Aleks Dragosavljevic
Production editor:	Deirdre S. Hiam
Copy editor:	Pamela Hunt
Proofreader:	Katie Tennant
Typesetter:	Marija Tudor
Cover designer:	Shawn Girsberger

ISBN 9781617298851
Printed and bound by CPI Group (UK) Ltd, Croydon, CR0 4YY

I want to dedicate this book to my long-time friend and mentor, Jim Milbery, fellow technologist (just don't let him code) and founding partner at ParkerGale Capital. Jim has had a huge impact on both my professional and personal lives (and even introduced me to my wife).
I would also like to dedicate this to my dear departed mother, who was with us at the start of this journey and read a few early chapters, but never made it to the end of the final product.

contents

foreword

Think Like a CTO provides comprehensive and insightful views on becoming and thriving as a technology executive in a modern-day world. This book provides first-time CTOs with a solid understanding of fundamentals while helping seasoned CTOs sharpen their skills. I love that this book covers all the major components of being a great technology leader while keeping "you" at the center of the book. If you've been a CTO for a little while, the checklists at the end of each chapter should act like a strategic guide and vision for you to start executing.

The role of a CTO is rapidly evolving across almost every industry and business sector. In the early 2000s, as the internet age was taking off, the primary responsibilities of a CTO were to manage physical servers, a software development team, and a couple of vendors, and oversee all of the software the company was using. Although those responsibilities still exist, how someone goes about managing, leading, creating, and executing strategic plans is completely different now.

Today, there is a stark difference due to advancements in technology, and the CTO is viewed as someone who can do it all. Not only can a CTO be responsible for all things tech, but they are also viewed as the primary decision maker and strategic visionary across all major components of technology. In addition, as technology shifts and evolves, the CTO must constantly have their finger on the pulse of change, ensuring that competitors and bad actors stay at bay.

One of my favorite sections in the book is chapter 6, "Team management." In my opinion, the people you manage and lead are the ones in which you invest considerable time and attention. Without them, you fail. Period. If you can focus on building a collaborative environment where people feel the autonomy and empowerment to push themselves, rapidly fail forward, and provide growth in a safe environment, you can accomplish most things. Technology is likely the least complicated part of the CTO role. It's the people that will make or break your success.

Whether you are new to the world of executive management and leadership or are a seasoned tech executive, this book is a must-have reference and guide. The learnings and insights Alan provides are remarkable solutions to challenges every tech leader faces. As a startup tech leader, you will find that this book will provide you with a clear sense of the responsibilities of your role as you grow and scale your team and company. As a CTO in a growing, small- to medium-sized organization, this book will help you navigate challenging situations and provide strategic solutions. For tech executives at large companies or government agencies, this book will be a guide to creating and executing your strategic vision.

I hope you enjoy reading *Think Like a CTO* as much as I did. The insights in this book are something tech leaders have needed for a very long time.

—ANKIT MATHUR, COFOUNDER AND
CTO AT ROUNDTRIP HEALTH AND FOUNDER
AT PRESS PLAY TECHNOLOGIES

preface

Chief Technology Officer is one of the most exciting and rewarding roles a technologist can take on in their career. The position can define a company, open up new opportunities, create new product lines, improve workflow, and have a huge impact across all departments.

If this were a game of chess, we would have the Chief Executive Officer (CEO) as the king and the Chief Financial Officer (CFO) as the queen, which is the most powerful piece on the board, being allowed to move in any direction and for as many squares as desired. This is true in business, too, with the CFO being involved in every decision relating to money either coming into or going out of the company. Where does that leave the CTO?

I like to think of the CTO as the rook (the castle), the next most powerful piece, because they provide the support for the rest of the pieces to move around the board, clearing paths into the distance. Yet with all this power and responsibility, it is a role that most are unprepared for, with many not realizing just how much there is to it, especially in today's modern architecture. Not only does the role oversee the research, development, and implementation of the company's technology, it also covers the execution, licensing, compliance, and continued security monitoring of the production environment. In a world of always-on-always-connected networks, linked devices of all shapes and sizes, and office, home, and remote workers, the challenges facing today's CTO are way beyond what the CTOs of the '80s and '90s faced.

If that isn't enough, we work in an industry that continually reinvents itself, undergoing seismic changes in our tools and processes every five years, from centralized computing (with mainframes) to desktop computing to the internet. Along with the web came the browser, evolving from a tool to view static content to a complete, rich platform in and of itself. We have seen the advent of mobile computing grow in power and functionality. We have seen cloud computing take over and evolve extremely rapidly to the point where a credit card can run a whole infrastructure of enterprise pieces that our predecessors couldn't even dream of. Storage is limitless, creating a whole new world of opportunities in data analysis, complete with machine learning and artificial intelligence.

Devices are getting smaller and more connected, with the Internet of Things finding its way into nearly everything that has power (and some that don't). Blockchain is promoting a world of openness and transparency in our interactions. Languages and frameworks are getting richer and faster. The average software developer is so far removed from the logistics of managing CPU and memory that some don't even realize they have limitations—if code runs slower, it is sometimes cheaper to increase the processing power than to spend time optimizing the algorithms.

In addition, hackers constantly threaten to attack our systems. Ransomware cripples more of our public services, clearly demonstrating how a poorly architected enterprise can bring a country to its knees. We witnessed this when hackers took out the oil pipeline on the East Coast of the United States in May 2021, resulting in gas shortages, with no stations getting fuel for over a week. This was not an isolated case. Imagine waking up as the CTO in charge of that pipeline technology on that morning—where do you even begin?

Whether you are a seasoned CTO, new in the role, taking over from someone else, or a CEO trying to determine whether you need a CTO (yes is the answer to that, by the way), there is a lot more to this position than most realize. No matter the size of the company, from a two-person startup right up to an organization with thousands of employees, the responsibility is wide.

This book was born from the need to fill a space in learning to prepare both the company and the individual for the role of Chief Technology Officer. I wrote it after many years of experience in the field, working with companies of varying size—from startups to SMBs (small to medium-sized businesses; typically not more than $100 million revenue)—as either full-time CTO or interim CTO for portfolio companies within and outside of the private equity space.

These companies had a wide range of activities, with little overlap. But they all had the same requirement when it came to their CTO: someone to envision, lead, implement, and maintain the product technology for the company.

When I started out, I had no idea what was expected of me. I asked around to all my contacts, reached out to existing CTOs, and spoke at length to many trusted sources about what I needed to do to succeed. One thing was clear: it was a far bigger responsibility than I first imagined. I had a lot of learning to do—and quickly. I made a lot of mistakes, mainly due to not knowing what I should be doing.

What I needed, and what you have now, is this book.

acknowledgments

Writing this book has been a labor of love. Two years in the making, through a global pandemic and several life events, it is finally ready. My ever-supportive, always-encouraging wife, Kelley, has been a rock throughout, lifting me up when needed, reviewing each chapter, and giving me candid feedback. It is an understatement to say I couldn't have done it without her. A huge debt of thanks goes to Kaitlin Powell, the most inspiring creative I have had the pleasure to work with as she stuck with me throughout all the iterations of the diagrams.

Big thanks go to my close friends, Jim Headley and Ryan Burch, for giving me the support and inspiration for many of the topics that have been addressed. Those who have contributed their expertise and insights, whom I have named throughout the book, thank you—it wouldn't be the same without your help.

Of course, I thank my parents, who pandered to the whims of a 10-year-old when spending a month's salary on a ZX Spectrum to see whether this "computer thing" had legs. Given I wore out the rubber keyboard on it, I think the return on investment has proven itself.

Finally, I extend a huge thanks to everyone at Manning, especially Dustin Archibald, who helped me craft and mold each chapter into a narrative that flowed and made sense. Behind every great writer is an even greater editor. I would also like to thank Deirdre Hiam, my project editor; Pamela Hunt, my copyeditor; and Katie Tennant, my proofreader.

To all the reviewers—Adam Dudczak, Adrian Bilauca, Adrian Rossi, Andreas Brodmann, Antonio Bruno, Aroni Pani, Burc Gunes, Chad Miars, Chris Heneghan, Chris Thomas, Christian Witts, Danilo Zekovic, Desmond Horsley, Dhiraj Gupta, Dorian Basuyau, Flavio Diez, Francesco Persico, Gavin Baumanis, Gordan Buckingham,

Hiroyuki Musha, Johannes Lochmann, John McCormack, John Wood, Jura Shikin, Kevin Pelgrims, Leonardo Anastasia, Matej Strašek, Matt Ferderer, Mike Over, Nicolas Modrzyk, Nik Rimington, Pavlo Hodysh, Pawel Klimczyk, Rick Oller, Seth Copeland, Shiroshica Kulatilake, Simone Cafiero, Stefan Mutschler, Tiago Boldt Sousa, Willem van Ketwich, William Rudenmalm—thank you; your suggestions helped make this a better book.

about this book

This book will answer some of the questions you may have asked yourself but dare not ask your CEO for fear of looking like you don't know what you are doing. After all, they hired you to take care of everything that they cannot, so they need to have the confidence that they hired the right person for the job.

Each chapter visits a major area of responsibility and takes a deep dive into those areas, outlining the considerations you should be mindful of and strategies to manage each. That said, this is not a technology cookbook. I am not going to recommend Java over C#, or Amazon over Azure, or the cloud over a data center.

Instead, I will give you the considerations that you should remember while making these enterprise-level decisions, because the decision you are making could have long-lasting effects, even well after you leave the role. I offer small case studies throughout to help illustrate the decision process. Each decision you make will be in the context of what the company needs and what resources you have at your disposal. There is no right or wrong—there may be a "wronger" way to do something, or a "righter" way, but a decision that is based on data and not gut instinct is always defensible.

This book will open your eyes to the areas of responsibility that a CTO may face in their career and give you the necessary skills to evaluate, understand, and execute for a successful outcome within the context of your company.

The CTO role is constantly changing, with new challenges to be conquered each and every day. This is why I love the role—boredom is inherently factored out from day one. As part of this, you need to keep relevant. We're in one of the most fast-paced industries possible, with new and exciting technologies popping up every day. How do you choose which to follow and which to ignore? How do you make sure your style isn't dated? How much are you expected to know? What level of detail are you expected to know? These are the questions we technologists ask ourselves all the time. But when you are making decisions for an entire company, the consequences are far reaching.

We all suffer from imposter syndrome—the feeling that we don't really know what we are doing and someone else always knows better. This is completely natural and more prevalent in the tech space, given how fast things evolve. Every time you read some news about the latest and greatest innovation, it makes you wonder if you are not keeping up or you are failing your team or company. Let me assure you that this feeling will not go away and you should learn to live with and embrace it. I will give you some techniques that you can use in your role as CTO to make sure you don't feel you are falling behind or backing a technology that will be out of date next year.

This book is filled with practical examples, illustrating the point at hand, complete with lots of real-world stories of the challenges that CTOs have faced and conquered. As part of my role at the MacLaurin Group, and now at the private equity firm New Harbor Capital, I work with CTOs across many different industries and in the private equity space, lifting them up, mentoring them, and advising them on specific problems they are facing.

Many of the situations I have been brought in to assist with could have been prevented with better planning and a little knowledge. The vast majority of this book is curated from these encounters—real issues, facing real CTOs—as well as my own experience growing a number of technical teams as a full-time CTO.

This book is aimed specifically at the areas that typically fall under the remit of the desk of the Chief Technology Officer. Because the role isn't as well defined as some of the more established executive roles, it is largely what you make it to be. A CTO can make themselves completely invaluable to a company if they see the opportunity they have to make the company run like a well-oiled engine.

So, whether you are working alone or are running a group of 100 engineers, you will discover in this book just what it takes to be a successful CTO.

Who should read this book

If you fall into any of the following categories, then you are reading the right book:

- An experienced technologist wanting to make that next step in your career to CTO
- Serving as CTO, first time in the role, and you want to be sure you are doing everything you can
- Seasoned CTO, your company is growing rapidly, and you are being asked questions that you simply have no idea how to respond to
- Taking over from a previous CTO, with the executive team looking to you for big, revolutionary changes

- A CEO/CFO trying to determine whether you need a CTO (and the sort of things they would do for you), and if so, how you hire for this role

How this book is organized: A roadmap

This book contains 15 chapters:

- Chapter 1 explores what a CTO is, the different types of CTOs, and the role a CTO plays in an organization.
- Chapter 2 deals with interacting with various roles in an organization from CEO to peers.
- Chapter 3 is about developing a vision for the CTO role in the organization.
- Chapter 4 defines some best practices for building your team.
- Chapter 5 shows how to recruit, interview, and hire team members.
- Chapter 6 deals with managing your team.
- Chapter 7 explains the process of performing annual reviews.
- Chapter 8 will help you make technology decisions.
- Chapter 9 deals with managing projects and communicating progress to the organization.
- Chapter 10 explains how to manage contracts.
- Chapter 11 is about creating and managing documentation.
- Chapter 12 shows some important considerations for securing your enterprise.
- Chapter 13 has additional considerations for your organization.
- Chapter 14 delves into managing company growth.
- Chapter 15 deals with identifying and reviewing your progress and planning for the future.

Depending on your company size, some of the chapters will not be relevant. They may be more appropriate for another time in your career or the company's evolution. However, even if that is the case, it does no harm for you to dip into the chapter and see what it would entail if there was an organizational change and suddenly you were faced with managing that area.

liveBook discussion forum

Purchase of *Think Like a CTO* includes free access to liveBook, Manning's online reading platform. Using liveBook's exclusive discussion features, you can attach comments to the book globally or to specific sections or paragraphs. It's a snap to make notes for yourself, ask and answer technical questions, and receive help from the author and other users. To access the forum, go to https://livebook.manning.com/book/think -like-a-cto/discussion. You can also visit https://livebook.manning.com/discussion to learn more about Manning's forums and the rules of conduct.

Manning's commitment to our readers is to provide a venue where a meaningful dialogue between individual readers and between readers and the author can take place. It is not a commitment to any specific amount of participation on the part of the author, whose contribution to the forum remains voluntary (and unpaid). We suggest you try asking him some challenging questions lest his interest stray! The forum and the archives of previous discussions will be accessible from the publisher's website as long as the book is in print.

about the author

ALAN WILLIAMSON has over 25 years of data and technology experience, with contributions to the core server-side Java API specification, creating the world's first CFML engine written in Java, which powered MySpace. He was the first UK Java Champion and has published several books in the Java space covering Enterprise Java, Servlets, JavaMail, and database access.

He has worked with and for private equity firms for over 15 years, building and growing teams, as well as serving as CTO for a number of portfolio companies. Alan served as Chief Technology Officer and Partner of MacLaurin Group, supporting portfolio company operations through CTO and Architectural Advisory. He has provided CTO executive team leadership for multiple private equity-backed organizations. He is currently serving as Partner of Portfolio Operations Group for New Harbor Capital, a Chicago-based private equity firm focused on midmarket founder-led companies, providing interim CTO and mentoring services.

Alan holds a degree in computer science with a specialization in digital control from the University of Paisley, Scotland.

The Chief Technology Officer (CTO)

This chapter covers

- What makes a Chief Technology Officer (CTO)
- The different types of CTO
- The evolution from engineer to CTO
- Determining whether a company needs a CTO
- Top qualities for becoming a great CTO

It is fair to say that, given you are reading this book, you already have a good idea of what a Chief Technology Officer (CTO) is. Yet, if all readers were to be polled on their definition of a CTO, we would get as many different perspectives as there are readers. Each description, though, is most likely right. This huge variety in interpretation is what makes this role not only challenging but exciting at the same time.

The closest counterparts, Chief Executive Officer (CEO) and Chief Financial Officer (CFO), are well-defined roles, with their areas of responsibility clearly understood: the CEO leads the charge, and the CFO writes the checks! Okay, a little disingenuous, but the point is, these roles are universally accepted, compared to the ambiguity around the CTO role.

For example, the dropdown list of job titles in online forms often lacks "Chief Technology Officer." Though this is changing—specifically in the field of insurance where *CTO* has started appearing in job title lists—are CTOs considered a higher insurance risk?

The CTO definition gets morphed and pulled, depending on the organization, with responsibilities ranging dramatically from company to company. At a high level, the CTO is responsible for the technology vision and execution of a company, though some companies don't even consider the CTO responsible for execution. It's not unusual for some large organizations to have a CTO with no one reporting to them. For this book, however, the assumption is that the CTO is responsible for both areas: vision and execution.

The different broad types of CTO will be presented so you can see which one you best identify/align with. This will help you position and firm up your goals for a successful career. As part of this, the qualities that define successful CTOs will be highlighted.

The remaining chapters will take a deeper dive into the key areas that the vast majority of CTOs will find themselves navigating at some point. Although not all chapters may be relevant to you, the area in question will be the responsibility of someone and that person will be your peer, so it is never a bad idea to get a feel for what they will be contending with.

1.1 *What makes a Chief Technology Officer*

At the highest level, the CTO is primarily responsible for the technical direction and execution of the company's main product, servicing the needs of the business for greater client benefit. The CTO usually reports to the CEO, but it is not uncommon for them to report to the CFO, COO (Chief Operating Officer), or even CIO (Chief Information Officer), depending on the size of the company and number of direct reports the CEO is comfortable managing.

Conversely, an area that does not typically come under the CTO is the IT infrastructure—in other words, the back office. Although the servers and software that make up your product would fall under the office of the CTO, the desktop computers, mail servers, phones, printers, and so on would not. They would likely fall under a separate IT director or manager, who usually reports to the CFO. Think of the CTO as usually focusing on developing, maintaining, and running the core platform, enterprise, or product line that services clients/customers—sometimes referred to as the front office.

That said, in smaller companies, it is not uncommon for this line to be somewhat blurry, and depending on your skills, you may find yourself managing items that are potentially outside of your primary responsibility. It is common in startups and smaller companies for the CTO to be doing everything, from ordering the laptops, to haggling contracts with the ISP, to replacing printer ink, to cutting and releasing code.

On the other end of the scale, it is common for an established (small to medium) company to operate without a formal CTO. It may have a development team, a support team, and a systems team, but no one is looking after and managing the technical strategy as a holistic initiative. This situation is easy to get into as a company evolves over years, not realizing it is more of a data/technology company than it may care to admit.

There is no fault here as most don't see how they could benefit from this executive role to unlock some hidden treasures within their operations. Again, if this sounds familiar, then this book will help you make the case to your management that this role needs to be filled.

Just as the CFO provides all financial and accountancy services for a company, making it all look rather seamless and effortless, a good CTO frees up the CEO and board to concentrate on the *what* aspect of a company, whereas the CTO focuses on the *how*. A good CTO should provide their company with the following:

- A stable, scalable, and manageable platform on which they can grow a company
- Informed leadership to keep the platform relevant and updated
- Opportunities for the business to explore new areas by unleashing the true power of the platform
- Operational confidence to provide customers reliability and predictability
- Creative ways to use technology for the benefit of the company and customers
- Ability to recruit, retain, and manage a highly efficient team

Although it is common and natural for a CFO to migrate to CEO, the CTO role is often one that developers and IT managers are ill prepared for. Most will look at the role, make some assumptions, and presume it to be just an extension to their current daily tasks. This type of attitude, though common, is doomed to failure.

There is a lot more than just running a team and cutting code, particularly as your company begins to grow, and even more so if your company becomes part of a transaction to be acquired by another company or private equity group. As noted earlier, the good ones make it look all so easy, as do most polished professionals, but that masks the years of experience and hard knocks.

The CTO will touch many areas of responsibility, including everything from architecture design and product design to recruitment, implementation, compliance adherence, security, reporting/communication, strategy/vision, and budgetary planning. As the company matures, other areas that a CTO can get involved with include board preparation for the CEO and/or board presentations, vendor management, outside investor preparation, receiving and managing due diligence requests, and even evaluating other teams/technology stacks if they are asked to integrate with a potential partnership or takeover.

What makes a good CTO is being able to adapt to the needs of the company they are servicing, or at least having the good judgment to know when they can no longer provide that role and step aside for someone who can.

> **VP of Engineering**
>
> It is worth noting that the line between VP (Vice President) of engineering and CTO can be confusing at times and is often the subject of many fireside discussions. It can be as simple as the company having a specific naming scheme for their titles, or there could be a clear difference, with a VP of Engineering reporting to the CTO, taking on the logistics of running the engineering team, and leaving everything else to the CTO. For the purposes of this book, many of the things I address are applicable to both roles, and I assume the VP of Engineering is on the road to becoming a CTO.

1.2   *Different types of CTOs*

How the definition of a CTO is made depends largely on the environment they find themselves operating in, so let us look a little deeper at some of the different common company types in which a CTO may work. At the end of each section is a small litmus test to see which one you most align with:

- Prestartup, in name only
- Startup, technology expert
- Established/mature company
  - First-time CTO
  - Filling the CTO's shoes

1.2.1   *Prestartup, in name only*

A typical early startup is maybe just two people—the visionary and the technologist. More likely than not, they are both early in their careers, maybe just graduated, with no real industry experience. Yet, they are chasing the rewards that only a dreamer with a will can achieve.

Here the technologist is banging out code on a daily basis, trying to keep up with the founder's vision of what they want the company to be. Many product pivots and redesigns are in the future as the reality of the creation starts to get into the hands of users. For gravitas, the founder has labeled the technologist as "Chief Technology Officer" on their business card (mostly to make up for the fact they aren't paying them an awful lot, if at all).

They are cutting corners to get something out; however, now that customers are starting to pay, their focus has to shift from product development to product growth. This includes worrying about keeping systems up, securing data to comply with regulations, and growing a team, all while still trying to code.

Although these types of CTOs are not in the same league as the world's best CTO (a contender for such a title would be Werner Vogels of Amazon), their stress and anxiety are no less real. They tend not to wish to give up control and feel threatened when they start to hire people, especially those who may be more qualified than they are. It's hard for someone who has pulled many a late-nighter, giving up blood and sweat, to admit they may not be the best person for what is next.

When larger investors, such as venture capitalists, get involved—because technology is a key component of success—they may look to bring in someone with more experience to take over. With a little guidance and mentoring, this needn't be the case because the existing CTO can be the right person. This may be you if you answer yes to one or more of these:

- When making technical decisions, there is no one to challenge or validate.
- You are the only person doing all the development.
- This is your first real job, even though you may not be getting paid fully.
- Very little process or structure exists in the business.
- Only you know how to manage and maintain the system(s).

1.2.2 Funded startup: The technology expert with money

The next evolution from the raw startup described in the previous section is the one that has convinced one or more investors (family, angel, or venture funding) to invest and build a business. Serious money is on the line, with a budget that makes everyone feel like they have already won. Most don't realize, however, that they are merely living off credit, which has to be paid back at some point.

The CTO has been charged with rapidly building a team to support an architecture that hasn't really been fleshed out yet. There is a need to produce something so the business can start to move forward, but the product team hasn't really solidified what it is they are doing, so it's hard to know what to build.

There will come a time when a product has been delivered, with paying customers expecting a level of service. The CTO now has to shift focus from pure research and development to support and execution. Keeping customers happy, scaling the growth while managing the next wave of product, is a skill that requires strong discipline.

As time continues, the preciousness of money will start to raise its head. The CTO has to choose the right technology that doesn't put undue stress on the finances but still has the room to scale its costs with the growth of its customer base. In the old days, much of a startup's investment was spent on costly servers and hosting. Nowadays, with the right decisions and strategic use of the cloud, these running costs can be a fraction of the total investment. Still, the wrong decision can see costs spiral.

Many CTOs who have found themselves in this position, who don't want to follow the normal rulebook, flounder (largely because they don't know the rulebook because this is their first role). There is sometimes a complete lack of structure because they feel it is modern and trendy to be completely freewheeling. However, structure and process are there for a reason: to maintain a consistent and predictable customer experience.

On the other hand, some CTOs so desperately try to make sure they stick to a given philosophy, paranoid of making a wrong decision, they end up stressing themselves into a state where progress is stifled because so much is on the line. This is decision paralysis—where the fear of making the wrong decision prevents any decision from being made.

These types of companies are in a financial race, trying to turn a profit before they run out of money, to flip them from startup to an established, cash-positive business, which is stressful for all those involved at the top. You may be here if you answer yes to one or more of the following:

- The company is less than three years old.
- No one in your department has been there for more than 18 months.
- You are now on your second (or third) platform evolution.
- The company is spending more money than it is bringing in.
- Product features feel like they are changing on a weekly/monthly basis.

1.2.3   *Established company: Their first CTO*

A successful established company, usually founder-led, has evolved to a state where they have decided they need to get a firmer handle on the platform. They have a sprinkling of development and support staff, maybe reporting up to the CFO. The systems are key to keeping the business running, but they are starting to show their age, falling behind, making it harder to either fix bugs or extend (the likes of Power-Builder, Microsoft Access, and Visual Basic are powering more of the world than most probably want to admit to).

The biggest, not-yet-realized problem facing this company is that no one is looking after the health and long-term viability of the technology platform. This situation is like living in a house for many years, forgetting how crucial things like the AC and hot water are, not realizing that as each year goes by, the systems are slowly aging, just waiting to fail spectacularly, leaving the house without an important service.

Sometimes the company gets lucky—management realizes they need to replace crucial systems, but they just don't know how. Maybe a plucky sales representative has convinced them all their problems will be solved by moving to an expensive off-the-shelf solution, yet the price of such an investment gives them pause for concern. The industry has seen many failed Salesforce/Microsoft/Oracle "solutions" that were made due to an ill-informed decision. It's not the platform's fault, but most times, people don't need the full suite, just a small part of it. The end of that spectrum is when the management doesn't realize just how much borrowed time they are on, being one restart away from going dark, and believe nothing needs to be changed—*if it worked today, it will work tomorrow.*

After talking around or seeking counsel, or maybe being told by their private equity owners, management have decided to hire their first CTO. The successful candidate has a lot of opportunities ahead of them but also is expected to prove their worth, because the attitude by some will be that they managed fine without this role up to now.

This CTO needs to be more strategic in their execution, acknowledging the nervousness that may come when introducing change or new systems. One of their primary roles will be looking to replace legacy systems, all without disrupting the current business. They will be faced with a lot of "*We don't do that sort of thing here,*" and although this could be a tough gig, it will be extremely transformational and rewarding. The role is ideal for a CTO who has a little more experience, or for someone who wants to step up to the next level in their career. This company type features the following characteristics:

- It's an established company, with paying clients and a mature product line.
- The majority of the platform is over 10 years old.
- Only a handful of people know how to keep things up; they don't know why they do some things but know if they do, then things work.
- Most of the company don't realize that they have as much reliance on the technology or data as they do.
- There's a lack of standard policies or practices, including no real focus on security or compliance.

1.2.4 Established company with CTO

Finally, the established company knows the value of having a CTO. This CTO might have been with the company from the start, having learned everything they know on the job, with no real guidance on what they should or shouldn't be doing. Things seem to be working for them, because the company is delivering on clients' expectations. Or the CTO has been with the company and the time has come for them to seek new challenges, so they are leaving a well-oiled machine.

Change of leadership in this position could mean a breath of fresh air with new challenges, or to simply keep things running as well as they are. Private equity companies tend to rotate out senior management if they feel the current managers don't have the experience or knowledge to take the company where it needs to be taken. In their world, they don't have time to wait and see because their hold period is around three to five years. This company is easy to spot:

- The company has had a CTO position for at least three years.
- The engineering department is established, with roles and hierarchy defined.
- Process and standard practices have been instituted and, for the most part, are adhered to.
- Road maps, strategic visions, and project plans exist.
- Technology is stable and understood by most in the company.

Of course, there is a hybrid of all these types, but each has a distinct type of CTO at some point in their career's evolution.

1.3   Determining whether we need a CTO

A common question that comes up among management is whether they need a CTO. Closely related to that—if they already have a CTO—do they replace them with someone who has different skills and drive? This decision can be inspired by noting how other companies within their space or size have a CTO on their management team, but they don't. Another trigger can be the nagging feeling that technology should be doing more for them than it is—the belief that things should be much easier (and probably cheaper) than they are.

If a company has technology beyond back-office IT systems (email, files, calendars, chat, etc.) that clients interact with or that are crucial to revenue generation, it is vital that someone oversees this delivery and continual improvement and evolution. Another simple test can be this: is there custom software that has been developed in-house without which clients wouldn't be able to engage what they pay the company for?

The question then becomes this: how do you present a case to management that this role is needed? This can be challenging, especially if you are looking to fill the role personally. As with any case that is presented to the business, the most successful are the ones where it is hard to argue, because they are data led, not emotionally led. Now, that isn't to say gut instinct doesn't play into decision making, but it should never be the only reason.

Let's look at the following questions, if answered in the affirmative, that point to the need for a dedicated CTO:

- Is there custom software being developed for clients or in support of clients?
- Has there been significant customization of a third-party platform (such as Salesforce or Microsoft Dynamics) to support clients?

- Do you lack usage data on how clients are interacting with your systems?
- Are you in an industry that has potential data compliance or laws to be adhered to (e.g., are you storing medical or financial information about or for your clients?)
- Is security treated as a necessary evil inside the company, with much sharing of passwords?
- Are you running and maintaining your own client-facing servers?
- Do you lack a sandbox or safe environment for testing and trying new software or configurations?
- Do you have a small team of junior or inexperienced technical staff with no technical leadership?
- Is the notion of software patching or upgrading foreign and hasn't been done in years?
- Do you lack documentation or asset/version management for the systems powering client production?
- Do you have no backup or real-time disaster recovery policy?
- Do only a handful of key personnel know how the systems operate, meaning that without them, the company would be in trouble in a catastrophic failure?
- Does support handle problems related to poor or outdated software?
- Are current systems beginning to show their age and not able to service the features clients are demanding?

A restaurant cannot run without a chef to look after and run the kitchen, making sure everyone is doing their role to provide diners with tasty meals. A CTO is the chef in the company, keeping an eye on everything that is needed to serve the food.

1.4   Evolution from engineer

The vast majority of CTOs I have had the joy of either working with, mentoring, or knowing have strong technical backgrounds, which makes a lot of sense. Many of them have strong hands-on experience, with a natural curiosity for all things new—great qualities that make for a reliable and strong senior engineer, even an architect. But does it make for a good CTO?

Unfortunately, not always. Although the role of a CTO looks attractive, it comes with a lot of hidden responsibilities that aren't at first obvious (something you will discover after reading this book) and most engineers struggle with. Not every CTO copes well with the burden of their office, because their engineering-leaning natural instincts have not translated to the new responsibilities. Why is this?

One of the biggest reasons is a lack of preparation for thinking both larger and longer term. Larger isn't about creating or managing larger platforms but considering how those systems live and operate in the context of the company and the end client. Longer-term thinking is in terms of five-year blocks—a natural cycle of the business. How is your platform going to look in five years? Will it serve the needs of the business while still being relevant?

These are all logical and simple on the surface, but scratch it a little and a whole level of complexity and interwoven problems makes this a problem that is never really solved, but requires a solution that has been built with flexibility and adaptability.

Setting aside all the soft skills that need to be mastered—knowing how to talk to peers who don't have an engineering background, preparing financial budgets for a project that has not yet been fully defined, hiring and maintaining a team full of talent—all while keeping the customer happy, there is a world of nebulous decisions and unknown outcomes, unlike the binary distinct world they have come from and are happy with.

It can be done. The most successful CTOs are those who know how to use their technical backgrounds to provide value and success for their company. The biggest tool that an engineer in a CTO role can have in their arsenal is the knowledge of expectations: you know what will work and what will not work, and how long it should take or last. These tools are going to make a powerful and consistent-performing CTO.

Words of wisdom

They won't thank you

I recall one of the best pieces of advice my long-term mentor and friend, Jim Milbery, founding partner of ParkerGale Capital, gave. At the time I was an architect, redesigning a platform for a portfolio company, and I had made the rookie mistake of thinking about today and forgetting about tomorrow. One of my selling points was that I was saving the company $10,000 a year with the redesign. That was a lot of money at the time. However, there was a risk (small) that the component might fail. Jim said that although the money saved was laudable, when things go wrong, try explaining to the board "but I saved the company $10,000," when they were bleeding customer goodwill. That was the lesson that showed me my decisions had farther-reaching consequences than simply running a platform.

1.4.1   The first 100 days

A common question asked in interviews for executive-level positions is, "What would you do in the first 100 days?" to get a sense of how thoughtful and strategic this person is. It is a great tool for the first-time CTO giving some serious thought to what they need to do and how they are going to tackle this new role. Seasoned CTOs starting a new role will also do the same thing before really getting started.

This following section looks at the things that start adding value before the 100th day comes around while not making any rash/reactionary decisions. As an engineer, you have to resist the urge to judge (at least out loud) and roll up your sleeves to start making changes. Engineers love to get their hands dirty as soon as possible—they see a problem and want to address it. Fight that urge.

0–7 DAYS

The first week should be spent getting to know the company from the perspective of the client. Learn precisely what the company does, the terminology used, the pricing model, the top and most important clients. Not too much detail is required here—the key is to get a good sense of how the company runs, what each department does, and who the key individuals are.

7–30 DAYS

The next few weeks will be spent getting to know the engineering department, as well as getting to know each of the departments that make up the company, in more depth. The engineering department will (or at least should) run in autopilot while you come up to speed. You may be pulled into various meetings, but the key to success here is to simply listen and observe, looking for how people perceive the engineering department and the types of personalities you are going to be interacting with.

From the field

Looking for tells

I call this phase the *going to lose for an hour* period, after Mel Gibson's 1994 movie, *Maverick*. He asks to sit down at a poker table and sees the players are a bit hesitant, so he convinces them he will just lose for the first hour—which he does. Then, once

(continued)

the hour lapses, he starts to play. When he wins at the end of the night, one of the men accuses him of cheating. Gibson's character explains, "What do you think I was doing for the first hour? I was watching your tells." The CTO role is a marathon, not a sprint—you have time to make your presence felt.

Understanding your environment is key. What are the problems facing the company and the department? What pain points do clients have that your new group could potentially look to help with? Getting to know each individual in the group is crucial. Understanding their backgrounds, their contributions, their frustrations, and their goals will give you the best view of what is facing you. Building that trust and connection will take time, but observing how they interact with others will give you a lot of intel.

As part of this, you will be learning how things are done, which technology powers which products, and who is responsible for what. Getting to know the projects that are currently being planned and executed will give you insight into how things are thought through and the appetite for the size of each initiative.

30–70 DAYS

The next wave is to dig a little deeper, get access to some systems, and start poking around for yourself. If custom development is done, then look at some source code to get a feel for quality. If you're at a data company, review various data stores to see how data is structured and maintained. Reviewing servers, or infrastructure, lets you see the reality of execution. In short, you want to lift the lid on the areas you have been learning about to see for yourself what state they are in.

This discovery phase will give you a lot of insight into the state and capability of the team. For example, it is amazing the number of times this area highlights that a crucial part of the system has no in-house expertise or support contract. As you are going through each area, note down any easy wins or quick fixes that could make a big difference.

At the same time, getting to know some established clients is a great way to get an outside perspective. A simple lunch or quick client visit will yield a lot of information that may not already be known inside the company.

Toward the end of this discovery phase, you will start to formulate a number of short-term plans, as well as get a feel for your vision for what the department needs to do for long-term success. You may look at the current list of projects and make some small adjustments, expanding or reducing their scope, based on what you have learned.

70–100 DAYS

In this phase, some execution will start—simple things, like putting in place various processes that might be lacking, or creating a better structure around areas that are a little fluffy. Your goal here is to have identified the key components of the company that are required to keep the lights on and what is required to shore those up, so any large initiatives you identify as needing further investigation don't detract from the company being able to function.

For example, you might find an area that has been neglected, and for all intents and purposes is considered legacy, that needs to be modernized because either the software is no longer supported or there is difficulty in finding resources to manage it. Although it is tempting to focus on the "new shiny" objects, it is vital to keep the "old dull" objects still functioning, because they are the ones paying everyone's salary.

You will have a good idea of what is what, and you will have met with the CEO a number of times, to understand them and to see what their vision of the company is. You will be starting to put more detail into your vision, but you need to get some project wins under your belt first.

By the time the 100th day rolls around, you should have a good feel for the state of the department, made some small incremental improvements/changes, and know where the company is heading. Now you can get to running the department and delivering value.

1.5 Top 10 qualities for a CTO

It's a common misconception that a CTO has to have a development background—someone who can get into the nuts and bolts of the platform. This is a fallacy. Although it is true that the majority of CTOs have development or computer science backgrounds, many have risen through the business management ranks and have a good grasp on how to manage processes and execute on goals. A good CTO is someone who

- Can lead and inspire through lifting others up
- Looks far down the road before making any decisions
- Communicates in a way that is confident yet nonpatronizing
- Listens to their CEO and board to understand their desires and goals
- Keeps themselves updated with the technologies that are most relevant to their company's industry
- Is not scared to fail and, should they fail, refuses to point the finger
- Doesn't try to do everything themselves and instead delegates to their team
- Knows they are not the smartest person in their team just because they are the boss
- Is confident to acknowledge and credit a good idea, irrespective of its source
- Has a vision that can be communicated and actioned

A CTO is no different from any other leader in business in that they need to have the same skills to motivate and inspire to get the best out of their team. It is important that this is not the only book you should be reaching for as you aspire to be better in your role—your shelf should contain at least one or two general leadership books.

The CTO has a lot of responsibility on their shoulders. They need to juggle multiple balls, operating at a level that is way beyond a senior engineer or even project manager. Realizing this difference is what sets the great CTOs apart.

Summary

- A Chief Technology Officer is someone who looks after the current and long-term future of the platform.
- For companies early on in their lifecycle, the CTO is more of a hands-on, doing-everything type of role because that is what enables early growth.
- As the company grows, the role evolves into more of a management/architecture role, delegating and looking outward more.
- For an established company, the role continues to evolve, shoring up the technology to permit growth and scalability while fixing some legacy problems.
- We created a checklist for companies that don't have a full-time CTO to make it easy to determine whether now is the time to take on that role.
- The first 100 days of taking on the role will define the leadership and thoughtfulness of the CTO, as they dig in to discover the challenges ahead and as they perform their own in-depth due diligence.
- Although many qualities make a great CTO, we identified 10 of them that all speak to making best use of the team around them and creating an environment where many hands can make light work.

Checklist

How many of the following items can you lay claim to having covered?

- Understand the role of a CTO
- The differences between a CTO and a Senior Engineer
- Identified how a CTO will benefit or work within the current organization

Managing up

2

Have you noticed how most technologists are, on the whole, extremely comfortable talking to like-minded technologists and find comfort in surrounding themselves in a sea of buzzwords and jargon? The phrase "birds of a feather flock together" speaks a lot of truth. This level of communication can be considered inward looking— talking to their own people, in their own tongue, comes naturally. Turning around and looking outward, we are faced with a foreign world with different words, language, and competing objectives.

Many new CTOs are ill equipped to deal with this world. They are thrown into an environment where a single misplaced phrase can send a whole team into a frenzied panic because how they interpreted it was so far from the meaning intended. Their words have a lot more meaning, and finding that common language to interact with the rest of the business is one of the keys to their success.

This whole area of communicating with peers, bosses, and the board comes with a lot of trepidation for technical people. It need not be so difficult when one realizes that the secret of working with each level is empathy—knowing to whom you communicate, their motives, desires, and concerns—makes your job of bridging the divide infinitely easier.

This chapter will look at the major stakeholders who you may run into and how to manage each situation to get what you need to be successful. If you are like me, it won't come naturally at the start, and you may find you kick yourself if you don't speak up or sound more confident than you are. It takes practice and, importantly, confidence in yourself.

2.1 *Partnering with your CEO*

There are many relationships you need to maintain, but one of the most important is with your CEO (or immediate boss, if you find yourself reporting to the COO, Chief Operating Officer, or CIO, Chief Information Officer). Without a strong trust and respectful partnership with your CEO, you won't be able to achieve your goals and vision for the company, no matter how good you are. This dynamic is different from the normal boss-employee setup because the stakes of failure or misalignment are so much greater. This section identifies the types of CEOs you may encounter and the challenges that each type brings and gives you the tools to make the relationship work.

My CEO doesn't understand

In my role mentoring CTOs in the world of PE (private equity), the statement, "My CEO just doesn't understand," comes around time and time again, resulting in me playing the diplomatic role, brokering common ground for the two parties to come together and communicate effectively. It all comes down to a failure to properly communicate, on a level that the CEO will feel empowered to understand. We techies have a natural tendency to go into too much detail too quickly. Most of the time, the person listening may not care about our detailed explanations. All they are thinking about is the result or implication of said event—how does this affect our customer?

2.1.1 *The office of the CEO*

Your first task is to stop thinking of the CEO as a single person. Instead, think of them as the representative of an office. Anything you say to them is open for them to use when another department seeks their council. That makes it sound all very legalistic and dramatic, but the key is the mindset with which you interact with this office. You are there to contribute to its productiveness and output. Recognize that when you are telling a CEO a given piece of information, you are instead giving them the sound bite with which they can communicate the same event, but in their language, to those who ask.

Missing mailbox

I once had a key third-party API suddenly stop working, which had a negative impact on clients. The problem was on their side—they had made a DNS change that resulted in resolution to the wrong address. Knowing this problem was going to be explained to many different people of differing backgrounds, I told the CEO that they had updated their mailbox and accidentally put the wrong number on it. This meant all deliveries were going to an unknown box, and while they were working on getting the right numbers on it, we were holding back all deliveries. It communicated every-thing I needed, and the CEO instantly understood the issue. Getting into the logistics of DNS resolution and time-to-live values was not going to advance the situation. I then saw the same metaphor repeated around our client success and sales team, and as a status update, I was simply asked, "Has the mailbox got the right number yet?"

Depending on the size/type of company, your CEO may not necessarily be at the top of the ladder. They may have to report to a board, private equity partners, or external investors. Each of these will have a particular detailed level of interest in the outcome of the company. Each one will ask the layer below for an update or pulse check. This is the ecosystem you are feeding with your statements and communications to the office of the CEO.

Try to use metaphors when explaining complex issues to both technical and nontech-nical people. Sometimes using a metaphor with a technical person can free them from thinking too much in the weeds. The nontechnical person may not feel inferior for not knowing a given subject yet still feel they can contribute to its resolution. You'd be surprised at how often something really useful comes from the strangest of disciplines.

We engineers and nerds love details. We love to surround ourselves with numbers and the finality of absolutes. We work best with no ambiguity. Businesspeople, on the other hand, inhabit a world of the abstract where there is no certain outcome given a set of known inputs. When we each go to our default communication style, we accuse the business of not giving us enough detail to do our job, and the business will counter that we didn't really understand the spirit of what they were asking. Neither party is wrong.

To succeed we must have empathy for their world, look on them as a partner, and give them the necessary sounding board that will make them more effective. Next, we will look into the different types of CEOs you may encounter in your career as a CTO.

2.1.2 *Types of CEOs*

Being a CEO is a tough job, with competing pressures to bring together a group of people to work in harmony for the production of a product or service to deliver value to clients, security for employees, and, finally, returns to investors.

Think of a company as an orchestral movement—although your string section is important, many other sections are involved in coming together to produce a harmonious sound, with the CEO conducting and coordinating the whole symphony. When it works, it is a beautiful thing to watch, but sometimes the CEO is just waving their arms around, throwing everyone off as they attempt to interpret their desires. Let us visit the various kinds of backgrounds of CEOs.

NONTECHNICAL CEO

In most cases, your CEO has come from a traditional management or finance background, with no direct technical experience. They will know of the technology as it relates to the end customer but not at the detail that you are comfortable with. That is perfectly fine, because that is why your role exists in the first place: to remove all the logistics and headaches from their desk so they can focus on the business of business.

Many a CTO can be quick to dismiss or underestimate this CEO type, believing that because the CEO doesn't have a handle on the technology and has maybe made a mistake or two in trying to describe something, they are not worthy of the CTO's attention. This is the most common type of CEO and is the one we will bump into the most, and they should not be taken lightly.

NONTECHNICAL CEO WHO THINKS THEY KNOW TECHNOLOGY

The next type of CEO (after the one who at least is well aware of their lack of knowledge) is the CEO who thinks they have a handle on the technology and talks confidently with buzzwords in a context that to the untrained ear sounds plausible. You've probably witnessed the type of person who nods knowingly at your updates, fooling you into thinking they are keeping up, giving you a false sense of security, but who has no real clue what you are really talking about.

> ### Getting off the bandwagon
>
> I am reminded of a situation where I visited a CEO in one company after learning they were now selling artificial intelligence (AI) as part of their offering, with much energy and gusto. Something didn't smell quite right, and after a short conversation, I discovered they had read all about AI in a newspaper and thought this was something they were already doing—but joining two database tables does not AI make. They had spun up the sales team and were all excited at being on the new frontier of innovation. In private, I informed them that we were not, in fact, offering AI. I felt bad

having to take the wind out of their sails, but they were grateful for the discreet course correction without making a fuss or making them look wrong in front of their team.

TECHNICAL CEO

Nirvana! At last, someone who speaks your language . . . but hold on a moment, Snow White—this apple may be poisoned. This CEO will have a good feel for what you do, but given they are no longer working in the technical space, it is easy for them to forget some of the challenges and quickly dismiss them as unimportant or trivial to address.

They may also want to question every decision you are making, from architecture to production to delivery to hiring people. It is healthy to question and challenge, but when you feel like everything you do is being questioned, it can be smothering. It isn't their fault—they have gone to their comfort place, the one place they know like the back of their hand, and in their own way, they think they are actually helping you out. A good CEO of this type will support you, lift you up, and help you with your own career development and make you a better CTO.

2.1.3 *Setting the tone*

Irrespective of the type of CEO, you have to find a way to successfully partner with this person who makes you, them, the company, and the client successful. The best way to do this is to lead them as much as they lead you.

KNOW YOUR CEO

The first thing you need to do is know the personality of your CEO. Particularly if you are coming into a company where you have no historical experience, it is important that you know this individual at a deeper level by doing the following:

- Find out their background (Google, LinkedIn, etc.) and what their previous experience is.
- Discover what motivates them, what makes them happy/sad.
- What does success look like for them?
- Are they a detailed/micromanage or a big-picture type?
- Have a conversation.

Basic information can be gleaned from direct conversations with them and through colleagues. When you are new to a company, it is perfectly okay to ask the question in the open: "Is there anything I should know about Person X that will help me be successful?" It shows a willingness to do your homework. Knowing how your CEO ticks will help you communicate more effectively with them.

Details matter

I recall one CEO who had a thing for the company name being spelled correctly—if people couldn't be bothered to pay enough attention to that detail, how could we trust them handling our clients? Silly as it sounds, that was his litmus test for attention to detail, and once the new CTO we were helping understood that, their communication style changed to continually demonstrate that details mattered to them, too.

THE CEO'S SUPPORT NETWORK

No one is an island. We all have our support network to reach out to and get help. CEOs are no different. They will have their own trusted advisors within a company—the people they can go to for sounding out ideas and thoughts. They may also have their right-hand person, completely trusted to execute many of their biddings. It is important you discover who this network is and just how much of the ear of the CEO they have. Their support of you and your vision may make later approval much easier, because you can use them as a way to test out whether you have your pitch right.

Know the rainmaker

I recall a time when the CTO for a portfolio company was having problems getting their plans approved. They reached out for advice. After digging in, I discovered that the key was winning over not the CEO but the CFO, on whom the CEO relied probably a bit too much. The CTO had failed to read the dynamics of the management team and did not recognize the power lay in the CFO, whose advice the CEO always sought. Once the focus was changed to that person, the CTO's success within the company rapidly improved. We'll go into dealing with the CFO later in this chapter.

Know who the real decision makers are in the company. Form alliances.

WHAT DO THEY WANT?

Sometimes the simplest way forward is to ask the most basic of questions: what do they want? Sitting down with your CEO and asking them directly how you can be successful for them is the easiest way. Ask them directly for an example of what level of detail they like, what their criteria is for when something should bubble up to their desk, what keeps them up at night, and so on.

Getting to know this should not be a one-time conversation. Rather, this should be part of your ongoing conversation (at least every quarter) to make sure you are continually delivering what is expected of you. As each meeting goes on, you will have interactions to reflect on. This will also build trust that you have the responsibilities of your department well within your grasp.

Kedric Griffin, senior director of engineering at EAB, notes nicely, "Faith comes from time, trust, and confidence in you. Way too often I have seen a technical person try to 'quick win' an argument by throwing out an opinion as fact. It only takes getting caught here once to lose all the confidence and faith you had built up with them."

REGULAR ONE-ON-ONE

You will probably meet with the CEO as part of the bigger management meeting, but it is important you meet with them one-on-one. These meetings should be kept regularly and should serve as a way for you to update them on the grander vision and strategies that are not part of the day-to-day grind of running the company. Use these meetings to understand their long-term strategy better to see whether there is something you need to change to accommodate that. These conversations can be hugely insightful and will make sure you and your CEO are aligned. A typical meeting may start with a quick high-level update from you, with maybe some pointed questions for them to address, and then allow them to tell you anything that will help you plan accordingly.

2.1.4 Tips for a successful partnership

There is no magic formula for making a relationship perfect. It takes hard work, experimentation, and patience to be a good partner for your CEO and organization. That said, you can do some things to make life a little easier on yourself.

LEAD WITH DATA

Emotions, feelings, and gut instinct can all be argued subjectively. Data is much harder to dispute. Make sure any decision you are presenting to your CEO is steeped in data that supports it. If you are looking to hire another team member, then show through data the productivity gain that will be had with this person on board. If you are looking to have a project approved, attempt to show the real financial impact on the business, for example, money saved in unnecessary support or licenses. Let data lead your conversation.

BRING THEM INTO THE HARD DECISION

There will be a time when you have to make a decision that may have a greater impact than you would like. No matter what way you look, there is no good path to take. At this point, after exploring all your options, you bring the CEO into this decision and lay out the consequences of each path, so they are fully vested in the decision with you. They may bring something new to the conversation that could remove an impediment, or they may agree with you that a decision has to be made. This is the "Sophie's choice" moment, named after the 1982 Meryl Streep movie, where she had to make a decision to save one child at the expense of another. Such a big decision should not be just your responsibility.

THINK SLOW, ACT FAST

We are human, and as such, we have a natural tendency to want to please, and in the context of business, that means saying yes to requests. It makes us feel good. We say yes quickly, particularly in a situation where we may feel a little more social pressure than normal, like a large meeting. Fight that urge. Take all requests under advisement and note that you will get back to them as soon as possible. You don't need to take a lot of time thinking about something, but you need the space to think through all the permutations before making your decision or recommendation. This practice will automatically stop you from being overwhelmed and committing to too many things you know you can't possibly deliver.

Once you have made the decision, act on it fast. Do not procrastinate or second-guess yourself. All the time you have spent thinking and poring over the decision should allow you to execute with no second guesses.

BUILD FOR INPUT/CHANGE

No one likes to feel they have no choice. If you present a proposal to a CEO that has only two outcomes, yes or no, then you have already limited your successful outcome by 50% before you even start. If you present with a variety of options that gives the CEO opportunity for input and control, they will likely be more willing to consider your proposal.

A common mistake is to present in an all-or-nothing tone. Instead, go with a phased, incremental approach, demonstrating wins along the way that the company can benefit from. This gives the CEO breathing room not to commit too much too soon before they fully understand the scope of what it is you are asking. Make the choices extremely relevant for the situation you are in. Not giving enough choices, or relevant ones, will have the opposite effect of what you are trying to achieve.

NO SUCH THING AS BAD NEWS

There will always be bad news that you will have to deliver at some time—the system is down, the database deleted (what?), or whatever it is. It will be uncomfortable and make for an uneasy exchange. The first thing to do is own it. If this is under your watch, then you are responsible. Own the problem, learn from it, and take the necessary steps to not repeat it. Second,

present the news without emotion or blame. Although it is tempting (and this happens more often than it should), do not name any person in your team who may have been responsible. We'll talk about this in a later chapter, but you have to stand as a team.

What types of bad news should be reported to the CEO? Assuming you haven't already discovered that by talking with the CEO, a good rule of thumb is if it affects clients or revenue, then it should be brought to the immediate attention of the CEO. They need to be in the loop as soon as possible. Never try to hide or mask a potential problem. Your worst nightmare is when your CEO tells you about a problem you already knew about. The fact they are telling you means it has popped up on their radar and you have just undermined all trust and faith they had in you by not transacting openly. A good example of this is if your client site is unstable or down. Don't wait—bring this immediately to the CEO (and company) and let them know you are on it.

Now that we have talked about building a partnership with your CEO, let us turn our attention to the Chief Financial Officer (CFO).

2.2   Counting on your CFO

You may think keeping a handle on costs and expenditure is not within the purview of your department—that is something for the Chief Financial Officer or controller to worry about. Although your company may not expose you directly to all the costs (e.g., it's common for salaries to be kept confidential), to be completely divorced from the financial aspect of your department is a dereliction of duty and will not serve you in the long run. This section lays out the reasons why you need to get a handle on this and how you can use this to your advantage to make better and more informed decisions.

The sad reality is that your department is most likely a cost center—it does not directly generate income. Yes, no doubt it is hugely important, and without your group, the company would probably not function. That doesn't matter. In accountancy terms, you cost the company money. The best you can hope for is to not cost the company too much. For every dollar you ask for, it is important to show the value that that dollar is going to provide the company in return.

Sounds daunting, but it isn't as hard as it seems, as long as you have a good working relationship with your CFO. The CFO is ultimately responsible for reporting all numbers to not only the CEO and board but also the government when they file the company returns each year. They have to stand by their numbers and justify everything going in and out of the company. Understanding what they need will allow you to align to their wants and, in return, make their lives easier because they will know they can count on and trust your budgets.

2.2.1   Getting a handle on your expenditures

The first thing you will want to do, particularly if you have inherited a department or recently joined an organization, is to figure out what your "burn rate" is. This is the amount of money that your department costs, if nothing changes, on a monthly and yearly basis. This number in itself is not enough—we need to contextualize it in a way that makes it painless to explain to the business.

An effective strategy that works well is to split your costs into three buckets as follows:

- Development
- Production
- Support

Depending on the company you are with, it may also make sense to break this down further into product lines or groups that best align with the vernacular of the business. You do not need an accountancy major to keep a handle on your costs—a simple spreadsheet listing all your costs will do perfectly. Every time a license is bought, or a service is signed up, you keep track of it and how much it is costing each month. Let's break down each area.

DEVELOPMENT

This is everything it takes to produce what the company considers "the product," which can include

- Staff costs (salary and computer)
- Software tool licenses (IDE, project management tools)
- Software runtime licenses (database, libraries)
- Hardware/cloud for development/testing
- Third-party vendors, such as contractors
- Training (courses, books, conferences)

When it comes to staff costs, it is common to just use their yearly salary, but a better guide is to use 120%–130% of their salary because this will take into account ancillary costs (such as benefits, equipment, furniture, and coffee).

> ### Making future budgets easier
> Consider breaking down roles into daily costs. For example, say a typical web developer salary is $100K (add 20% overhead—$120K), which works out at $10K per month, or $500 per day (assume 20 working days in a month). When a future project demands 14 days of a web developer, you won't need to hunt around or guess at a rate—this will cost 14 × $500. Your budget suddenly got a lot more informed.

Knowing how much it costs to produce a product gives you the greatest insight for budget and growth planning. When your CEO asks if they can have something faster, you have insight into how much that extra speed is going to cost the company. Again, be data led with your decisions, not instinctual (instinct should confirm what the data says).

PRODUCTION

Anything associated with servicing the client comes under this category, including the following:

- Staff costs (client setup or onboarding of client data)
- Hardware/cloud costs
- Software runtime licenses (database, libraries)
- Third-party services (domains, APIs)
- Security audits

Popular cloud services like AWS and Azure make it easy to tag your resources, which will allow you to allocate costs to production and development. Likewise, runtime licenses are usually different from development licenses and can cost significantly more. Staff costs may not be applicable, depending on your environment, but if it takes effort to onboard a client, then this has to be factored in.

Ideally, you want to try to get to a number that is closely tied to the number of clients. This will allow the business to properly factor in the cost of delivery and get a heads up on potential costs should they scale up client acquisition. Some organizations get to a level of granularity that they can tell precisely how much each client is costing/consuming their infrastructure.

SUPPORT

Finally, there is support. When something goes wrong or a client needs help, how much is that costing? How much effort is spent just maintaining the system, like keeping log files monitored and backups validated?

This cost should be in line with your production costs, so when those increase, so do your support costs. Support desk costs should be broken down into an hourly cost if possible, so you can see just how much servicing a given type of ticket/issue costs.

Many older, legacy systems cost an inordinate amount of support, due to a lack of adequate features for the modern-day environment. In one system, we discovered 60% of all ticket requests were password reset requests, and because we had the hourly cost of support, it was straightforward to put a real financial amount to what this was costing. While putting the budget together for approval, the decision to have a password reset mechanism installed became a trivial matter and showed an ROI (return on investment) in the first month of going live. Budgeting is an area that is addressed later in this chapter.

Support desks often do not properly track everything that is useful for analysis. One often overlooked data point is the actual client (or product line) the ticket was raised against. This can often unearth some real surprises, like how one particular client is taking a much larger percentage of support than usual.

Do not discount the time and effort it takes to service client requests. This is your window into how you can improve your systems and make it really easy to have a conversation with your CFO to reduce cost and friction at the same time. An example of a monthly breakdown for, say, production could be as simple as table 2.1.

Table 2.1 **Example monthly breakdown**

Area	Monthly
AWS cost	$ 15K
DevOps (one person)	$ 2K
Software license (JIRA and GitHub)	$ 0.5K
Support (two persons at 10K each)	$ 20K

2.2.2 *Reaching out*

The area of finance is usually foreign to the new CTO and can be quite intimidating at first. Create a good dialogue with your CFO and ask for their input. You may not be seeing all the bills, and it is perfectly acceptable to ask to see them, as long as they relate to your group. Just don't go asking for the CEO's salary!

Once you have compiled your initial expenditure tracker, go and review it with your CFO. You may be double-counting expenses (e.g., the Microsoft Office license may be a group license for the company and is allocated under a budget outside of yours), or you may not be capturing everything the CFO has assigned to your group.

A good CFO loves to see a department lead who has a good handle on their own expenditure because it makes their job easier. It is always good practice to meet with them periodically to review your expenditure sheet (maybe once a quarter) because they will be able to tell you precisely how much over or under you are with your numbers.

The secret to a good relationship with your CFO is no surprises. The CFO is responsible for all costs within the company, not just your department. They want predictability and dependability on your numbers, and if you can prove you are someone who can be trusted with your figures, when it comes to budget approval, your life will become so much easier.

Too many CTOs let themselves down by not having a firm grasp on their costs and get caught off guard at key moments where a little information could have made everything go so much smoother.

If you don't know your burn rate at this precise moment, then that is your litmus test. You are missing out on a lot of information that could be very useful to have in your back pocket.

2.3 *Working with peers*

How well do you know each of the different departments that make up your organization? Given how pervasive technology is, a CTO should not be caught off guard not knowing exactly what each and every department does in the overall operation of the company.

James Headly, founder/partner of MacLaurin Group, in his role of mentoring of CIOs notes "The CTO must be well versed in the needs of all of those members of the organization and work closely with the business owners. They must not look myopically through the lens of a developer, but must partner with the business as they move this society forward."

This section goes over the importance of having a good working relationship with your peers and knowledge of their worlds that will ultimately help you succeed.

2.3.1 Know your company

Let us define what a peer is, for the context of this section. A peer one is one who sits on the same level, organizationally speaking, as the CTO. If your company isn't that formal yet, then these are the people who are in the same meetings as you and who report to the CEO. These are the people and their departments who you should know.

At a high level, you probably know what the sales department does, but do you have any appreciation for how the department is made up, what problems they face, what pain points they have, and their metric for success? You don't need to know how the department operates at a detailed level, but you do need to have a good appreciation of what it takes for them to be successful.

It is not uncommon for a CEO to have a particular favorite or synergy with a given department. This is usually due to one of the comfort zones. If a CEO has come from a sales background, for example, they will have a greater appreciation of their sales group and may spend more time with them. Do not see this as anything more, because a good CEO loves all their departments equally (ideally, that is; it doesn't always play out like this, but it is good to go in with that attitude until otherwise proven wrong).

You are the leader of one of the few departments (HR being another one) that every other department in the company relies on. The technology that you are responsible for interacts with the client, and every department is focused on delivering value for the client in one way or another. Your successes (and failures) directly influence how every other department is going to engage with the client.

> **Out to lunch**
>
> One of the pieces of advice I give to CTOs is to get into a rhythm of going out to lunch, at least once a month, with each of their peers. Get to know them on a personal level. You will be surprised at what you can learn while you both break bread over lunch. Another subtle way is to invite department leads to come and talk at one of your department meetings, to give some insight into their group.

It is therefore vital not only that you know how they work, but also they should know how you work. Every person in your department should have this same appreciation and be part of the onboarding process.

2.3.2   Speak their language

Even in a small company, a different lexicon can exist to describe various entities within the business. We all know how important it is to keep these differences to a minimum, but vocabulary vernacular has a tendency to evolve. As soon as one person uses a word confidently in a meeting, it enters into the vocabulary of that department and can leak out into the wider company.

You say potato, I say potato

I recall at one portfolio company I worked, there were two terms flying around to describe a customer: the project ID and the campaign ID. Some departments would use one, claiming they had no knowledge of the other. It took me a good few months before I realized it was the exact same entity—there was no difference at all. Never be scared to ask the basic questions.

A common language is important, but understanding the meaning of differences can make your departments' interactions with those external to yours so much easier. Get to know what phrases and definitions each department uses, and when you need to interact, use their language without imposing your own.

2.3.3   Find their pain

Every department has its own internal workflows and business rules, working hard to service clients. Sometimes they get into a rut, knowing there is probably a better, more efficient way, but what they do know they know extremely well.

In my experience, small suggestions or changes to a department, once you have truly gotten to know how they work, can truly revolutionize their workflow. It is a wonderful way to build bridges, get easy wins, and gain a greater insight into their function.

A little knowledge can go a long way

Sometimes the easiest of solutions can make the biggest impact. One group kept their team workflow in a spreadsheet, so anyone could easily see the current state of a given client. This spreadsheet was emailed around as each person made an update. You can see the problems already—the spreadsheet sometimes went back in time if someone updated the wrong version in their email and forwarded that.

Tempting as it is to overengineer a solution (e.g., recommending a customer relationship management [CRM]), the easiest and simplest solution was to move the group over to Google Sheets in the short term. A single spreadsheet eliminated their biggest pain but was still familiar so their entire workflow was not disrupted. Do not underestimate the reliance the corporate world has on the humble spreadsheet.

Look for opportunities to help and bring some wisdom, particularly around human-intensive processes, where the potential of introducing errors is great. If you can help to eliminate human error, then everyone benefits from this. Let the solutions evolve; don't automatically overburden them with completely new workflows and disrupt their job.

2.3.4   *Think strategically*

Once you have gotten to know how all your departments work and have formed good relationships, you can start working together to make things work easier. Some companies go through regular reorganization, where new departments are formed or people are moved—with the CEO usually trying to change things up for a better outcome. However, the people who best know what really works and doesn't are you and your peers—those who are in the daily grind of running the business.

Now, this is not an opportunity for a land grab to make your department larger or more powerful. This is about common sense changes that just make for a better workflow overall. Sometimes you can find pockets of mini departments inside of a bigger one that would be better served if they were elsewhere. These mini departments have usually evolved from a single role and, over the years, become bigger and bigger and have just stayed where they are because no one thought of moving them.

A common department that evolves from the mists is customer support, which can often be strewn across different departments, each one functioning in a narrow area. With the right conversations and negotiations, these mini departments can often be brought together and put under a single leader to better serve the client.

If you and your peers' suggestions make sense, it is an easy sell to the CEO, who should approve it. A good CEO will not get in the way of a reorganization, because they trust their senior management team to make the right decisions.

A well-oiled engine is one in which all the parts work together as they should, with no single component causing problems for others. As the leader and visionary for your company's technology, it is vital you understand your company and what each department does to service

your client. Failure to do so will make it harder to build alliances and support for executing your plans.

2.4   Taking over from another CTO

One of the hardest things you will do in your career is to take over from an existing CTO. As the old carpenter lament goes, "The one before you was an idiot, and the one that comes next will think you were an idiot." We technologists are always quick to judge, particularly if things aren't done how we would do them. There is also the opposite: that the CTO before was the best but moved on to greater challenges. Never assume one or the other.

This section goes over some of the dos and don'ts to successfully transition from one administration to another—yours.

2.4.1   Celebrate, not disparage

As obvious as it may seem, the one thing you should never do is disparage any of the decisions and processes of the historical CTO, however tempting it will be, given some of the things you may see as you start to understand what you have in front of you. You don't want to look like the "blame CTO," where you are quick to point the finger to take heat away from you. Do not worry—everyone knows you are new and not responsible for any sins of the past. You do not need to remind them.

The best thing to do is to celebrate their progress. After all, no matter what you think of some of the decisions, they have successfully navigated the technology where the company is profitable enough to offer you a salary to continue growth. You will be lacking the historical context for some of the decisions; they are where they are. Don't be quick to judge.

It is sometimes not a case of they didn't know a better way (though this is true a lot of the time—*they don't know what they don't know*). Perhaps they were forced down a given path by a CEO that felt they knew better and the CTO didn't have the skills or data necessary to persuade or encourage a different path. The point is, you will never truly know why, so there is no point in looking back, only forward. Whatever problems there are, they are now yours to resolve.

> **From the field**
> *You did what?*
>
> I have often bumped into very creative solutions, and instead of disparaging them, I celebrated their creativeness and ingenuity, while inside in my head, I was screaming, "What were you possibly thinking?" I had one portfolio company where we were hiring for a new CTO to take over from someone who had been there from the start. This particular gentleman did not trust the various standard version control systems (CVS, SVN, or Git). His solution? He built and maintained his own standard and forced his team to use it. On one hand, I had to celebrate the inventiveness, but upon digging in, I discovered it was nothing more than a fancy zip layer and wasn't version

control as we know it today. I used the excuse of moving to Git so we could use the built-in tooling to the developers' IDE without making a fuss and drawing attention to how weak their "version control" was. Everyone saved face. You don't need to draw attention to your wins or seek adulation for being smarter. Just do it and move on.

On the other side of the spectrum, you can find yourself looking at a solution that you are unfamiliar with, maybe not knowing the technology stack, but you can appreciate the use of the technology. This is a wonderful opportunity for you to learn, especially as you look at something that is operational and being used in the field. You won't always inherit a mess or a team in disarray.

One of the burdens of being a technologist that we all suffer from time to time is rewriting something because we have no clue how it works. As a CTO, you have to resist this urge to change just because you don't necessarily know or prefer the way it is working. Don't fix what isn't broken.

2.4.2 Speak to the outgoing CTO

If you are lucky to have the opportunity to talk with the outgoing CTO, this is something to welcome and run toward. Maybe the CTO is moving on or is retiring, but if you get this chance, however rare it is, you should embrace it with both hands.

It is a huge opportunity to be able to ask the right sort of questions that will make it easier for you going forward. You don't want to ask questions that will have them on the defensive, because this really doesn't give you any insight except to satisfy a morbid or intellectually superior curiosity. Questions that will make your life less complicated include these:

- *What kept you up at night?*—This gives you an insight into the sort of ongoing things that they were concerned about but didn't have an immediate solution— usually things you would never have thought of.
- *What pressure did the business place on you?*—An example of this is whether there is anything seasonal that you may not be aware of, that you have to pay particular attention to, or if there is a stronger voice than others directing your output.
- *Who is the most important client?*—Every company has that one special client that they will bend over backward for; getting a line of sight of who this is will make sure you don't accidentally step over any legacy goodwill.
- *Which client placed the most overhead on your department?*—Conversely, which client gave them the most trouble, either in the amount of time they took or the complexity of their systems? This could be a particular feature that was developed for just them that at the time was a good idea but has created many headaches going forward.
- *Who in your team did you rely the most on?*—Probably one of the most important questions, this gives you an insight into who they relied on to keep the lights on. So, when it comes to evaluating the team, you should take special consideration for this person or persons.

It is important to give the outgoing CTO all the due respect and credit they deserve (even if they left a horrendous mess that you now have to resolve). You want them to know that you will honor their legacy, and should you ever need to reach out, they will feel good to take your call. This is why it is important that you never disparage them, no matter how safe you think the circle you are talking to is. You never want them to hear, from whatever avenue, that you are saying one thing to their face and another to the team.

Yes, it is common decency, but too often the existing CTO has cut off all opportunities to lean on historical knowledge by simply running their mouth off in what they think is a safe environment. Resist the temptation, even if others are quick to point the finger of blame.

2.4.3 *Discover the team*

A CTO is only as good as the team around them, and to discover just how good the former CTO was, you can evaluate the team they assembled. If the CTO had been there for a long time, and they personally hired everyone, you may have a loyalty problem to crack. The team may see you as an enemy, someone who ousted their beloved leader. The key to winning this moral battle is to not make too many changes quickly. Keep celebrating the previous CTO, while slowly making subtle changes. With each change, you let the team get used to it, until they wonder how they ever managed without you. Successful CTOs can turn around a complete team using this technique while still honoring the previous management.

Another problem you may encounter, particularly common in founder-led companies where the CTO had been there from the start, is that the team is relatively weak technically but yet paid way above their equivalent salary working elsewhere, having been rewarded for longevity and not achievement. This area of inflated salaries is addressed in the recruitment chapter because it is a very common problem. For the technical side, assume they have not yet met their full potential, and design a program that will allow them to show what they are capable of. Do not write them off too soon, but give them a runway to show you they are worthy of being on your team. Maybe they have just not had the right inspirational leader to show them the way.

Overall, when taking over from an existing CTO, try not to make too many changes too quickly, and take the time to learn the environment, who the key players are, and build bridges. Things don't need immediate attention, and you have time to properly assess the situation and plan accordingly where you are going to put your mark and move the company forward.

2.5 *Presenting to the board*

Depending on the size and stage of growth of your company, formal board meetings may be held regularly throughout the year. This is not your typical company or project meeting and shouldn't be treated as such. Nor is it a meeting of all the C levels in the company. Most of the time, it is only the CEO and CFO that attend the full meeting from the company, with the rest of the attendees being investors.

In this section, we are going to go through what you need to be considerate of and how you prepare, should you be invited to participate. It can be a very intimidating experience because the decisions made in this meeting can be far reaching and lasting, and, therefore, it is something you don't want to get wrong.

> **DEFINITION** A *board meeting* is a formal gathering of directors, investors, and guests, held on a periodic basis (usually quarterly) that has a set of rules and processes to review the strategic direction, major initiatives, and financial well-being of the company. Board meetings have a set agenda with formal minutes taken that are logged as the official record and reviewed at the start of the next meeting. If anything needs to be voted on, this is the environment where this happens, with the weight of each vote detailed in the shareholdings.

2.5.1 Know your audience

The members of the board are not typically involved in the day-to-day running of the company but, instead, focus on the longer-term goals and making sure the company is still going in the right direction. They are usually major investors or shareholders, representatives of an investment fund (e.g., a private equity partner), and outside invited board members who have experience and deep domain knowledge useful for guidance.

Although this group may know one another, more often than not, this is the only time they all get together in the same room. They will not be very technically literate (at least not to your level) because they are more focused on the business side of the company. Getting intel on this group of people is not difficult because they are usually included on most company About Us web pages or have a profile on LinkedIn, giving you all the hooks to do your own searching.

Also, speak with your CEO/CFO to gain a little more insight into each of their personalities. Which one is the silent one who rarely speaks? Which one is the snarly one who questions everything? Which areas do each particularly have a fondness for? Which one has the real authority to make decisions? Knowing who you are about to present to will make your time with them more productive and prevent you from making any rookie mistakes out of the gate. Treat the preparation like you would for an interview.

2.5.2 Format of the meeting

Board meetings are formally documented as minutes. These are not like the output of courtroom stenographers where every word is captured, but instead, minutes capture all decisions, who committed to any deliverables, and the results of any votes. The minutes of the previous meeting are reviewed at the top of the current meeting. Each meeting has a formal agenda, which is the running order, and for the majority of board meetings, it is usually a slide deck that has been shared with all attendees a couple of days beforehand.

Meetings can go on for a couple of hours, right through to being a multiday event, with an evening dinner in between. If you are asked to be part of it, assume you are not going to be there for the full thing. You will be invited to come in at a designated time, present your piece, then leave. You may also be invited to the evening dinner, or premeeting drinks, which is usually an informal meet-and-greet affair for everyone to get to know one another.

You may be invited to attend the full meeting. For these, you are expected to be engaged in the full discussion, contributing where necessary. This is not an opportunity for you to check email or chat while it is not your area. You have been asked to attend for a reason, so give them the reason your contribution is invaluable.

NOTE Devin Mathews, founding partner of ParkerGale Capital, notes how rare it is for a CTO to actively participate, but one that asks questions, supports, and helps their peers is hugely appreciated and usually invited back.

Your CEO will be able to help explain the format if there is any special thing the board does. Now, it is fair to say, the CEO is probably the most nervous, because this is the meeting where they are rated by those who can replace them. So, anything you do will reflect on them.

2.5.3   *Your role*

You are being invited to present to the board for a specific reason. That reason is one you should not guess at, but talk in depth with your CEO about what it is they are looking for. The CTO is not often invited (unless you are a full technology company), but when they are, it is for a very narrow reason, usually around major platform initiatives or product changes. Keep your presentation at a high level, and do not go into too much detail. Focus on the customer and the business, and always relate everything you present back to one of those constituents.

Provide context for what you are presenting, remind the board where you are supposed to be at this point, and if you are not, explain why; do not simply shrug it off. You are not going to win their hearts and respect if you just say everything takes longer and costs

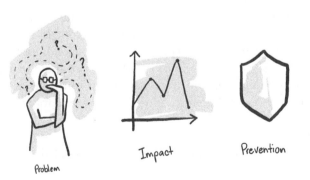

Problem   Impact   Prevention

more and that is just the nature of technology. Be transparent on why things are on or off track.

You can also be asked to present to the board if there has been a major outage or security breach that requires more explanation. The tone of this presentation is a little different from a normal one, because this is one of those times you may have to fall on your sword and take the responsibility that your office dictates. Present these types in the PIP (problem, impact, prevention) format as follows:

- *Problem*—What happened to cause the problem? Explain in business terms they can relate to.
- *Impact*—What was the impact on our clients/employees/partners?
- *Prevention*—What has been learned and instigated to prevent repeat issues?

Whatever you are being asked to contribute, review extensively with your CEO so they are fully aware of what it is you are about to offer. They are best to judge if you have the right level of detail for the audience and do not like surprises, particularly in this forum.

2.5.4 The dos and don'ts

Here are some pointers to help make your board participation successful:

- Know the agenda of the meeting, and understand the overall message your CEO is trying to convey.
- Do not disagree or correct your CEO/CFO if this is not your area. Make a note of it, and follow up afterward. There may be a context you are missing.
- Keep your presentation on point and focused. Find ways to explain complicated initiatives in a way your listeners can relate to.
- Don't be intimidated into making any rash decisions. Take their question, and commit to following up with an answer within a couple of days.
- If reporting bad news, never blame, disparage, or name anyone.
- Be prepared to go into detail and field questions that may come out of left field and not feel on point. You may not be aware of what else has been discussed.
- Do not take your laptop, or use it sparingly if you have to give a demo, closing the lid as soon as you are done. Hiding behind a laptop, pretending to take notes, looks like you are disengaged. Take notes the good old-fashioned way, with a pen and paper, to show you are engaged.
- If you are not involved in the whole board meeting, leave as soon as you are finished and questions have been fielded. Ask the CEO (or chairperson) if it is okay to leave; don't hang around and be told to leave.
- Be on your guard in the informal meetings. These people are very adept at making you open up and tell them something you probably shouldn't.

Although board meetings can be extremely stressful and formal affairs, they can be fun and informative at the same time. Don't ever treat them as routine, and relish the opportunity they afford you to gain visibility into a very influential and important group of people.

> **View from the other side**
>
> *Making a good impression*
>
> As a founding partner of a private equity firm, Devin Mathews is no stranger to board meetings. His popular podcast, *PE Funcast*, has a number of episodes on how CEOs, CFOs, and CTOs can make a good board presentation. When I asked him what a CTO can do, his answer was simple: "Don't just tell, show." Too many times in his experience, the CTO does not show the product for which they are responsible—it's like owning a chocolate factory but never getting to taste the end result. Demonstrate progress and let the product show where future development or improvements needs to be made. They say a picture can say a thousand words, but a software demo can speak a thousand slides. It also gives the CTO an opportunity to show their pride in their team's effort, simply through their body language—a useful side effect for those struggling to find the right words.

2.6   Communications

It is important to set your stall out early and think about how you are going to present your office to the rest of the company as well as to the outside. This is an area that is often overlooked by the new CTO, and some struggle to find the right cadence or opportunity to use a potentially great opportunity to build alliances and bridges. This section addresses the sort of things you should be communicating and how you can start.

2.6.1   Internal

The goal of communicating with the company as a whole isn't to make yourself look intelligent or show off your knowledge. It is to help others better succeed in their roles and to demystify what it is your group does, making you and your team more approachable in the process.

A number of reasons you can use to send off a company-wide email/Slack/Team message follow:

- *A new release of your software*—If you are releasing either an internal or client-facing update, take your release notes and contextualize them into terms that are meaningful to the company, without assuming any buzzword knowledge. Give people talking points that they can easily convey to customers.
- *If something has gone wrong*—This is an area that should never be ignored. If something has gone wrong, no matter whose fault it is, get out in front of the messaging, taking one or more of the PIP strategies. People will start to trust and respect that you will be open and honest and be in a stronger position to answer any queries they get from outside.
- *Something technology related in the mainstream news*—This one is a little more nuanced. If something has been published, say a security breach or hyping up new technology, in the mainstream news, chances are, most people will not really know what it means at the same level as you. So, if it's at all related to anything you do, take the time to write up an explanation in terms they can understand and send it out.

Another thing you may consider is to have an open invitation to everyone in the company to any of the brown-bag lunchtime sessions (where you bring your lunch and eat together) you run that are geared around teaching or introducing new technology. You just never know who you might attract who may be a potential hire for you in the future.

Helping contextualize

Security breaches

There was a period of time when certain security breaches hit the likes of the BBC and CNN. There was little detail on the how, but the technical news outlets were giving some detail, and in this instance, it was due to someone not securing the S3 file storage service from AWS. The mainstream news suggested the cloud wasn't secure and we should be wary. Taking this opportunity, I wrote an explanation of what they had done, explaining that they had left all the files outside of the gates instead of inside, and it wasn't the fault of the cloud provider, but of those managing the security. Knowing this question may be asked by clients to our account managers, I also noted the processes we put in place to make sure that could never happen with us because we didn't allow anyone to create such file spaces and we had tools monitoring for that sort of open security. People will tend to remember this far more than if I had just sent this out of the blue with no context because it was relatable to something they were reading and seeing in the news. As the old saying goes, never let a crisis go to waste. If something is on the minds of people already and you can help contextualize it, then do it.

Whatever path is open to you, be sure to use as few buzzwords and technical jargon as possible. If your department is quite large, then encourage or ask one of your team to send out the bulletin instead, particularly if it aligns more with them. This is a great way to have more voices be heard and show you are not just a single person but a team of highly skilled individuals.

2.6.2 *External*

You should also consider communicating outside of the company. Look outward because crafting your message for a nontechnical audience helps you hone your messaging skills. This helps to promote both your own brand and that of your company but also helps you meet new people and attract new talent to your team.

Speaking at local user groups is a wonderful way to get to know

the local community and learn who is who. I recall one client that had weak in-house SQL Server knowledge. They took a small group out to the local SQL Server user group. We sat and listened to some speakers. We got to know our fellow attendees and discovered a couple of local companies that ended up helping us. We saw them firsthand before we even considered engaging them. The same can work in reverse for you.

How many times have you looked up something on the internet and discovered the key to a specific problem you have been chasing, thanks to someone posting to Stack Overflow or some other site? Now ask yourself, have you paid that back? What content have you contributed to the common intellectual library so others may learn from what you have discovered? It is highly likely that most people reading this have probably taken more from the library than they have put in. You are not alone.

Consider empowering your team to post answers on Stack Overflow, or run a company blog that helps promote things you have discovered, particularly if it is something you have learned about an open source piece of software. Take care not to post anything confidential. The topic of open sourcing code is covered later in the book, but this is another avenue that can be used to your advantage.

Developing external connections is easy to do and, although it may seem a waste of time, you just never know what it will yield in the future, whether learning of new vendors and providers or finding that next hire. To do nothing means nothing will come from that avenue. As the old joke goes, *Why do I never win the lottery? Well, you could start by buying a ticket.*

2.7 *Internal politics*

At some point, you are going to come up against office politics both within your own group (which is more controllable) and at a company level. I suspect you have heard a number of times that a company is just one big team and they have no politics, only to discover they really are a dysfunctional group and have plenty of inner issues—they just don't call it "politics."

This section goes through some of the common scenarios and calls out some techniques to help you handle them. This is not by any means an exhaustive look, and it is recommended to read some books specific to team psychology.

2.7.1 *The major types*

Office politics can be defined as the absence of data that is replaced by emotion. We work in an environment where our goal is making things better for our customers and employees while creating wealth. You would think with everyone rowing in the same direction, there wouldn't be time for conflict or personal emotions. We're only human, and emotionally led sentinels who sometimes forget that getting on with our fellow person is one of the best things we can do for our own well-being as well as others'. Let's take a look at some of the types of emotions or politics you can often encounter.

FIEFDOMS

A common form of tribal behavior often found in large organizations is the fiefdom, a term from the early 1800s that describes the control and assertion by a single person over a given area. In business, this can translate to one or more persons who serve to satisfy their own goals, first and foremost, before considering others in a semi-loose alliance. Like an unofficial club, where membership is exclusive and no rules ever written, it is hard to prove their existence, yet their presence can be felt.

These can be toxic to any company in any guise, no matter how innocent they seem. Even if it is innocent and it's just good friends looking out for one another, others will perceive there is more to it and start making conclusions.

BULLYING

It's hard to believe bullying is still a thing, with mature adults in a professional setting, but it happens more often than not and comes in many forms. It is important to recognize it as different from being assertive. A bully will often exhibit inconsistent decisions or actions and be intimidating, irrational, and very rude.

> ### The shouty persona
> One of the worst examples I witnessed was in a meeting when the then CEO of a company barged into a conference call (I was one of the callers) and completely chewed out the CTO, cursing and swearing, about something that wasn't even that important or emotional. The CEO had no idea who was on the call—it could have been a client. In this case, the private equity firm, upon learning of this outburst, was not at all impressed and immediately fired them. Turns out this CEO had a history of such bullying, and it was rather unfortunate (for them) that the whole thing was recorded as part of the conference call, leaving the CEO with no excuse.

PASSIVE AGGRESSION

This is a form of aggression that expresses itself when people don't deal with the underlying issue directly. Instead, they exhibit detrimental behavior, like dragging their feet, expressing different views from others, or being resistant to the issue at hand.

An example of this can be when someone disagrees with an action being taken, fails to speak up, but voices their approval to the group as a whole. Outside, they undermine the initiative, noting how it is doomed to failure and they wouldn't have done it that way had it been their decision.

INFORMATION HOARDER

This is the person who believes that if they share valuable information with others, then their role somehow will be diminished and, therefore, sharing puts them at risk of termination. This type of person is discussed in later chapters, but it can be frustrating when trying to navigate a given issue where they are getting in the way instead of helping.

2.7.2 Mitigating politics

As technologists, we like processes with clear steps—do this, and then that will happen. Dealing with the emotions of others offers no if-then-else logic. There is no foolproof way to deal with naughtiness, but we can try to mitigate it. When someone comes up with a magic wand that makes office politics disappear, they will be a very rich individual. Until then, let's look at some ways to make life a little easier:

- *Recognize it in yourself*—Do any of these traits feel familiar in your own personality? Before expecting a change in others, we must first start with ourselves. Ask a trusted colleague or friend for feedback.
- *Call it out*—When someone is presenting themselves in a threatening or passive-aggressive manner, call it out there and then. With a simple phrase like, "Wanna try that again, this time without the aggression/sarcasm?" I have found I can disarm the most hostile of situations with a little humor and directness because it shows you are not intimidated.
- *Avoid ambiguity*—Try to stay out of the abstract as much as possible when dealing with people who exhibit this behavior. Ambiguity gives them room to change their mind but pretend it was what they were wanting the whole time.
- *Clarify and confirm*—When someone is in a shouting or intimidating mode, seek clarification and specific examples of their grievance. Do not move or concede on a single point until they clarify precisely what it is they are angry about and you have confirmed you have understood that. Emotions and stress can sometimes get the better of us all, and sometimes being calm and collected is all it takes.
- *Welcome criticism*—If someone criticizes you or someone in your team, deal with specifics. Ask for an example of precisely the issue at hand. By pushing back for detail, you take the natural urge to be defensive out of the situation, until you understand what it is you are dealing with.

No one is perfect. We all make mistakes and sometimes let emotions creep into our dealings with our colleagues. All of these techniques are just means to try to bring some rationality into an emotional situation and get to the root of the difficulty. This doesn't always work, sadly.

If you find yourself in a situation where nothing seems to be working and you are convinced you are not the problem, fear not: there is a solution—leave. Life is too short to be in an environment where you are not happy, productive, and making a difference. It is not a failure if you have tried.

24-hour rule

Jeff Hanner, data warehouse manager (retired), had a wonderful way of making sure things didn't fester and be allowed to erode relationships over time. He gave people 24 hours from the time of the so-called infraction to address it head on; after that, it was never to be mentioned again. This little rule headed off many misunderstandings then and there. It's a rule I have since adopted myself, even if the other person doesn't know it—if someone has wronged me (or, at least, I think they have), I will let it go if I have not taken steps within the window to better understand any wrongdoing.

2.8 Change management

The art of introducing change to any organization is a whole discipline in itself. Often I have come up against initiatives that have failed because an overly eager CTO has failed to communicate and allow the business to warm up to the change they are facing. The success here is to recognize that change is going to affect the whole business, and to start, you need the support of the CEO and all the department leads to make this a successful switch.

By bringing together your senior management and communicating the impact and potential short-term downsides, you are setting everyone up for a less painful change. Do not blindside or misrepresent the potential disruption that change can bring. This is why the support of your leadership team is crucial.

Stephen Tallamy, CTO of EditShare, notes that "each functional leader can have specific areas of ownership but can easily see the areas required across the business to be successful and can help each other line up for success. This alignment at the leadership level permeates through the company and can really reduce the noise when making significant change."

The following will address some of the things we have to be mindful of to make sure our projects and initiatives succeed.

2.8.1 Boiling the frog

Have you heard the old proverb on how to boil a frog? If you place a frog into a pan of boiling water, it will instantly reject the heat and jump straight out. Instead, if you place the frog in a pan of cold water and slowly turn up the heat, the frog will adapt and adjust, and before too long, it will be sitting in a pan of boiling water.

Leaving aside the ethical treatment of amphibians, this is a good way to think of how to manage your change. If you release a new piece of software and force everyone to use it, without much training or prior warning, they will revolt and jump straight out of the pan.

This may seem counterintuitive to us technologists. We embrace and welcome change. Our industry naturally reinvents itself every five years, and we are trained to work with this cycle. Most (nontechnology) people, however, don't like too much change. They simply want to do a good job, get paid, provide for their family, and know they can come back tomorrow and do the same thing again. Any sort of change will be a disruption to this cycle.

We must slowly introduce change in a way that feels like we are slowly turning up the heat where most people won't notice the change in their environment. As a business, we can't afford the inconvenience that too much change at once can bring to servicing our clients. Therefore, we want to do this in a way that isn't too much too soon.

In many ways, the agile way of project management (an area that is discussed in a later chapter) promotes the release-a-small-release-often mentality, which lends itself beautifully to the goal of slowly boiling our frog. We are giving people time to warm up to the new change.

Real example

Microsoft Windows 10

If you want a master class on change management and slowly boiling the frog, look at Microsoft and what they have done with Windows 10. Instead of big changes, (3.1 → NT → 2000 → XP → Vista → 7 → 8), Windows 10, released in 2015, is still with us. Slow, incremental changes have drastically changed the program over the years, but because it still feels like the same version, we accept it willingly as a nonevent. They are slowly boiling the frog (i.e., us) without us realizing it. Granted, at the time of writing, they have since moved to Windows 11, with the cycle starting again: small-big changes.

2.8.2 *Excitement committee*

When you are involved in any project that has far-reaching consequences across one or more departments, you must bring everyone along with you. You can't simply turn on the switch and force everyone to do a different process. Each department has its own business rules and workflow, and everyone in that department knows how that works. However poor or inefficient it may be, it largely works because clients are being serviced.

Kelley Powell, CEO of the MacLaurin Group, believes every large initiative that has the potential for a lot of change should create what she refers to as the "excitement committee." This is a collection of representatives from across the business who are part of the project from the start. They are your diplomats and advocates as you develop to make sure you are still heading in the right direction. These people are your prerequisite to success, notes Powell, because they will be able to describe the change that is coming way better to their own group than you could possibly.

Communication early and often helps prepare for your coming change. Do not be tempted to overpromise and have people believe this will solve all their problems. Likewise, do not disparage the current way of working, because this will create resentment, for, as ugly as a baby may be, the mother believes it is beautiful.

2.8.3 *Valley of anguish*

There comes a time in any large project's delivery where the fear and disruption are so great, leaders begin to question whether they should continue. Everyone starts out excited at the potential, so you get much contribution and support.

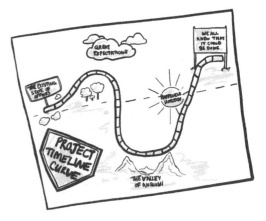

Then as the project continues, things are unearthed that challenge some of the easy wins you were looking for and take a little more time to work through. As they are identified and resolved, time marches on, and the business may start getting a little impatient.

James Milbery, founding partner of ParkerGale Capital, calls this phenomenon the "valley of anguish." Milbery argues that technology leaders need to be fully aware of this cycle and be ready to help the business come out the other side for a win. In his experience, the successful CTOs are those who can truly appreciate the impact that any change can have on a business, and they work with the leaders of the various departments to minimize that anguish as much as possible.

Milbery is also a fan of the "burn the ships" strategy when a project gains enough traction. This strategy made sure people couldn't return to their homeland upon reaching new shores—leaders would physically burn the ships to force people to adapt to the new world. In software terms, this is identifying that moment in time when the older/existing systems are turned off and can no longer be used.

The last thing you want is to be maintaining two systems, causing more support and problems, confusing all. As part of your change management strategy, you need to identify the criteria when you can "burn the ships" and get all business leaders to agree on it.

2.8.4 Consequences

Change is an important and crucial aspect of the evolution of any company. However, we have to appreciate the consequences that change can have on a business. It is more than just introducing a new piece of software; it is about challenging all the business processes that have been established, the training of employees, the onboarding of clients, and the inherit company know-how that has been built up over the years.

Build a change process into your vision and remember the frog—it really doesn't enjoy being dropped into boiling water.

Summary

- Having a good working relationship with your CEO. Knowing their motives and criteria for success will make the job of aligning your projects for you to be successful easier.
- Meeting with them regularly will help you stay aligned and give you instant feedback to make any corrective actions needed to stay successful.
- Communicate in a language that will help them succeed and communicate with others upstream without getting bogged down in details.
- See your CEO as your partner, not necessarily your boss, making their job easier by giving them the confidence you are dealing in specifics and not just winging it.

- Be mindful of the cost and expenditure of your department and projects by working closely with the CFO so you are never blindsided.
- Getting to know the other departments and their heads will give you a full picture of all the parts that make the engine run and allow you and your team to be more sympathetic to their success criteria and how you can support them.
- If you are taking over from a CTO, celebrate their success, and never disparage their decisions. There is no point in dwelling on the past: you are not responsible for that, but for the future, you are.
- When asked to present to the board, be prepared, and get involved. This is not a chore or a distraction but an honor to have the position to influence the direction of the company.
- Knowing how to communicate with the company and with clients will give you more perspective and allow you to be more approachable and take away the mysticism of technology.
- Recognizing the typical types of internal politics that can arise will help you head them off before they become part of the culture and will allow you to transact openly and transparently.
- People dislike change, but as part of your remit, you are at the forefront of continually improving systems and products. Building in the time it will take to bring others along with you will yield a higher acceptance level.

Checklist

How many of the following items can you lay claim to having covered?

- Identified the type of CEO you have and understand what detail they prefer and how best to work with them
- Booked regularly scheduled meetings with your CEO
- Have a good working relationship with your CFO, with regular updates on your budgetary needs
- Created allegiances with other peer leaders across the business and understand their goals and issues
- Understand the internal power dynamics and politics that power the company's decision-making process
- Prepared for a board presentation, knowing the board members and their drivers
- Created a cadence on how you will communicate to the company as a whole as CTO
- Got a handle on the needs of the business when it comes to change and how best to introduce a difference in working

Visionary planning

The CEO is charged with not only running the company but leading the company. Leading is looking forward, anticipating the needs of the market, and taking steps to be out in front instead of being reactionary to external events. Your role as CTO, the leader of enterprise technology, is no different. It is not enough to merely keep the lights on; you have to make sure they stay on and continue to shine bright for a long time, irrespective of what else is going on. The company is looking to you to make sure they are capable of delivering value and growth for your clients. Taking

45

time to create a vision, hone it, plot the course, and communicate that journey will give the business the confidence it needs to know they are in good hands with you.

To help illustrate the concepts, let us introduce our fictional company, HomeMax PLC. Let's say the company has been around for over 40 years, providing home warranty insurance for residential homeowners. They are running on legacy technology, built in a mixture of RPG and Cobol, all driven through terminal software against a Db2 database on AS/400s. They have never really had a formal CTO, with the founder instead directing a small team of developers. They have recently been purchased by a private equity firm, who are keen to expand their market and have brought in their first CTO to drive the technology transformation.

3.1   *The grand vision*

Your organization most likely already has a vision or mission statement. The difference is subtle but important—the vision statement is the goal of the mission, the end result, whereas the mission statement can be considered the action-orientated vision statement, detailing why an organization exists, what types of services and products they are offering, and what makes them unique.

From the field

Example vision statements

To give you a hint of a good vision statement, let's look at some from larger well-known corporations. LinkedIn sets its stall out with "Create economic opportunity for every member of the global workforce," whereas Disney has "to entertain, inform and inspire people around the globe through the power of unparalleled storytelling," and Microsoft has "a computer on every desk and in every home." What is common to these is that all include very easy-to-understand, jargon-free statements. Our Home-Max company's vision statement could be "Gaining peace of mind about your most valuable asset."

A CTO should have their own version of a vision statement that is focused on the output of their group yet supports the overall vision and mission of the company. This is called the "grand vision." This is what you are working toward, why you are heading in that direction, and will define what you and the business will be able to do once you get there (a small detail a lot of people often overlook). Although it is great to say you are heading to a given point, it is also important to remind people what you are going to do on arrival.

Your vision should include two to five years out from where you are now. Anything longer will be hard for people to relate to, because the business may change or pivot or even be sold before your vision is realized. A good vision is one that can be delivered and celebrated. You never want to be the leader for whom "tomorrow never comes." Of course, your vision will need to evolve and change as the business and the technology landscape changes, and how this is accomplished will be explored later.

Important to note here: if you are taking over from an existing CTO who has crafted a well-oiled machine, your vision here may be to simply keep this going in the same direction, to continue the evolution. Fortunately (or unfortunately, depending on your viewpoint) our industry never stands still, and there is always room for improvement at every turn. You will have plenty of opportunities to add your improvements.

When you are putting together your vision, you need to be conscious of two different audiences: the business and your own group. The business wants to know what your vision means for them, in terminology that is devoid of as many buzzwords as possible. Consider this the "what" (and "why") part of your vision. Your own group wants to hear that, too, but they will want some meat on the bones, a lot more detail, and how that is going to be achieved. This is the "how" part of your vision.

3.1.1 The "what"/"why" part

The business is interested in what your vision means for them. This includes the rest of the company outside of your group: board members, investors, and even clients. If your vision is not able to speak to each of these groups and give them a benefit, then your vision isn't any more than a project goal (or just paying down technical debt). A vision can speak to the economic benefits, the major features of a platform, or the opportunities that can be opened up.

From the field

No data left behind

In one of the portfolio companies for which I was CTO, I had to define what my vision was going to be after observing the business and their values (a data-led decision culture). To support the vision of the CEO, I focused our group on making sure that the business had all the possible data available to them for making informed decisions, so I came up with the simple statement, "No data left behind." I even had the art department create a huge banner in the font and style of *Back to the Future*—it looked stunning (handy having a full art department in house). Given how cheap data storage has become, there were no more excuses for not logging or retaining data. This was something that had bitten the company in the past, and going forward, everything we did was to support that statement and make data accessible to the business. Every time we released a new feature or version of the platform, we could easily speak to the execution of our vision and how it was opening up understanding and opportunities as more and more data was amassed.

A vision statement does not need to be overly complicated or nuanced. It must say that those listening can internalize it and see how it will help them. For our HomeMax company steeped in legacy technology with a desire to move to a web and mobile environment, instead of relying on their call staff to field every claim and update, the vision statement could be "A self-driven, customer data–centric platform."

3.1.2   The "how" part

You and your group have to deliver on your vision. This is where you need to go into more detail on what it means and how things will change/adapt to be in support of that vision. A successful vision is one that everyone understands and can build into each area they are responsible for. For every decision that is made by you and your team, ask whether this takes you a step closer or a step farther away from your vision. Is the new hire you are about to make, the contract with that service vendor, the technology stack decision, moving you closer to your goal?

Your vision should excite your group, be something for them to get behind. To test the commitment of your technical team, ask "Do they [your group] believe in your vision?" If they do not, then selling your vision to the business is going to be nearly impossible. If the very people who are down in the trenches, working daily on client problems, bugs, or feature initiatives can't get behind your vision, then chances are you've got your vision wrong, or you have not articulated or broken it down to a point that feels real.

From the field

A cloudy vision

One CTO I encountered was proud of their vision statement: "We're integrating machine learning into our analysis." A grand vision for sure, but upon questioning him, it lacked detail. They had not thought about what it meant to the business and how their clients could benefit. His own group was not told of the "how" part (the "why" was already missing), so they were left chasing a shadow, trying to solve a problem that didn't exist. The issue here was that the CTO had jumped onto the machine learning bandwagon because it sounded cool. He knew he had a lot of data in his databases and thought this would help his career. There was no thought as to whether this was the right thing to do. New technologies are good for the right application—not for everyone or everything (don't get me started on the number of blockchain visions we have had to shatter!).

3.1.3 Define success

One of the beautiful things about a clear and well-articulated vision is that it gives you something to run toward and, importantly, rate your own progress against. A CTO without a vision is a captain without a destination—you have to know where you are going to know when you have arrived. By defining your vision, you can start to place smaller milestones as part of that and treat each one of those as small wins and celebrate those with your group accordingly.

Although a lot of CTOs don't have visions, the ones who do get a little fuzzy when probed on what their success looks like. They speak in generalities with wide-ranging statements. It is a good idea to firm up on your success criteria so there is no dispute when you reach it.

Let's look at some examples of some visionary statements with breakdowns, with some of these applying to our HomeMax company. These are supporting the overarching vision statement as advertised to the business, which is to give the customer more control.

Table 3.1   Visionary statement examples

Statement	What	How	Success
Deprecate all hardware and move exclusively to the cloud.	Remove the overhead of maintaining physical assets so we can move to a pay-as-you-go model that will accelerate the onboarding of new clients.	Stop purchasing hardware, start learning cloud alternatives, and identify the areas where we can have early wins without putting the business at risk.	When the last server is turned off and the reliance on the office/data center is zero.
Move toward an API-driven architecture.	Make our data/services available in a secure and reliable fashion, which lets our customers directly integrate with us without transferring files.	Identify the touchpoints our clients need to send and receive data, as well as how we move data around internally, to free ourselves up from data overhead.	Client interacting without needing to send or attach files; self-servicing using the API.
Replace the legacy system.	Move the system to a modern, supported architecture that will enable us to react to the requests that clients have been asking for with significantly less effort.	Extract all the business rules and responsibilities of this system, and then start designing one or more systems to take over in a phased approach.	When the legacy system is finally turned off, supporting no more clients.
Empower the client with a modern web and mobile interface.	Remove our call center from managing all interactions, instead letting customers do it themselves.	Using a modern web framework, talking securely to backend APIs.	Seeing a dramatic reduction in the number of calls being actively answered.

The rest of the chapter goes deeper into planning and how that supports your overarching vision.

3.2   *Engaging with clients*

As you begin working on your vision, one of the most important constituents you should have first and foremost in your mind is the client. This starts by identifying who your client is. A client is the person or group that consumes your primary output. In large corporations, this may not be the company's main client but an internal group. Nevertheless, whoever they are, they are the reason for your existence.

Understanding your client, their motives, their wants, and their goals will help you better deliver your product. These are standard business school principles. Yet many assume this methodology is the exclusive purview of the sales and marketing group, to be applied at the company level. Many don't see the parallels that operate at a departmental level, especially one like the CTO group, who is responsible for the technology with which the client will interact.

3.2.1   *Know your client*

Depending on the company, you may not get direct access to your clients. Instead you have to go through an account manager or sales engineer. This is probably a good thing, especially for the new CTO who maybe isn't versed in talking with the client. The last thing the CEO wants is running the risk of losing a large account because an overeager CTO has promised too much or let slip something they shouldn't.

The best piece of advice when it comes to talking with clients is don't jump on anything—just listen. Offer no solutions, no promises, no assurances; just listen. You want to get to know how your client interacts with your systems and discover any pain points. A good set of questions to get you started includes these:

- What system/service is the primary point of contact with our company?
- If you exchange data, where do you source that data?
- What happens to the exchanged data once you receive it?
- Typically, how do you use the service each day?
- What is your team relying on to be available for them to be successful?
- What aspect of your processes are you looking to improve or change in the near future?

The answers to these questions will shape how clients see you, and what may seem intuitive to you and your team may be difficult or cumbersome to others.

For the given sample setup of questions, let's look at some answers that would apply to our HomeMax company from the perspective of a homeowner, shown here:

- I can only interact through the call center helpline.
- If I have to change or update my information, I have to read it out over the phone.
- I have no idea whether the agent has received my data until I get a confirmation at renewal time.
- I need to interact only when something has gone wrong and I need to start a claim. I also need to call regarding the status of a claim.

- I want the call agent to answer in a timely fashion.
- I want to be able to make changes myself, upload photos to support my claim, and look up on the status without having to make a single call.

Clearly, the end customer has an expectation that they should be able to drive a lot of the experience themselves at their pace and time. Not unusual, but what this tells the CTO is that we aren't necessarily at the stage yet of needing to offer new products or features. Instead, we need to remove the friction of interacting with the company by going through the phone.

From the field

Solve the problem, not the symptom

For one client we worked with, the relationship with their clients was top notch, with an over 95% retention rate. The account manager was happy, as was the client they dealt with. The layer below wasn't quite as pleased—too much management over-head was the cry. They had a high turnover of temporary staff that would log in to the client's portal, and the time it took to set up and dismantle user accounts was a pain. The new CTO reached out to introduce themselves, as part of taking over. Upon hearing this complaint, he promised nothing but started asking other clients what their experience was like. Before long, he had single sign-on as part of his vision so clients didn't have to worry about user management.

Additionally, knowing where your client is going will be hugely beneficial to your vision and plans going forward. Say, for example, you discover that the majority of your clients are based on the Microsoft stack and their plans are to move into the Microsoft Azure cloud service. Although you may not have made any decisions as to which cloud provider you are going to use, it does make a lot of sense to go where your clients are, to remove as much friction as possible. The point is, you wouldn't know this without first talking to and getting to know your clients.

3.2.2 *Your counterpart*

For larger accounts, it is recommended getting to know your counterpart—their CTO or VP of engineering, if it makes sense. One of the biggest advantages is that this relationship creates a channel to resolve any issues before they become larger issues, and it also gives you an insight into their thinking and plans. Using this relationship, you are best positioned to make sure your vision and plans support theirs.

This special relationship can yield positive outcomes at a time when confusion runs rampant. How many times have you been in a situation where you have been told a client has asked for feature X, and when you hear of this request, it baffles you? This request has come down the chain and been reviewed by product development, and this is the only way you are assured. Yet something doesn't quite sit right with you. Who do you ask?

Remember the Telephone game you may have played as a kid? Sitting in a circle, you whisper something into the ear of the person on your left, and they have to whisper it to their left and so on, until it gets back to you. What you hear back in your right ear is not what you originally said. Yet as it was passed from person to person, they have interpreted and used their words to relay what they thought they heard. Business is just one big Telephone game.

This is often how client requests find their way to you and why your knowledge of how they interact and your special relationship can kick in to save the day to seek the clarity that your senses were alerting you to. Sometimes you have to ask them the basic question: what are you trying to solve?

Clients are not mythical creatures that are always right and must be obeyed. They are people with businesses like yours, trying to solve problems for the benefit of their clients. Whatever they are wrestling with may become your problem, too.

A situation where this typically crops up is when clients go through growth spurts and find themselves now being more scrutinized, for example, requiring compliance or accreditations as they reach a certain level or enter a new geographic market. Helping a client not do harm is probably one of the most important and beneficial side effects of being their partner.

From the field

I worked with one client whose primary data exchange was creating a file and then emailing it to the client on a daily basis. The main issue was that this file had a lot of sensitive data in it going over a transport mechanism that is inherently insecure. The client was adamant they needed it by email. The CTO at the company was still new and didn't feel he had the authority to refuse this request to the client. Once I had regained control over my heart and brought its rate down to normal upon hearing of this, I gave the CTO the necessary talking points for opening up the conversation with the client to understand why they felt they needed this information by email. Turned out, the email was just a means for the user to easily save the information to a network share on their side. Because the user was already interacting with their portal each morning, the CTO added a file download feature, so they could fetch it from there instead. Everyone was much happier because data was now being logged and transferred over a secure channel, with no one losing face.

Some clients will be more technologically advanced than you; some will not. For those ahead of you, aspire to be more like them and learn from their vision. For those behind you, find ways to help them so they don't accidentally open themselves up to unnecessary exposure.

Your vision should incorporate, or at least give some consideration to, the downstream consumption of your services. This way, you are staying relevant and preventing potential headaches before they happen.

3.3 Long-term planning

As I have noted, if your vision can be executed in a few months, then it isn't a vision but a project. A vision is a multiproject endeavor that may take many years to complete. Visions are typically revolutionary in nature but can be evolutionary if the company is in the midst of transformational change.

Although not unheard of, it is rare for a project to be so large that it takes many years before you have any sort of deliverable. If you find yourself in this situation, assume you have missed something and go back and challenge yourself to find smaller deliverables, even if that means you have to take a slightly different path.

The following section looks at what it takes to start turning your vision into an actionable plan that will be palatable to the business.

3.3.1 Timing is everything

Large visions take a lot of effort to plan, schedule, and implement. A good vision comes from necessity as opposed to something to do. Good examples are reimagination projects where legacy systems are put through a heavy modernization and upgrade (like our HomeMax company). These can be multiyear undertakings while at the same time trying to maintain and support the existing system. When tackling such a potentially disruptive, yet rewarding, project, you have to be very conscious of how the business is going to react and how strong their appetite is to support you, both financially and in terms of their patience.

Failure to secure either means you are doomed to failure before you cut a single line of code or turn on a single service. You have to think like the business: what would you need to be convinced of before signing off?

First thing to consider is your company's schedule. Are you a seasonal business? It is rare to have a company that hasn't got some period of the year that is a no-go change period. For example, retail companies (on- and offline) will most likely want no major changes or releases around heavy trading periods like the sales after Thanksgiving or the Christmas season, whereas educational companies don't like to see any change at the start of the academic year or around exam time. Identify what these periods are, and make sure you plan accordingly. For organizations that have these seasonal times, when these times are taken into account, they can remove three or four months engineering time away from new developments, per year, because resources have had to be redeployed to support systems.

Do not underestimate the time it takes to context switch between projects for your team, particularly if the team has been off the project for a couple of months from November through January, factoring vacation into the mix.

The second thing to consider is the tolerance for the company to wait for your vision to be realized. To be clear, whatever they say at the start, they will never have the same patience as you to wait for delivery. You no doubt have heard the query, "How do you eat an elephant?" implying the project is so large you can't conceive of how it is going to be done. Yet the answer is simple: "one mouthful at a time," which is a nice way of saying that one has to split the problem into smaller, bite-size chunks.

Your vision is the same; you need to break it down into bite-size chunks that the business can feast on and feel a sense of progress. Identify the areas that you can break up that you can deliver to the business. These should be items that the business can get some real benefit from immediately.

From the field

Try a skip and then a jump

I was brought in to review a CTO's plan by the private equity company who were a little nervous about the plan's ambitiousness. The plan was a good one: it was a modernization project to reduce their data center reliance and start to use the benefits of the cloud. The issue was the CTO was taking too big a leap, going from a very traditional server mentality to a cloud native architecture—too much change, with a huge risk associated. I suggested that the plan needed some smaller steps to warm up the business and give him some wins to build confidence and faith in his vision. This included identifying the older servers and moving them to the cloud instead of renewing the hardware. Yes, it wasn't completely cloud native, but by reducing the hardware reliance, we were marching toward the vision, letting the business see benefits along the way while warming everyone up to this new world of virtual computing, which bought him the time to continue moving forward.

When a business can see benefits from your vision early and often, then their appetite to continue to support and fund you will not diminish. In the rare (usual?) times you find yourself slipping, having deliverables under your belt will give the business confidence they can trust you longer than normally may have been tolerated.

The weakest position you can find yourself in is one where the project feels like it is getting larger, taking longer, with the release date getting further and further in the future. Your leadership will be put in question, and the business may lose confidence and cut your funding altogether. Yes, this is a worst-case scenario but not rare, even with all good intentions.

I hereby name this

I can't tell you the number of times I have sat and listened to an excited CTO tell me of their vision, detailing all the benefits, noting the challenges and the rewards at the other side. Yet, when I ask them what they are calling it, I get a blank stare. Name?

We name things to give them personality, to give them emotion. We grow attached to things that are named, and we, therefore, want them to succeed. It is why I gave my three boys their names, instead of simply Child #1, Child #2, and Child #3, which, to be frank, would have been way easier. A good project name will breathe life into your vision and let everyone become emotionally invested in it.

Don't be too clever with your naming, because this is just an internal name, but every so often, a good name can find itself out in the wild, so consider thoughtfully. I find it a good thing to make it a collaborative exercise so everyone feels they have a chance to weigh in. Sometimes these can be around a theme, such as *Lord of the Rings*, or the classic *Star Wars* can be a rich field for the picking (large warehouse projects have a tendency to be called the "Death Star").

A good name, such as Project Gandalf (which I have seen used for a legacy transformation project—the project was in two phases: Gandalf-the-Gray and then Gandalf-the-White) or Codename Borg (to describe the building of a large data warehouse), all kept with their narrative to help people imagine and keep focused on the overall goal. One of the best names I came across was the Gump Platform. It was a system to manage Internet of Things (IoT) devices, and one of its primary requirements was to keep running all the time (recall Forrest Gump was advised to just keep running).

3.3.2 Keep in mind

As you are looking to lay down the plan of your vision, you should be thinking through the following things:

- *What is the overall problem you are trying to solve?* Identifying the problems you are trying to solve will make answering the "why" question easier when asked by the business to justify your vision.
- *What are the benefits to the company and/or client?* Highlight the rewards to the business and client that your vision will bring. It could be an ability to be more flexible to client wants or opening up new opportunities.
- *Is this time sensitive?* If your vision can start anytime, then great. But if there are better times in the years than others, then highlight this and use this as an opportunity for greater planning.

- *What are your criteria for success? Are they aligned with the business?* Identifying the metrics for success is crucial to knowing when you have finished. Think about how the business will interpret your initiative and how they would rate the success. Remember, your pain isn't necessarily their pain.

- *Who are the main people you need for success?* If there are key personnel you need for your vision to be successful, how crucial are they to the running of the day-to-day business, and how can you backfill or minimize their absence?

- *Is this principally a modernization/reimagination project?* Are you looking to modernize an old piece of legacy systems? Although this may solve a lot of your problems, clients and the business may be quite happy, so you have to think a little more creatively about why you are looking to change the status quo.

- *What impact will this have on the continuity of the business?* Large initiatives are always a distraction. What will this mean for both your department and the business? Even if you are planning for additional resources, someone has to manage them, and they will take away from keeping the existing systems operational.

Being prepared for the impact of your vision helps you think through all the considerations, so when pressed by the business, you can show you have considered all their concerns. It is okay not to have all the answers. Identifying an area where you need more input is welcomed more than bluffing through an answer at the time, only for it to come back to haunt you later.

3.4 *Incorporating seismic shifts*

Have you noticed how we are in one of the most dynamic and changing industries? What was considered bleeding edge last year will have now matured and become accepted as mainstream or faded away and been forgotten. We are in an ever-changing environment that sometimes feels intimidating and leaves you with the thought that you are always playing catch-up. This is normal and to be embraced.

Making the right decisions on a particular technology is itself an art and an area that is addressed later in the chapter. But for the focus of this topic, we will look at how you incorporate a changing environment into your long-term plans. In a multiyear journey, what was considered potentially risky at the start of the project may have become the norm two or three years later. The last thing you want to do is to deliver something that is already dated before it is released.

3.4.1   Decision paralysis

Agonizing over whether a given path is the right one is to waste time and deny the opportunity to change direction. When it comes to technology, any decision is better than making no decision. What is right at the time, given all the data and reasoning, will always be the right path.

> **From the field**
>
> *Starter's guilt*
>
> No one likes to think they have made the wrong decision, so when a CTO decides on a given path, they sometimes have what I call "starter's guilt," which is not dissimilar to buyer's remorse—that feeling that you have made the wrong choice. We all feel it at some point and wonder if someone else would have made the same decision. Related to imposter syndrome (a subject I deal with later), it is that feeling that the whole project's success hinges on that one decision, and if it is the wrong one, it is all doomed. Don't worry—no decision is irreversible or, at least, can't tolerate a small course correction.

Allow me to let you in on a little secret of long-term, big projects: things do change, and often, as we learn and discover more. It is okay to change and rethink some of our initial assertions. The key is to find a framework or method that allows and welcomes change without resetting the clock back to zero. This section proposes a thinking framework that lets you accommodate change without jeopardizing the project as a whole.

3.4.2   Identify the pillars of your vision

We all know the importance of a good foundation for the stability and strength of a house built upon it. In our world of technology, we, too, must have a good foundation on which we can build and have our company succeed. If we have a shaky foundation that is intolerant to external forces, no matter what we build, it will always be a weak point.

You need a good foundation—pillars, if you will—that will support your project. The advantage of thinking of your foundation as pillars is that any given pillar can be replaced as long as the others continue to function to keep supporting your vision.

Sit back and think about what your pillars are. These are the biggest components that you need to rely on to support your vision's execution. Let's look at some examples to help illustrate this.

Assume you have decided that as part of your vision you are looking to move to an API-driven architecture so business units and clients can get at the data and services they need. The pillar here would be the mechanism through which you are going to provide the API endpoints that is both secure and scalable. Let's say you decide on HTTP REST endpoints with JWT for your security token. This does not limit your language or framework, but it has narrowed your thinking to a methodology so you can focus on your implementations.

Another example is that your vision has deemed that collecting and managing data is a large component, and you need to be able to store large volumes without any degradation in performance. Your pillar here is the storage and management of data. Let's not start too hard—create a data lake (which is a fancy term for a big storage area that can take any type of data) in which you can park data and then decide later on how and where you are going to transform the data. For example, AWS S3 is a great starting point.

Identifying the areas, or pillars, is not the science or business rules you have to create but the areas that ideally you would like to outsource (which includes using a framework or library) to give you services without the headache or housekeeping. These are the services you can think of as the commodities that your vision relies on.

3.4.3   *Watching the pillars*

Once you have identified the pillars, you should actively keep an eye on their evolution. You are looking to see how they mature and become accepted to see how you can incorporate these into your vision without too much disruption. If you have identified a pillar correctly—something that is not specific to your business, yet you rely on—then somewhere someone is trying to commoditize that.

> **From the field**
>
> Cloud, another word for commoditization, is when a process or technology gets to a point where its role, innovation, and competition in a space reaches a given state of acceptability. Web and mail servers are two good examples. More recently, databases have moved into that world, when running and maintaining your own cluster of database servers is just too costly compared to buying database-as-a-service from one of the big cloud providers. In the old days you would have had a whole team of DBAs maintaining backups, optimizations, and failover, whereas all these are just a click away in a browser window. Some see this as a loss of control, but in reality, it means you have a whole swath of technology you no longer have to manage.

Talk to any (traditional) architect and they'll tell you a good foundation is one that is accessible. If you find one of your pillars is going through a seismic shift and has settled in a different direction, then you should allocate a splinter team to investigate whether this indeed is the time to pivot over to the change. A splinter team is a small team that is spun up for a few days to dive deeper into a very narrow area—to fetch the intel to allow you to make more informed decisions. If you have designed your system properly, this change should be relatively seamless without too much fuss (I discuss in subsequent chapters how best to insulate yourself in a good design that tolerates change).

For long-term initiatives, it is expected that you are going to have to take a number of steps back to be able to leap forward. That said, this should be embraced only for large foundational pieces. Changing frameworks or languages is not in the same vein as the foundational pillars. These are more disruptive and can risk the success of the project as areas need redevelopment. Such decisions are equally as important to make from the outset but are more macro in their level. How you make these decisions for your team at the time is described in a later chapter.

3.4.4 Looking for simplicity

Hopefully, one of the goals of your vision is to reduce overall complexity and overhead. Anything that gets you closer to that should be investigated and embraced. The last thing you want is to increase housekeeping responsibilities that are not germane to the core business.

> **From the field**
>
> *Sunk cost*
>
> Like a good poker player will tell you, once you see your hand is no longer going to win, it doesn't matter how much money you have bet so far, pull out. In business this decision process is called *sunk cost*. It's that feeling that because you have invested so much so far, you should see it to the end, even though you know the chance of yielding success is thin. I have seen this many times, and usually it is either AWS or Azure that has gone and changed the game. I have seen teams come up with sophisticated, elaborate systems only for AWS to completely "null and void" their efforts with a pay-as-you-go service. The question then becomes, should they stick with what they have developed or move over? At first the answer is always stick with what you have—let the service shake out and take the time to confirm it has everything you need. As soon as it does, then switch over, reduce your operational burden, and move on to the next challenge in the project. Life is simpler the fewer parts you have to manage.

Back in the days when big data was all the rage, the vogue tool of choice was Apache Hadoop, a system for managing large datasets across multiple machines in a redundant manner. It was a great tool but a nightmare to manage and maintain. Yet it was really the only game in town for managing datasets that would not sit on a single hard disk. It was such a hotly demanded skill set, and those who had Hadoop skills commanded a large fee. Overnight this subindustry disappeared when the cloud providers offered their big-data-as-a-service offerings (Amazon S3 service, for example). Although a huge blow to those who were specializing in this area, it was a huge gain to the companies that were looking to use this area without the Hadoop overhead.

Things will and do change. At the time of writing, the industry is going through one such seismic change when it comes to managing servers, by encouraging you to even ditch that basic of requirements: "serverless computing"—the art of not needing to manage any servers at all. A lot of internal projects are being thrown out as the serverless world proves itself and gains acceptance. A strong vision plan allows for change and embraces it as a win for overall reduction in complexity.

3.5   *Elevator pitch*

One thing you need to be able to do, without thought, is to explain your vision to anyone who asks in a succinct and easy-to-understand manner. Think about all the different skills sets and backgrounds of the people within your company. Think about how you would explain your vision to them, knowing they will most likely be impacted at some point, so they too can share in the excitement and be part of the journey. This can be a very difficult thing for some, trying to de-geek their explanations, so that anyone can understand. It is a skill that, once mastered, can be used over and over again in all aspects of your role as a technology leader (especially as you try to explain what it is you do to your mother—"he works with computers" is as far as my mother could explain to her friends).

There is a common phrase in business that we call the *elevator pitch*. This is basically a short description that can be explained in approximately 30 seconds in such a way that anyone listening can understand what it is you are saying. This became a popular way to ask whether you had honed your idea for your startup in such a way that if you bump into an investor, you can easily explain it to them and hopefully wow them into investing.

History

Elevator pitch

There is no consensus on where this term originated. Some claim it was the 1990s; others date it to the 1970s, with one story right back in the 1850s when Otis developed the original elevator. The one I prefer, because it feels more relevant, is two *Vanity Fair* journalists, who could never pin down their editor in chief to pitch story ideas. To solve this, they would join her in the elevator ride and pitch her their thoughts.

This section discusses what makes a good elevator pitch and how you can practice it so it doesn't feel forced or unnatural. Although we refer to this as your "pitch," it really is your outline, because hopefully by the time you are explaining it to others, it has been approved by the CEO/board and you are well on your way to planning and execution.

3.5.1 Creating your pitch

When you ask a new CTO what their vision pitch is, often a terrified look forms, and then they begin to ramble, spouting lots of great words, all of them horrendously detailed with too many technology buzzwords. All very natural—let's try to address this.

The issue isn't the content but the presentation and getting it into a format that feels natural, rhythmic, and, above all else, engaging. Let's go through a few steps that will help you start to craft your vision into a series of statements that will have even the most technology-challenged listener lean in and ask for more:

1 *Write up to five items that describe the benefits of your vision for either employees or clients*—These are the gains that the business or the client will be able to use upon your vision's delivery, for example, a greater insight for a client to measure success to compare year-over-year data.

2 *Write up to five internal features of your vision*—This is the list of the features you may consider to be internal to the company, or even your department, that are more technology focused; for example, reduce the overhead while increasing capacity of data management by moving to a cloud-managed database.

3 *Step away from the list and leave it for at least one night*—This is important; everything requires time to cook, so let your brain process these items while you sleep.

4 *You have 10 items, so remove all repeated or implied items to get down to a list of six*—Assuming you've done step 3, this will be easy because the list will look so different when you see it in another light. Find the items that are really saying the same thing, but using different words, or are implied (e.g., if moving to the cloud, it is implied that you are also reducing your hardware reliance).

5 *Step away from the last six for at least an hour*—A final check will make sure you have the right six items, before you focus on them.

6 *Rank the six in the order of importance*—Now order them in terms of importance from a business perspective.

7 *For each of the six, create a technical sentence and a nontechnical sentence*—Start with the technical sentence, because that will feel more natural, then try to write another version that is more business orientated with no buzzwords or jargon.

8 *Find the opener, the grabber*—We need to find that opening sentence that engages the listener and has them excited to listen to you for the next 20 seconds as you run down your list. This could be a problem statement you are looking to solve ("We need to onboard a client in hours instead of the months it currently takes") or by trying a parallel to something they know ("Imagine becoming the Uber of home warranty by empowering our clients to self-serve for HomeMax").

It is that simple. Does the final list feel right? Have you hit all the big points? Now let this all marinate for a while before you start practicing it out loud.

3.5.2   *Practicing and honing the pitch*

Until you've said it out loud, you won't know whether it sounds right. Find some people who you can trust (both technical and nontechnical) to try out your opening lines. You won't have it right the first few times. Do not be disheartened by this—this is something that will become better as you practice.

The opener should always be the same, but depending on the audience, you can change around the technical and business versions of each feature item you identified. At first, it will feel unnatural and forced. The more you do it, the more familiar the words will sound coming out of your mouth. Each time, you will find subtly different ways of saying the same thing as you read the body language of the person standing in front of you.

As you do it more, the less robotic and scripted it will be. Your natural personality will come out, and the excitement you feel will be obvious in how you pitch it. Repetition will get rid of all the "first-night" nerves and allow you to relax into the words so when you have to present it, without notice, it will come out in a way that will engage the listener and have them probing for more information.

Success is measured by seeing the person get as excited as you do, engaging you in a series of questions, seeking more detail. Your pitch will bring people along, have them support you so you are given the time to do what needs to be done. As an example, here is what the pitch for HomeMax could be:

> *By letting our clients manage their own data on their mobile device or browser, we are going to reduce the overall burden on the call center while increasing the data quality and promoting engagement. Moving to a scalable, modern architecture, we are opening the opportunity for greater integration with third parties to further offer products that would complement our offering, for example, offering a yearly home service to address the smaller items before they become big problems.*

In this very simple pitch, we've indicated we are going to reduce overall running costs; we are going to address one of the biggest areas of concern, which is quality of the data; and by promoting or teasing the cloud, for example, we are showing we are setting ourselves up for new markets and products.

3.6   *Putting together a budget*

One of the hardest things you may find yourself doing at some point is creating a budget for your vision. A budget at its most basic level is how much this is going to cost the company. We all know software and IT projects are notorious for their overrun, but keeping a firm grip on the costs will make sure the business will stay with you as you journey through the implementation and delivery. This section covers the major components of a budget and how you keep yourself honest so when you need to react, you can easily do so without too much fear.

3.6.1 What to include

A common problem with budgets is a lack of detail. The biggest omission, interestingly, is the cost of in-house personnel. The rationale here is that because this is a cost to the business already, then why include it?

You can appreciate why that line of thinking is flawed. The issue isn't that the business is already paying for the cost but what the personnel were hired for in the first place. If they are going to be working on your vision, either partially or full time, that means they are potentially not working on something else. Is there an area of the business that will no longer be served and will need back support? Highly likely. Either way, the cost of each person working on the project needs to be accounted for. Be sure to include the increased cost of salaries (and any bonuses you wish to reward) year over year, because most companies look to increase salaries a given percentage each year (2%–5%, depending on performance/inflation).

> **From the field**
>
> *Cloud-deflation paradox*
>
> The cloud brings a huge economic gain if used properly. For projects that span multiple years, be sure to build in inflation—the economic reality that most things cost more year over year. Most cloud services strive to drive down the cost of services. Experience tells us that, though this is the case, the savings are usually lost as we increase usage. Because we think it's cheaper, we use more than we probably need, believing it's well within budget. I call this the cloud-deflation paradox.

The second omission is the resources required for the project. This should include hardware, software licenses, third-party services, and cloud resources. Including them is not enough; they must properly reflect and align with the progress of the project. For example, if you are doing something in the cloud, then the cloud costs for the first few months will most likely not be the same in the middle of the project, let alone near the end. Think carefully how and when the costs will change.

You are looking to set a realistic expectation for the business as to how much this will cost over a given period of time. Never slip into the habit of putting together numbers that you think your CEO wants to see, because you are concerned about sticker shock (the initial shock at the cost of the project). No good ever comes from such a poor budgetary start.

3.6.2 Lay out the budget

Your budget doesn't need a terribly complex model; a simple spreadsheet works, with the months going along the top and the expenses detailed in each row, broken out as monthly costs. Once you have gotten your first best guess completed, the next person you want to review it with is the CFO. They will be able to go over each line item, confirming or adjusting each cost to make sure you are properly representing all the costs.

Once this review is completed, this will be considered your best-case scenario, the one that has captured all the costs as accurately as possible. Now you are ready to start putting together some what-if scenarios so you can react when pushed on your budget by the CEO or board.

A common tug of war goes on, where the business wants a project fast, good, and cheap. Yet, we can generally deliver on only two of those at any one time. The business, therefore, has to choose which two they wish. If they want it good and cheap, then they have to be prepared for it to take longer. If they want it fast and good, then they should expect to pay more for either higher quality or more resources. They don't opt for fast and cheap, as most know in their hearts that it is a foolish dream, but that doesn't stop them from asking.

The fast-good-cheap model is actually a good one to model two additional budgets because this will also allow for some scope creep (where the requirements change slightly). Take your original budget, and assume you are challenged to make it faster (we are always going to assume we want good, no matter what). What do you need to spend to have faster delivery? Is it increased personnel costs or bringing in short-term contractors? How much faster can you really make it? Remember, as Warren Buffet said, "You can't produce a baby in one month by getting nine women pregnant." Some things take as long as they take for a reason. But be prepared when asked, as hypothetical as it may be: if money were no object, how fast can you deliver this vision? This is a question that our friends in private equity often pose, because they are generally on a tight timeline, and the only thing they can control is the flow of money. Another area you can negotiate on is the number of features being requested—is there something in the project that, if wasn't necessary, would make things easier/cheaper?

You also need to look at the fast-cheap option. When looking at this, it isn't necessarily that they wish it were cheaper; it could be a simple reflection of a limited amount of in-house resources available because they are critical for other pieces of the business. Here is where you can remove a significant number of features, highlighting which items you are going to remove, to be able to satisfy this budget model.

Keeping these models/options will allow you to determine what your upper and lower limits are. It will also map out the costs over the year(s), and when the CEO or CFO looks at the budget approval, they will be able to align this project against competing costs and determine the best time to give you the green light.

3.6.3   *Keeping track*

It goes without saying—yet it is worth saying—that this is not a one-time thing. Once you have been given the green light and have started out on one of the scenarios, you need to keep all budgets up to date, at least on a monthly basis. Get into the habit that at the end of each month, you review all expenditure and marry that up against all the invoices and costs to make sure you are on track.

Your project manager (make sure your project software can track resources) will be able to tell you just who and how long each resource worked on the project. Did someone contribute more time than what was planned? Keep an eye out for overbudgeted, underutilized resources. These can lull you into a sense that you are coming in under budget, but in reality, they may have been on vacation or had to work elsewhere and couldn't spend the time that was planned.

Keep the other scenarios up to date, too. There is a strong possibility that once the project has started and after a number of successful deliverables, management starts to get really excited and the CEO asks you to accelerate your plans. If that is the case, if the funding tap is turned on a little more, you need to be able to see what that can do for your deliverables. By keeping your alternative budgets aligned, you will be able to answer that question, and as things change or evolve, prospects may turn out to be more attractive than they looked at the outset.

At least once a quarter, review your current budget with the CFO. They will keep you honest and make sure the numbers are realistic. A well-laid-out and updated budget, even though it can and will change, will give the CEO and the board the confidence that you can be trusted with numbers.

3.6.4   *Return on investment (ROI)*

It is not uncommon, particularly for visionary-type projects, for the business to ask for the ROI. What this means, in simple terms, is this: for every dollar spent, how much will the business receive in return? This metric is extremely hard to accurately predict but not impossible.

For projects that are looking to replace or upgrade legacy systems, this will be the cost savings. Include any software licenses or support contracts no longer required to maintain, hardware upgrades, and, importantly, the reduced management costs for managing the systems. This is the easiest one to estimate.

For other types of visionary projects, where you are making significant changes to the way the business operates, opening up new markets is a little harder to come up with a number for, especially if you are preparing the business to have a launching pad for greater product diversity or depth. In these cases, you need to reach out and get the input of your peers to see whether they can help you figure out the reduced costs or opportunity for increased revenue.

Sometimes it is a collective gut feeling that it is the right thing to do, so the ROI is not a justifiable metric to measure against. By collective, we mean the whole management team is behind you on this. In the case of our HomeMax company, the ROI could be calculated from the reduction in the head count in the call center and reduced cost of buying, maintaining, and hosting the physical hardware.

3.7   Near-term planning and expectations

Getting started with any big project can always pose a problem. Yes, everybody's excited, everybody's expecting big things to come from this, but the problem is that with any large project, there's a lot of preparation that needs to be done. This is usually stuff that is more behind the scenes (code layout and flow, cloud formation, initial architecture design, etc.) that has no real visible components (or at least to the business), and after two or three months with nothing to show, the business can get a little nervous.

> **From the field**
>
> *Every house needs a good foundation*
>
> One of the ways I have managed these types of situations in the past is to draw analogies to building a house. The business is usually excited at what they can do with each room, how they are going to decorate, and how they will fit out the kitchen. I temper eagerness by saying we're at the point of digging the foundation. Once that is done, I then say we're at the plumbing stage or getting the electric cabling done. As the project continues, I liken that stage with house construction—drywall going up, internal doors being hung. This sets the expectation and allows those not familiar with software projects to truly get a sense of project progress.

The thing we are getting ahead of is anticipating when business fatigue starts to settle in—the point in time when the business looks at your long-term project, forgets it was going to take this long (or if slippage has started), and begins to question whether continuing is worthwhile. This phenomenon, the valley of anguish (named by James Milbery, founding partner at ParkerGale Capital and described in chapter 1), charts the business enthusiasm for a long-term project, and if you pay attention to where you are on the curve, then you can head off the anguish.

This is the point where the business may have some naysayers, whispering in the ear of the CEO, that they have lost (or are beginning to lose) confidence in the success of this project. This is the time when the old legacy system is looking extremely attractive—better the devil you know is the attitude.

Your role is to make sure they never sail into the valley of anguish, but if you find they are there, you have to show them a path out. Let's look at how you do that.

3.7.1   Communication

Keeping a tight rein on the project, making sure everything is captured along the way, is the first step. The vast majority of large projects slip—it's a fact of life—but to not document why they are slipping and not communicating this is doing nothing but setting you and your team up for failure.

The business needs to know when things happen and the reasons why. Many CTOs do not like to deliver bad news and tend to gloss over when things get too far behind. This is the wrong attitude, and instead, you should look at the business as your partners who have as much of a vested interest in your success as you do. Slippages usually happen due to unforeseen business logic cropping up or having to tend to the daily running of the business. These things need to be communicated, and you may find assistance coming from the strangest of quarters.

Don't forget to celebrate the successes, each and every milestone that comes along. Be careful with the scope of your celebration. By all means celebrate the smaller ones, such as successful sprints, internally with your own group, but when it comes to the business, the general advice is to not to get too excited outside of reporting progress is going well. The time you want to make a bigger deal of celebration is after you have delivered some value that the business can start to benefit from. This is when your project will start to prove its worth (and head off any undue negativity).

Speaking of delivering to the business, make sure you have built in significant time to your overall project plan for training and support of the business as they start to use your deliverables. It is natural to get all panicky about time slippage because resources have been consumed for a number of weeks as you onboard the business and work through some of the kinks. This is to be expected and should be planned. The worst that can happen is that the time is not used and the business takes to it like a duck to water, and you get time back on your project plan—a nicer problem to have.

Creating this communication plan for a variety of audiences (e.g., senior management may get a different level of detail than the whole company) and determining the cadence to which you will issue it will get you into the habit of delivering good or bad news. It can be as simple as an email, with high-level bullet points, or a quick slide or two at a standing management meeting.

3.7.2 Controlling the narrative

Although this is sounding like a political campaign in many ways, it is not too dissimilar to how one controls messaging. In the absence of information, people will fill in the blanks themselves, for better or for worse. The longer the reach of your vision, the more you have to temper expectations.

At some point, your vision will take on a life of its own. What is meant by that is that this project will start to be the salvation to all problems. Any issue, client concern, sales opportunity—your vision will address it. The promise of the new world, where no issues exist, is a very alluring dream, and you will be surprised at how quickly this can take hold. In project management circles, this is the ultimate destination of what is known as *feature creep*. Feature creep is when smaller features keep being added on, because they don't seem to be big, so it won't make much difference just to slip them in. Akin to the straws that are being added to the camel, at some point there is going to be that one straw that will break its back. Feature creep can destroy a perfectly good project—by the time it is delivered, the expectations are nowhere near what the reality is, even though you may hit every goal you set from the start.

Although standard, strong, project management principles will help a lot with this problem, you still have to make sure this is communicated outside of your group. A way to do this is to reset expectations in every periodic update, so people are reminded what it is you are delivering, and what it is you are not. It does no harm to address any misconceptions there and then. This is especially important to help reset expectations through the organization and unofficial circles. Better to deliver small disappointments that a given additional feature or solution isn't going to be in the first wave of releases as and when they come instead of having to defend the potential failure of a project to live up to its hype because you were too polite to correct misconceptions.

Summary

- Creating a vision that will drive long-term value lets you get out in front of any changing dynamics.
- Breaking apart the "what" from the "how" lets you better focus on different audiences.
- A good vision will have easily measurable metrics for success.
- Knowing who your immediate client is and creating a special relationship with them to know their pain points will give your vision the validation it needs.
- Visions are not short-term projects; they are a series of projects, lasting many years, in some cases.
- Knowing how to weave your vision into the timeline of the company will reduce adoption friction.
- Given how long it takes to complete a vision, building in adaptability for changing technology is crucial.
- Creating and practicing your talking points, so you can easily communicate your vision in a very succinct and engaging manner, will make it easier for people of all levels to buy in to where you are taking them.
- Aligning a budget with your vision eliminates any economic surprises in the future and sets expectations properly.
- Setting a communication plan to keep all constituents updated will help head off any questioning of the validity of your vision when it seems like there is still a long way to go.

Checklist

How many of the following items can you lay claim to having covered?

- Created a long-term vision and laid out how you are going to get there
- Communicated your vision internally, at various technical levels
- Detailed the business benefits your vision will bring
- Created a timeline of when you hope your vision will be implemented and what will be available
- Identified the necessary technology improvements that will let you stay relevant with your vision
- Practiced and delivered your elevator pitch so others can quickly know your vision
- Able to deliver a detailed review and progress report on your vision on very short notice

Building a team
4

This chapter covers

- The different ways you can grow a team
- Evaluating resource types
- Recognizing the business events that result in hiring
- Identifying areas where you can start to source candidates
- Writing a job description to attract the best talent

No matter how good you think you are, no matter how fast you work, at some point you are going to need the efforts of others to make up your team. Whether you look to external firms or hire your own team members, a wide range of options is open to you. The modern workforce is made up of a variety of third-party contractors, offshore teams, onshore teams, and full-time employees, all working together to build and run your platform.

But do you know which type you should consider and which one will work for a given circumstance? It is not an easy problem to solve, because many different variables are at play, including availability, experience, budget, and the type of work to be done.

This chapter presents how to take the mystery out of this whole area. The one piece of advice for CTOs is that you should never see recruiting as a one-time event; you need to make it a part of your routine, with the mindset that you are always hiring. You never know when someone just might leave your team or you need to scale up quickly; bench strength is a wonderful tool to have in your back pocket. The most successful CTOs are skilled at bringing people on nearly immediately, because they have built up a great pipeline of candidates.

Once you have your pipeline sources prepared, you need to have a good description of the role so the would-be candidate can read it and be inspired—often an area left to the HR department, using a standard template, which never comes over as exciting. If you wouldn't apply for the role, why would you expect others to? This chapter also explores what makes a great, punchy job description. You are only as strong as your team—tend to its future growth now.

4.1 Different types of resources

Hiring your own team isn't the only way you can source your team. This section covers the popular mechanisms that successful CTOs use to build out their engineering team, for both short-term and long-term projects. As any CFO will tell you, hiring a full-time employee (FTE) is an expensive endeavor and one that should have a lot of thought, reasoning, and data to back up why this role is required. We will go into some of the metrics for knowing when to do that later on in the chapter. You can draw on the following five methods to resource your needs:

- Full-time employee
- Contracting individuals
- Outsourcing to vendor
- Onshore resourcing
- Offshore resourcing

Each has its strengths and weaknesses, dependent largely on your budget, time frames, and access to quality candidates. Let's have a deeper look at each of these.

4.1.1 Full-time employee (FTE)

The FTE is probably the most widely understood resource, the team member who is directly on your payroll, who has bought into the overall vision of the company, and who is there to do more than just produce work. They help shape and cultivate both themselves and other team members. These are your most valuable loyal assets, because they persist beyond a single project and help manage other employees. They have a vested interest in keeping quality high and clients happy, and generally making sure the company is profitable.

An FTE is an excellent resource when you need someone to interact directly with clients or someone who thinks much longer term and may be involved in more than one project at a time. If you need someone to help grow or manage a team, or to help shape the company direction, an FTE is the ideal choice. The FTE will be on a fixed salary (usually including health care/pension if in the United States), with an optional performance-related bonus each year. The FTE is a candidate for receiving stock options or shares, depending on the size of your company. This resource will also be protected under different federal/state/local (depending on the locale) laws regarding their employment status and will go through an annual review as part of their career growth.

You are investing in this resource to help them grow into their career and for you to hopefully benefit from that investment as the years continue to make this person more valuable to you. Conversely, terminating an FTE requires specific protocols/laws and communications to be adhered to and can take a little time (I discuss performance management in chapter 5). This chapter also goes into much greater depth on how to attract, interview, and onboard full-time employees.

4.1.2   *Contracting individuals*

A contractor is someone who charges you a fixed rate (daily or hourly) and is focused on a specific task or project. They are sought through recruitment agencies or staff augmentation companies, who take care of the final payment to the individual, whereas you deal with a company who will invoice you each week or month.

The contractor can be terminated extremely quickly, for any reason (the project may be coming to an end, or their skills are no longer required), assuming you haven't agreed to a minimum requirement. If you find a contracting company looking to fix you into a given period, look for a more attractive rate. Like any business, they are looking to keep customers engaged as long as possible and have their own techniques for making sure you keep their contractors.

A contractor is someone who has temporary status—they will be out of the company as soon as their task is done, and subsequently they generally don't get involved or invited to company meetings or events.

It is a common misconception that one should assume each contractor a contracting company sends you is top-notch quality and, as such, many companies do not interview potential contractors before hiring them. This is a big mistake. A contractor still needs to be interviewed; however, you should focus less on their soft skills and more on their hard technical skills. You are bringing them in to do a specific job, and they should be able to produce from day one. For contractors who operate as independents, make sure you ask for and check references. In some countries, specific laws prevent you from hiring a single contractor in an extended role for too long, citing that they should be considered full-time employees with all the benefits that entails.

The perfect type of role for a contractor is one where there is a specific task that needs completing, for example, designing the user experience for the mobile app or producing the necessary jobs to extract data from each database into a warehouse. The task, which has a defined start and stop, has a need for a skill set that isn't going to persist beyond this engagement.

There is a special kind of contractor here that is worth pointing out: the contract-to-hire individual. This is like a "try before you buy" sort of arrangement—if you find after a period of time the individual is really working out and you have a full-time role for them, you can convert them to an FTE (for a small fee). This path can work out really well for companies that have not yet figured out whether or not a given position is full time.

4.1.3 Outsourcing to vendor

This is an area that used to be the purview of larger organizations, but economics have driven the costs down to the point where smaller companies can benefit from it as well. You bring in a company to handle everything associated with a given area. Examples of this include IT management of employee desktops, printers, and networks; database management; and, more recently, cloud management and security.

The vendor is responsible for the resourcing and training and providing continuity for 100% coverage. You never need to worry about resources moving on and leaving you with a gap. Contracts with vendors are usually over a much longer period of time (6–12 months) and come with specific service-level agreements for them to respond to.

A whole chapter is dedicated to this area, and, if used correctly, this arrangement can save a company significant costs without the overhead of maintaining a team for continuity, training, and in-house expertise. An area that you would consider a commodity (like you think of electricity or office management), which, should it fail, would have a significant impact on the business, yet would feel a distraction to maintain and manage as a dedicated team, is a good candidate for using an external company.

4.1.4 Onshore resourcing

Onshore resourcing is when you look to a consultancy company to help you with one or more pieces of your project. They are generally located locally, or at least within the same country. This is an extension of the contracting model, except the company in question has its own in-house resources who do the bulk of the work for you, at their own offices. You are typically assigned an account or project manager who will liaise with you and your team to identify the work required and make sure things are going forward in a way everyone agrees on.

The onshore company will provide all the necessary expertise as and when the project demands it and usually has a wide range of skills on staff to be able to bring in the necessary people. This arrangement gives you the advantage of tapping into this pool of expertise without you having to plan for it.

This type of employment is ideal for standalone projects, with clear outcomes and deliverables. Depending on the size of the project, the company may dedicate a resource to stay on-site with you and your team throughout the project, so they can react quicker to any changing requirements. Although this results in a higher cost, it can be beneficial if you don't have a dedicated resource on your team to manage and liaise with them directly.

Such engagements are priced on a fixed project cost or a fixed monthly retainer basis, depending on the complexity. The big advantage of this type of engagement is getting the necessary skills to manage and resource a project, with you getting the results. The downside is, although you retain the intellectual property right (IPR) of the resulting project, you don't benefit from or have much input towards any of the learning along the journey to get to the final product.

Sourcing good onshore companies can take some trial and error. If you have a very defined project specification (and it doesn't need to be too detailed), the best way is to put this out to tender to a number of companies. This is when you invite a company to quote for the work, based on the specification.

Ask around for recommendations from your peers. If you are new to the area, keep an eye on the user groups and university recruitment fairs to see which companies keep popping up. The larger, more reputable ones will have a local presence and tend not to do a poor job on their own doorstep because a poor reputation can travel quickly.

When reviewing tenders, do not always go for the cheapest price, especially if there is a huge delta between the different bids. Look for at least three to five bids, and if there is a larger than 20% price difference, remove those outliers instantly from the contenders. You should ask for the resumes of some of the people who will be working on your team. These will probably come back to you anonymized (to protect their employees) but will give you an idea of the experience and skills of the people working on your project.

4.1.5 *Offshore resourcing*

The final resourcing type you can look to is offshore, which, as the name suggests, is considered to be anywhere that is not your own country. Classic examples include workers in India, Eastern Europe, and Latin America. When compared with US-based workers, the cost of such resources is considerably cheaper. The lure of fractional costs can be very seductive to any company looking to reduce costs, but as they say, there's no such thing as a free lunch, and to that end, there are a number of things to be wary of.

The first thing to realize is that you are going to have a team that is not only remote but most likely outside of your time zone. With some countries, you can lose a whole day if an issue arises or confirmation is required before moving forward. So, you need someone local who can be the liaison between the local and remote teams, bridging that gap, and this usually requires that person to work some of their day outside of typical local hours.

The second thing is finding the right company to work with. This requires trust and confidence that you are going to get what you pay for. Chances are, you are not going to make the trip out to the company to vet them, because that is going to be very expensive and time consuming. Instead, you have to rely on recommendations from peers and reviews on sites such as LinkedIn. Be prepared to kiss a number of frogs before you find your ideal partner.

The secret is leveling your expectations. Do not expect your offshore team to be as thorough or have the same attention to detail as your own local team. It isn't that they produce poor or shoddy work; it is just that they don't have the context for the daily happenings that can shape a product.

Start your engagement with small, quantifiable tasks that will help you gauge the quality and time expectations. This will allow you to build a more detailed project plan.

In my experience, offshoring has been hugely successful when you have the architecture and principal design completed and you have the necessary infrastructure to let a remote team develop code that is then automatically checked and confirmed through code-quality tools. Testing is another area where offshore resources have excelled historically, particularly for projects that can't have automated test suites and still require human interaction.

Expect to spend far more time managing a remote team than you may first realize. Many engagements fail because of a lack of proper oversight and management from the domestic side of the relationship.

4.1.6   Comparison review

Table 4.1 pulls together the major features and downsides in a single view.

Table 4.1   Resources comparison review

Type	Strength	Weakness	Compensation
Full-time employee	▪ Long term ▪ Client facing ▪ Aligns to company vision ▪ Promotes loyalty ▪ In person	▪ Costly over time ▪ Hard to remove ▪ Can lead to too much reliance on an individual	▪ Fixed salary ▪ Health care + pension ▪ Stock options/ bonus
Contracting individuals	▪ Short-term projects with specific deliverables ▪ Terminate fast ▪ Great for short-term expertise requirements ▪ Simple billing model ▪ In person	▪ No loyalty or vested interest in the company vision ▪ No long-term view; focused on the project at hand	▪ Fixed hourly/daily rate

Table 4.1   Resources comparison review *(continued)*

Type	Strength	Weakness	Compensation
Outsourcing to vendor	<ul><li>Long-term commodity type of servicing</li><li>Continuity of service while resources are rotated</li><li>No on-the-job learning</li></ul>	<ul><li>No team building</li><li>Narrow in what they can do for you</li><li>No in-house expertise on the given subject area</li></ul>	<ul><li>Fixed price per contract</li></ul>
Onshore resourcing	<ul><li>Long-term, defined projects</li><li>Engaging a team, not an individual</li><li>Good when a project requires a lot of short-term expertise</li><li>Complete outsourced management</li></ul>	<ul><li>No learning or expertise; only the resulting project</li><li>Only for larger projects</li><li>Requires greater definition of the project</li><li>Harder to find/vet the right company</li><li>Loss of control of individual resources</li></ul>	<ul><li>Project price or monthly retainer</li></ul>
Offshore resourcing	<ul><li>Low cost</li><li>If different time zone can increase your time availability</li><li>Once found, the right company can scale up and down resources quickly.</li></ul>	<ul><li>Time zone issues</li><li>Very hard to find/vet the right company</li><li>Much harder for dispute resolution</li><li>Cultural differences may impact project quality.</li></ul>	<ul><li>Fixed price per contract/resource</li></ul>

These are the broad strokes of the type of resources. Many hybrids of these models offer you both individual contractors and teams, both on- and offshore. Before going down a given path, make sure you have a strong sense of what it is you are looking for and how best to look for that partner that will help you succeed. Of course, exceptions to every rule can be found.

4.2   *Knowing when to hire*

The whole hiring process is a tricky business at the best of times, but knowing when to start can be even harder sometimes. This section covers some of the metrics and trigger points to watch for that will help you decide when the time is right. Although the advice is always to hire based on data instead of instinct, that merely moves the problem: what if you lack data to properly back up what you know in your heart is the right move? This section shows how you get data to confirm that your heart is right (or, conversely, show how now isn't the right time after all).

The following three broad categories generate hiring events:

- Project development
- Attrition
- Team exhaustion/back support

It is worth noting that extraordinary economic situations drive a shortage of quality candidates. If you know you are in such a situation (which should be easy to gauge by reading the trade press) and you happen upon a great resource but don't have an open position, ask your CFO if you can squeeze something out of the budget so you don't lose them. If you don't ask, you will never know.

4.2.1 Hiring events

Let's take a deeper dive into the three main hiring events that will shape the growth of your team.

PROJECT DEVELOPMENT

From a data perspective, if you have a strong project plan, this is one of the easiest methods to justify the need for a new addition. Your project plan will not only tell you the type of resource you require but also when and for how long, though that is only part of the problem. It is rare (and, in my view, unhealthy) for an organization to hire someone for a very narrow skill set.

Instead, look for someone with two to three core strengths, with a suite of secondary skills. For example, say someone is strong in cloud architecture and Java, with database, messaging, and security as secondary skills. This person will be a lot more useful for a project team over a longer term than bringing in a separate individual for each of those skills.

You have to look at the skills required for your project. Pull out those that naturally fit together, are industry accepted, and could be found more or less in a single person. This hire will tick a number of boxes at the same time and is much easier to justify to your CFO/CEO as part of the project budget.

It is perfectly acceptable (and encouraged), as you build up your team, that disciplines overlap. This not only gives you bench strength but also promotes and stimulates healthy collaboration so the best solution will be presented. Remember, an idea is good only if it can stand up to scrutiny. If you don't have people on your team who can offer constructive feedback, you are doing your project a disservice. Later, I introduce the discipline matrix, which gives you a small framework to let you map out the skills you have within your team.

New projects are a great way to expand your team, both to bring in new resources and promote or move around those already in your team. You have to make sure you don't starve existing projects of resources if you move people to a new project. Do not make the naive assumption that a given person can simply do both—that is a challenge that any CFO/CEO will most likely ask of you: "Can't you simply do more with who you have?" It is a fair question and one you should be prepared to address, no matter how much it offends you. If you have a good handle on your team's current workload and how much extra help you need, then the data will show whether you need another person. The assumption here is that your data will show you are already at capacity, which is why you are asking for another resource in the first place. A later chapter goes into team management to keep a track of these metrics.

When hiring, primarily around the needs of a given project initiative, consider the following:

- The disciplines required and how that maps to an individual
- How this individual will be used after the project: will they no longer be required, or will their skills continue to be required?
- Will this role benefit more than just this project but also potentially other areas you are responsible for?

ATTRITION

A team will naturally experience attrition, or shrinkage, through a number of "life" events that can include retirement, moving on to other opportunities, and (sadly, one

I have had to deal with personally) death. Hopefully, you will never have to worry about the last one, but the situation where a member of your team changes jobs is common in our fast-paced industry. This can come out of the blue at times, with a very small time frame for reaction—most employee contracts have a notice period of around two to four weeks, depending on seniority and locale.

When such an event is forced on you, it is a good time to pause for a moment and take the opportunity to reshape your team. A hole has been left. Now you have to make the decision on how you are going to fill the hole, if at all. Questions you should be asking yourself include these:

- *What were the top two things you were counting on this person for?*—Don't be too detailed—you are not writing a eulogy. Think about the top couple of things you relied on this person for and how they will now be taken care of.
- *Loss of skills*—Do a stock check of the disciplines and the level of expertise that have been lost. How important were they to the success of your team?
- *What in-house knowledge has been lost about either internal or client systems?*—The longer someone has been with you, the more in-house knowledge they will have naturally garnered. Was this knowledge documented anywhere, and, if not, how much did you rely on it to resolve issues and placate clients?
- *Was this a full-time role?*—The natural inclination is to say, of course, it was a full-time role, but think about whether this role had run its course and, although the person kept themselves busy, were they truly productive?
- *What was the person lacking that could have made them more productive?*—Sometimes you have the wrong person in the role, someone who maybe lacked some key discipline or personality trait that would have made them more successful—for example, someone in support who doesn't like talking to clients.
- *Impact on overall team moral*—Think about the impact on everyone else in the team in the absence of this person. Will it have a positive or a negative impact? Did they inspire others (or, conversely, cause more problems than they solved)?

Although it is a loss, and a huge distraction at a time you probably least wish it, be prepared for when it comes, and be ready to think through the necessary corrective action. Sometimes your decision may be not to rehire for the role immediately but to pull back and wait. A well-structured team should be able to cope with a loss without an interruption in the short term.

Be prepared

Not a case of "if" but "when"

No matter how good your current team is, or how loyal you believe everyone is, as Abraham Lincoln said, "This too shall pass." In other words, things always change because nothing lasts forever. I have sometimes thought that I had my "dream team" many times in my career, but each time, forces outside of my control have forced a change, and I had to mold a new "dream team."

You have been given an opportunity to weigh what you have lost and determine how you are going to evolve your team. The last thing you want to do is to try to find a replacement. No matter how good (or poor) the person you are replacing, you will never find their exact equal, and to measure a new hire against that is not setting up the future for success.

TEAM EXHAUSTION/BACK SUPPORT

A given team can comfortably handle only so much work before exhaustion, fatigue, and burnout occur. It takes effort to keep this situation from happening because it is easy to get caught up in the daily grind of execution and support of the business. Here are some of the tell-tale signs that your team may be needing some extra capacity to bolster your productivity:

- *Project/sprint deadlines are being missed more than hit*—We all know deadlines slip and sprints have things pop back in the backlog—we are the eternal chronological optimists. When you look at your postmortem/retrospective, pay particular attention to the reason for slipping. If resources being pulled away is a common reason, your projects are doomed to fail before they get started if you can't keep resources focused on the task at hand.

- *Overall PTO (vacation) is not being used*—PTO (personal time off) is important for the health of all teams. We all need to recharge our mental batteries and focus our brains on something non-work-related. If you find your team is not using up all their PTO, do not assume they love their job too much to leave. It may be because they don't feel they can take prolonged periods of time because there is too much to do, which leads to the next flag to watch out for.

- *Panic/stress when key individuals take PTO*—When individuals do take their PTO, especially for a week or more, is there a heightened stress among others in the team/business because this person was relied on heavily for their knowledge and skills that no one else has yet managed to pick up?

- *Overreliance on a single individual*—If you look at your team as a whole, who do you rely on to the point that if they weren't there (for whatever reason), you would have a serious problem on your hands? Every team, at some point, has had that one person who is the only one who knows how to restart a given piece of server/ software, or handled that account, or had their own toolbox of scripts to solve a given problem. Sometimes this situation is known as the *key person risk.*
- *Prolonged late-night and weekend work*—Having to work late every so often is the nature of our business. Whether we are dealing with a client issue or releasing software at off hours, a good engineering team is one that is flexible. However, if you find you are needing to ask your team to work late (or work weekends) on a continual basis, you are effectively asking them to work two or more jobs.

Spotting this problem is harder than it looks. Interestingly, we seem to see it in other teams more quickly than we can in our own. The first thing that will help is enlisting others in the team to keep an eye out for these traits and for them to feel comfortable bringing it to your attention. Second, the partners or spouses of your team will be the first to see any stress or absence quickly. If you have a line of sight into that, don't dismiss any complaints or concerns that come your way—a happy home life is a happy work life.

Your role as the leader is to determine whether what you are seeing is a blip or a pattern. If it is a pattern, you have all the data you need to make the case for more resources to your CEO/CFO.

4.2.2   Discipline matrix

You are now getting a better handle on when to hire. You find data is indicating that you need to expand your team. The question now becomes, who should you hire? What skills can you bring into the team that will relieve the pressure and let you get on and produce results? It is easy to quickly rattle off, "We need another Java developer," but given the number of disciplines highly skilled engineers have these days, being this fast to decide may be limiting your options.

Look to build and maintain a discipline matrix or, if you will, your human capital assets. This is a list of all the types of broad disciplines that your group requires to successfully execute projects and business objectives, rating what you currently have with their strength/knowledge. Let's look at a small team for illustration purposes.

Discipline	Current					Avg. current skill	Total skill	Need	Delta
	Cormac	Noah	Joseph	Dillon	Preston				
AWS	[7]	0	0	0	0	[7]	[7]	10	-3
Java-Script	2	5	5	2	1	3	15	20	-5

Discipline	Current					Avg. current skill	Total skill	Need	Delta
	Cormac	Noah	Joseph	Dillon	Preston				
Java	2	0	0	8	0	2	10	5	+5
HTML/CSS	0	8	8	0	0	3	16	15	+1
MySQL	0	0	0	8	8	3	16	10	+6

Here there are five core skills, and for each member on the team, give them a competence score out of 10 against each skill. This is a rudimentary scale, with the following meaning:

- *10 to 8*—Primary discipline with a senior/advanced knowledge
- *7 to 5*—Primary discipline, but considered junior; requires guidance or mentoring from a senior
- *4 to 3*—Secondary skill that compliments primary discipline
- *3 to 0*—Knows enough about the skill to assist and provide backup, but not a core competency

Mark any skill that is exclusive to an individual with brackets ([ ]) to make it easy to see that they are the only resource in the team with that skill. Then total the skills to give a general competency value for that team, with an average score.

The Need column is subjective and one that can change, depending on the projects and tasks you have ongoing and coming up. You may want to split this out into a number of columns: per project, next six months, and six months and beyond, for example. What you are trying to do is get a feel in a data-led, unemotional manner for where you are weak and, should you decide to hire, what skills you really need.

In our contrived example here, we see we have two concerns that immediately stand out: our AWS skill is meeting our requirement, but we are reliant on a single resource. If Cormac decides to move on, we really have a problem. The other area where we are lacking is JavaScript and, based on our gap and given the people we do have who are juniors, a senior hire here is appropriate.

Keeping this skill matrix up to date is vitally important and should be a collaborative effort. It will identify where people's strengths and desires lie, including giving you an insight into anyone who could benefit from more training to bring them up to the level you need. As is discussed later in the chapter covering team management, training your existing team, either with new skills or upgrading their existing skills, is an area many companies fall behind on, not realizing the huge payback that a relatively small investment can yield.

> ### Know your team
>
> *Human capital audit*
>
> When I start working with a new CTO or team, the first thing I do is ask for everyone's résumés so I can start building the matrix. Depending on the formality of the review process, I ask to see previous reviews to see how people are evolving through the years. Then I sit with the principals and ask them to review my findings, which usually results in them completely readjusting every figure I create—that is okay. It's so much easier to edit than to create. One thing that is consistent is the surprise the data paints because the team is usually not as strong in a given area as they thought they were. This is particularly relevant for companies in the private equity space—PE hates to see single resources that are propping up the business, because that represents too much risk for them.

4.2.3   *Impact of not hiring*

Now, just because you have all the data indicating that you are understaffed, that does not automatically mean you are going to be approved for the hire. Every department always wants more resources, and although their request may not be as scientific as yours, the CEO/CFO have to weigh all the options to make sure the funding for this role is there and the return on investment makes sense. A company may put a pause on hiring for many reasons, ranging from poor cash flow to uncertainty in future contracts, or they are going through a buy/sale process.

Whatever the reason, it is your responsibility to illustrate the impact of not moving forward. This includes the projects that may not be completed in the time the business requires, or the risk that comes with losing a key resource, especially if they are critical for a given area.

Present this data not as a threat or an ultimatum but as the reality you are facing. You will, of course, do what you can with what you have to be a success, because you are a professional who does not want to see anything needlessly fail. If one of the impacts is a delayed product feature or project, ask for help in communicating this delay to the client or department that was waiting on your team's output. This action promotes the idea that you are all in this together, and when you ask for extra resources, you are doing it for a reason and not just to increase your head count.

4.3   *Sourcing candidates*

You can source candidates and attract them to your organization in many different ways. This section goes through the common avenues, detailing each of their strengths and weaknesses, depending on where you are in the hiring process.

We are going to look at the following:

- Referrals
- Recruitment agencies
- Headhunting
- Graduate fairs/internships
- Self-serve online

4.3.1 Referrals

Assuming you are doing everything you can to create a wonderful working environ-ment, the best advocate for helping you increase the team is your current team. Encourage them to reach out to their network of people to see if they know of anyone who meets your requirements. It is common to offer some referral bonus ($500–$1,000) for any successful hire as a result of an introduction.

Do not limit this request to just your current engineering team but enlist the help of the whole company. Organizations have great success historically, with a well timed email to the company, inviting people to dig into their networks. You just never know whose sister, best friend, or son works with someone who thinks they might be looking for a new challenge. You literally have nothing to lose.

A word of caution: treat anyone you attract through this process like anyone else—no short cuts or special considerations. If you treat everyone equally, you will have no issues or social guilt if the person doesn't work out or fails to make it through the interview process.

Advantages:

- Timing is everything, can be quick to find someone
- Inexpensive

Disadvantages:

- No guarantee of any candidates
- Can make things awkward for the referring employee if not handled properly

4.3.2 Recruitment agency

The traditional recruitment agency is always a good source of immediate résumés, tak-ing a percentage of the first-year salary of the hired candidate. Not all agencies are the same, and it is important you do your research and get to know the agency, how they source and validate candidates, and whether they specialize in a particular niche. Sadly, a number of agencies are just keyword matchers, so no matter what résumé is in their database, you will see both good and bad candidates if they match the criteria.

A good recruitment agency is your partner in this process, as echoed by Lori Jen-nings, founder of Jennings ProSearch. They are there to sell and promote your oppor-tunity, weed out the candidates who are not qualified (skill-wise or personality-wise), prepare the candidate for the interview, and work through the selection process. Some of the best agencies should truly feel like a partner. Some even accompany the candidate, waiting outside until the interview is done.

Jennings gives good advice when engaging with an agency such as hers, which includes knowing the standard metrics, such as time to fill, completion rates, and retention times. Though it goes much further, she continues, "Are they constantly talking to people in your role across companies understanding your challenges as a CTO? Can they help advise you on compensation? Do they understand what motivates candidates at your level? Do they have a strong network of candidates who will take a call from them?"

Doing your research

Mystery shopper

It does no harm to see how an agency handles and treats candidates, and the best way you can do that is to have someone register their interest with the agency for a particular discipline and see the quality of roles that are offered. This is a trick I have performed a number of times to weed out the charlatan résumé pushers from the ones who know their trade. Some of the jobs I have been asked to apply for are so far away from the core competency of my résumé, I wonder if they even read the résumé in the first place. You want to know, if you are paying a one-off agency fee of up to 20% of the salary, that you are getting the quality candidates you are assured you will get.

Advantages:

- Quick to present a number of qualified candidates
- Prequalified before you even have to review a candidate

Disadvantages:

- Takes effort to find the agency that understands your needs
- Rarely do any technical validation
- Can be very expensive with rates from 10%–25% of the first year's salary

4.3.3 *Headhunting*

Headhunting is the process of soliciting the interest of someone who fundamentally isn't actively looking for a role but is passively keeping an eye on any opportunities that may come along. Although some agencies specialize in this, they are still a recruitment agency by another name. You and your team interact with people from many different avenues in the daily course of your professional life—people you have built a relationship with, or someone whose work you know, prevalidated, if you will. You have a wider network of potential candidates than you may first appreciate. Channels can include these:

- Any service or vendor company you have been working with, where making an offer to a key individual wouldn't violate any contractual obligations or intellectual property/trade secrets.

- Open source projects are a rich hunting ground of experts, where their body of work can be seen publicly.

- Who better to get than the person who wrote the book on the subject? The majority of book authors will happily take your email at the very least and have an exploratory discussion. If they are not looking, they will usually know someone who is.

- In the same vein as book authors, those who have published articles or maintain popular blogs on your subject may be open to having a conversation.

Advantages:

- Already prequalified—they know their trade or skill to a high degree.
- If you have already been working with the person, you know their personality will work with your team.

Disadvantages:

- More opportunistic than strategic.
- Search is very narrow.

4.3.4   Graduate fairs/internships

If you feel you have the organizational structure that can onboard a fresh graduate and give them the necessary guidance and mentoring, attending your local university graduate fair can unearth a rich picking of fresh candidates. All universities and colleges have some sort of recruitment fair, at various stages throughout the year, and they will be more than happy to have you be involved. This is a long-term strategy, because graduates do not become available until they graduate (naturally), which is usually at the end of the calendar year and at the end of spring.

This process can take up to a whole year, depending on when you first interact with the students. This gives you the opportunity to build and cultivate a relationship with them, see how they get on throughout the year. (Did they make the grades they thought they would? Was their end-of-year project in a field that interests you?) You are not looking for perfection here, so do not judge too harshly—this is not a typical job interview. Instead, you are looking for that diamond in the rough, that personality type, that passion, that appeals to you. Is this a person who, with the right mentorship, could be a top-class resource and make an impact on your industry?

Too many times organizations see graduates as a cheap form of employment, treat them like seasoned resources, and then despair at their poor performance. Even the most pedigreed racehorse needs training—they don't win races straight out of the gate.

A number of opportunities for you to get to know and work with students before you potentially hire one—a "try before you buy," if you will—include these:

- *Corporate project sponsorship*—Most engineering courses require students to conduct a yearlong project that makes up a significant part of their final score. Professors have a hard time coming up with unique projects year after year, so they welcome input from the local professional community. This is a great opportunity for you to assign a project that may be worthwhile to you and have them work on it, while you guide and mentor them throughout the process.
- *Internships*—Internships can give a young person real insight into how your industry works and help them with their remaining studies. Internships can last just for a summer or for a full year, depending on the course. Consider assigning an intern to an experienced member of your team, so they can learn and help out. There is great success to be had hiring the real stars a year later then they graduate.
- *Sponsored hackathons*—These are special coding competitions that some engineering schools run, to let students work together to compete against teams to see how well they can evolve and bring a project to fruition in a short period of time. They are hugely fun and bring out the best in people as the gamification of coding comes into light. Schools are always looking for corporate sponsors to buy pizza, breakfast, coffee, drinks, and so on as the event runs.

Walk the talk

Up all night

One of my fondest memories is when we were one of the sponsors of a 24-hour hackathon at Virginia Commons University (VCU). This was an event that brought in teams of four to six engineers (including neighboring schools) that took over the engineering hall for 24 hours so they could produce a working project that would impress the judges. I wanted to get the maximum out of this event, and I put together a rotation schedule where, as a company, a member of our team was on-site at all times throughout the event to help the students. I wanted them to know we were in the trenches with them. One of my personal rules is that if I ask you to work late, for whatever reason, I will be there with you. This was no different, so I spent the full 24 hours with the students, going through sleep deprivation with them. It was an absolute hoot.

Advantages:

- You get to know the students over a long period so by the time you are hiring them, you know what you are getting.
- It's a great way to give back to the community and help, even if you don't hire a single person.

Disadvantages:

- Very long term; think in terms of at least six months
- Requires mentoring and patience as you train them

4.3.5   *Self-serve online*

Finally, you can take matters into your own hands and use one of the many different online resources to source quality candidates. Resources like LinkedIn, ZipRecruiter, Indeed, and Stack Overflow are some of the bigger players in the space. Results will vary, depending on the time of the year and the type of role you are recruiting for. No magic formula works each time; what works one day for a given web recruiter can fail the next.

You are hoping to align the planets, where that ideal candidate happens to be looking at the precise time you are advertising and is inspired enough by your position that they will take the next step and inquire.

A word of caution when using an online resource: you will attract the attention of recruitment agencies, who will attempt to sell you their services. Those soliciting you like this will send you the same candidates who would have found you anyway through the big online recruitment sites at a fraction of the cost.

Charges are usually a few hundred dollars a month, with a host of upsell packages to further promote your position. Depending on the role, certain sites are more favorable than others. For example, if you are seeking a developer, you should lean to Stack Overflow, whereas if you are seeking more of a noncoding role, then LinkedIn should be your choice.

Advantages:

- Complete control over the wording and presentation of your role
- Very cost effective

Disadvantages:

- Not guaranteed
- Generates a lot of noise from agencies and window shoppers (who just apply to everything)

4.4   *Creating the job description*

So, you are all geared up, and you have the approval to hire talent and get them onto your team. You have been asked for a job description. This, at its core, is a one-pager that describes the role. For the whole process, this is the most important document you are going to produce. This is the verbiage potential candidates are going to read and be inspired enough to take the next step and apply. If this doesn't work, then everything downstream is moot. Seems obvious doesn't it?

This section covers some of the reasons most CTOs fail at this most basic of tasks and how, with a little copy editing and wordsmithery, you can polish that diamond buried deep in the rough. Your goal is to produce something that makes job seekers run to you when they read it.

> **Adapt**
>
> *The "Lou Adler" approach*
>
> The ideas that I present here are heavily inspired by the recruitment specialist, Lou Adler. His whole approach is to sell the opportunity, not the tasks, be goal oriented not activity oriented. I have adapted his approach slightly for our technical space, but if you read his books and watch his videos, you will see a common theme. Check out his book, *Hire with Your Head* (Wiley, 2007).
>
> This is one of the most underappreciated parts of this process, and I can't tell you the number of teams I have worked with who complain they find it hard to recruit. When I ask to see their job description, the reason presents itself clear as day—you catch more bees with honey. If you can't inspire, then you are just wasting money chasing dreams.

4.4.1 *Basic structure*

Depending on your company's size, there may already be an existing standard template that HR uses. We are going to be bold and pretend it doesn't exist. Let's not be boxed in with standards and process just yet—that will come soon enough naturally.

The outline of most job specifications uses the following familiar template:

1 Title
2 Description
3 Minimum requirements
4 Required skills
5 About/legal information

Absolutely nothing wrong with this. It conveys everything required, but, if we are honest, we are concerned with only the first four sections, because the last one is usually a standard company blurb. Yet, if there are only four elements, how do people get them so wrong?

As we go through each of these sections in detail, think of the person you are looking to attract. If the ideal candidate is similar to someone you already have on your team, think of this person as you go through this process. Think how they are going to react when they read each word; will this leave them with a positive view, or have you just padded out a sentence for the sake of sounding clever and lost their interest?

Now, you may notice one is missing from the list: the pay scale. Although this is a vital piece of information, you may get pushback from management. They may feel it could create issues with current employees, who may discover they are being underpaid for the same role. Don't let this situation happen; it will never end well. Advertising a pay scale will create trust and weed out those who are looking for a specific range.

4.4.2   Title

This is the most important piece of the whole document: the title. This is the first thing your potential new hire is going to read. This title could be read over the phone, in an email, a tweet, or a search result. In whatever way, it is the first thing they are going to read and your first (and maybe only) time to catch them. The advice here is simple: don't be too clever; keep it simple. Let's look at some examples of titles:

- VP of Engineering
- Senior Web Developer
- Head of Digital Transformation
- Cloud Architect
- React Mobile Developer (Jnr)
- Project Manager
- Scrum Master

As you run your eyes down that list, what did you discover from each job title? Did you get a sense for the actual role and the seniority/experience level required from each? Are there any titles for which you had no clue and just read a bunch of words?

People hiring tend to be too smart with the title. Although Environmental Community Liaison Associate is a fancy way of saying Refuse Collector, it won't attract the people who can do the job because they will not recognize what it is you are selling and will move on to the next opportunity.

In the previous list, Head of Digital Transformation is too vague and could mean anything, including roles outside of our technical space. Cloud Architect is not too bad, but it could be better by specifying the cloud provider and the level required, so Senior AWS Architect would say so much more.

Stick to standard industry titles, no matter what titling your company uses internally. Remember, you are not attracting people from within—you are casting your net into the wider sea, and you have to play by their rules.

Build as much metadata into your title as possible without going overboard. React Mobile Developer is a good example of speaking intelligently and directly to your intended audience. You want a mobile developer, and because there are many frameworks and languages, state up front what you are expecting so people don't have to read further to know whether they are suited for it. By the time someone decides to read further, they already know if they are qualified. The same goes for the last two. Yes, Project Manager is a known title, but if you are already working with Scrum, for example, then say it up front in the title; don't waste the opportunity. People naturally head toward familiarity, especially when they are contemplating such a life-changing change.

4.4.3 Description

Here we are, the entrée, the big act, the main part of the job specification that will give the candidate all the information they need to know whether they are taking the right next step. Like the title, time and space matter. You want to grab the person's interest within the first sentence, or the second one at a push. By the time you are reading the third and subsequent sentences, you have them sold. From here on in, you are adding detail and color to your opportunity.

The first sentence is desperately important, because you will never have control over where your job appears as it propagates throughout the various channels. Think about all the places where you get a snippet, like an email preview in an inbox, a tweet, or a LinkedIn post. All have small windows to tease you into the fuller content. This sentence, therefore, has to convey everything that is good and exciting about the role and really grab the reader. Here is a short of list of dos and don'ts for your opening sentence:

- Do not talk about your company.
- Do not repeat what your title has conveyed.
- Do not waste time with unnecessary surplus words.
- Do describe what it is the candidate will be doing.

Too many times a job description wastes too much space talking about their company and how exciting the opportunity is before they even get to discussing what it is the candidate will be doing. There is plenty of time to talk about the company and all the benefits that come along later in the job posting.

Let's look at a couple of examples of good openers that get straight to the point:

- Title: Cloud Architect

  First sentence: Lead the team transforming our traditional data center to run exclusively in AWS to provide resilience and self-scalability for our web infrastructure.

- Title: React Mobile Developer (Junior)

  First sentence: Join and learn from our seasoned mobile developers as they transform our digital offering through our signature Android and iOS apps.

- Title: Project Manager

  First sentence: Organize, educate, and manage our engineering team projects as they embark on our continued growth.

Once you have grabbed the reader's attention, you can start adding to the description by detailing the areas that would excite them to learn more. Again, avoid overly marketing-type words (like *exciting, fun, fast-paced,* or *energetic*), and focus on words that convey something real. Most of the time, such oversell words are implied.

The Lou Adler approach is to appeal to the reason someone may be looking to move from their existing role. Most people move to better themselves professionally. They are looking for something that excites them and takes them to the next level. It is a sad reality that it usually requires a new job to get that promotion or step up in their career. Adler calls this the "stretch goal"—make the job sound a little harder than they are currently doing but not too hard that it is out of reach. Make it appealing that they can step up to the role and that this is the opportunity they have been looking for to finally prove themselves.

From the field

This is my time

Powerful and yet simple—it is this technique that we use when searching for CTOs for the clients we work with. The most successful hires we have made are not the ones who have been doing the job already but the ones who feel they are ready for that next step in their career and want to go out and prove themselves. They have been preparing for this for a long time but have just been waiting for the right chance.

The remaining description should be talking directly to the person you want to hire. Talk in their language, because they will understand what it is precisely you are referring to, and you will be creating a bond directly with that person. It is okay to talk about other fringe benefits in the description, such as international travel, working with clients, or anything else you think would really appeal.

While you are writing this, keep in mind the person you are talking to. Imagine you are writing them an email or talking over the phone to that person. That is the language you are seeking.

4.4.4 *Minimum requirements*

This is your classic bullet list of minimum requirements that the candidate must have. As an employer, you are setting a filter for the things you think the candidate needs before even thinking of applying. As a prospective employee, they can run through the list and automatically take themselves out of the running.

The best job descriptions are the ones where this section is kept to a bare minimum. A lot of companies get this section wrong, including items that are really not required. How many times have you read, "Minimum experience of *x* years," for example? Think about that for a minute—you want someone who can fill the role, so does it matter how long it took them to figure it out?

This area should be reserved for real, demonstrable, non-negotiable items you need to have. A good example is that the candidate is legally permitted to work in your jurisdiction or has a certification if you are recruiting for a highly specialized area (e.g., security clearance). These two items should be moved to the next section, required skills.

4.4.5 *Required skills*

One of the most misunderstood sections of a job description is the required skills list because it has evolved over the years to mean "most of what is listed here is required."

Most people reading this list will run their eyes down this and, if they meet at least 75% of the items, will still feel compelled to apply—as they should.

Although it is tempting to go overboard here, be masterful on how you construct this list. Remember who you are talking to, and ask yourself whether the thing you are listing is implied and necessary. An example is listing that the candidate is proficient in, say, Microsoft Office when you are recruiting for a developer role. You can safely assume that if they can code, then handling Word or Excel isn't going to pose a problem for them.

Do not treat your candidates like idiots. Talk to their professional side. List only the items that are relevant and, as a rule of thumb, anything you would talk to them about in an interview situation would be here. This is the list of things that they need to have to be successful in the role, and again, they may not have everything, but the right candidate will be able to learn quickly on the items they don't have.

It is okay to load various requirements with words like *demonstratable* or *working knowledge*, because they give the reader an indication of the depth of the skill you are asking from them. Resist the urge to put years of experience here—again, as noted earlier, years do not equate to more knowledge. You can look to see how long they have been in the industry by their career history—this should be enough for you to gauge how experienced they are.

4.4.6   *About/legal information*

Finally, you have a section that your HR/Legal Department can have free reign over—well not quite. A little tempering here does no harm. Large corporations are guilty of turning this area into effectively the Terms and Conditions that no one reads. Why waste this valuable real estate?

Use this to describe your company, its products/clients, and why this is a good place to entrust with someone's career. Yes, list the classics—you are an equal opportunity employer—and if you have basic benefits, such as vacation, pensions, health care, all should be here. If you have a work-from-home policy, that, again, should be listed here. This area isn't about the role but about the organization in which this role is located. By the time the reader is this far, they have already made up their mind whether they can do the role you are seeking and will be making the decision to apply.

Summary

- There are more options than simply hiring full-time employees; contractors and third-party vendors can augment your team's needs at different times, each with their strengths and weaknesses.
- The different events that can happen within the business, including people changing jobs, death, or, more usually, growth within a company, can result in you needing to hire.
- Make sure your team does not burn out: get help for them before they decide to leave.

- You can use many different avenues to source candidates.
- Writing a job description is more of an art form than science. Getting it right takes time, effort, and lots of testing.

Checklist

How many of the following items can you lay claim to having covered?

- Identified the different types of resources and the circumstances you can scale them to
- Created the necessary metrics, which are reviewed periodically, to know when to hire
- Have the knowledge at hand to know the level of your team's technical competence
- Crafted a pipeline to source new candidates through at least two separate channels
- Have job descriptions prepared for each of the disciplines within your group

Interviewing, choosing, and onboarding

This chapter covers

- Interviewing and evaluating candidates
- Making the candidate feel special
- Scoring candidates to make it easier to compare and contrast
- Making an offer, and then saying no to the others
- Onboarding the new hires

When you do reach the decision that you need to grow your team, you have to go through a whole sourcing, interview, and evaluation period. Then, once you have decided to make an offer, you have to communicate this to both the successful candidate as well as the others who didn't make it over the line. It doesn't stop there—your chosen hire still has to show up and start working. You may be surprised at the number of times a candidate goes through the acceptance process and signs the papers, yet never shows up on the start date.

In this chapter, I present how to take the mystery out of this area. A good piece of advice for CTOs is that you should never see recruiting as a one-time event; you need to make it part of your routine, with the mindset that you are always hiring.

You never know when someone might leave your team or you need to scale up quickly; having bench strength is a wonderful tool to have in your back pocket. The most successful CTOs are skilled at bringing people on nearly immediately, because they have built up a great pipeline of candidates.

You are only as strong as your team—tend to its future growth now.

5.1 The interview

The interview phase is one of the most daunting parts of the recruitment process for interviewer and interviewee alike. In my experience mentoring new CTOs, this is an area that many are weak in, and whereas most think they are good at it, few actually are. In this section, we are going to go over the overall process, including covering how to interview, suggesting a framework to help you rate candi-

dates, and reading the unspoken signs that are often overlooked. This is by no means an exhaustive look. Many books and online resources take very deep dives into the interview process.

The one thing you can be assured of, though: no one technique fits all. You will evolve your own style and will most likely be very poor at it to begin with. Fear not—practice and honest retrospection will have you interviewing like a professional.

5.1.1 Getting into the right mindset

Put aside your stress for the moment, and instead focus on the stress of the person you are going to put through this process. The candidate will most likely be very nervous and not necessarily present themselves in the best light—ironic, considering they are desperately trying to show their best side. The outcome of this process could be life changing for both them and their family. Not only are they trying to impress you and your team, they are also seeking to determine whether this is a place they want to work with. Can you offer them the environment that will have them getting up in the morning excited to get started?

Therefore, it is important you treat each interviewee with all the respect and due consideration possible. Treat them like you would a potential client. If you use that as your starting block, you will then create a positive experience, which will hopefully allow them to relax a little and let their natural personality shine through.

Depending on the size of your team, you may not be the candidate's direct manager; it may be one of your subordinates. It is completely up to you on how you want to manage the recruitment of these indirect reports. That said, you shouldn't be the primary interviewer if this is the case. If you have given the responsibility of managing people to someone, then you should feel comfortable letting them choose the people for their team. By all means, be part of the process—either sit in with the small group when interviewing in person, or talk to them one on one for 15–30 minutes at the end of the interview to give you the opportunity to meet them, and for you to do the last sell on what a great group of people you have working here and why this should be their own choice. If, on the other hand, this person would be a direct report, you should be the primary interviewer with at least another person from your team or company helping to give you a second pair of eyes and ears.

People tend to remember their interview, not only because of the high-stress touchpoint but also because it is their first time meeting you and your team. You want to create a lasting impression, even if you decide this person isn't suited for you. One of the things you can do to prepare is to think back on all the interviews you have done so far in your life. Although you may be a cofounder, working in a startup straight from school, not having done a formal technical interview, you will have most likely been interviewed for something at some stage. Every bit of experience counts. Think back on that interview—how did it make you feel? What question caught you out? What question did you actually enjoy answering? What was the atmosphere like? These are all good data points that will feed into you becoming a better interviewer.

Never treat the interview as a necessary evil or an hour you have to get through. Although it may be an hour to you, just another person in a constant stream of candidates, the interviewee will have been stressing and worrying about every piece of the process, thinking what to wear, what to say, how to conduct themselves, all in an attempt to put their best foot forward. Give them the respect, time, and latitude to have a good experience, irrespective of the final decision.

5.1.2   *Your objectives*

A good interview should be a two-way engagement, with each party interviewing the other to see if this role is indeed for them. In reality, this seldom happens, with the interviewee not showing enough confidence in themselves to even up the playing field. You should not take advantage of this but see this more as the norm than the exception. The interview process takes a lot of time and detracts from all the other things that are on your plate. Therefore, it is essential you make the process as productive as possible and for you to achieve your objectives.

What is it you are looking for out of this interview? Ultimately, you are looking to expand your team, for this person to add value and productivity to your output. Specifically, you want to know whether you are going to make this person an offer to join your team. For this to properly work, and to treat everyone fairly, you need to lay out a series of specific objectives this person must satisfy for you to be able to make an informed, data-led decision.

The best way to do this is to have a common scorecard that all interviewers can rate the candidates against. The scorecard is simply a list of areas, specific to that role, to which you will assign a number, 0 to 5 (with 5 being the highest). Zero to 1 denotes they are completely lacking in that area, whereas as a 4 or 5 means they have more than enough experience or skill for what you need. The items in this scorecard should be pertinent to the role and be focused on the areas you listed in your required skills from the job description.

Develop a scorecard for each role, and make sure each of your interviewers understands the context and goal of each area before the interview takes place. A sample scorecard is presented toward the end of this section.

It is too arbitrary (and clinical) to simply reject or hire a candidate for reaching a given total. Instead, the result should form the basis of your decision and help give you a framework to remind yourself on how a candidate performed in given areas. Chances are, you're probably interviewing a series of people over a short period of time, so you will want to make sure you have a mechanism to properly capture each candidate's performance.

Now that you have a way to capture the data gleaned from the interviews, let's take a look at the interview itself. Over the next few sections, we will build up this list of objectives and create a scorecard that you can have your interviewers discreetly (or postinterview) populate.

5.1.3   Phone interview (or preinterview)

It is a good idea to have a preinterview call with the candidate before you go through the expense of meeting them in person. This initial interview need not be terribly long or in depth—no more than 30 minutes. The purpose is to get a feel for the person and their applicability for the role you are looking for them to fill. From a technical point of view, the questions should be very low-ball ones that allow the candidate to feel good about the role they are applying for. Build up their confidence and take away any nervousness they may feel about making it through to the next stage. If they are lacking on some of the basic questions, you can remove this person from the intake pool quickly and not waste any more time.

You want to assess their personality—simple things, like, did they take the time to find a quiet area in which they could talk to you versus sitting on a crowded train (or, even worse, at the checkout line in a supermarket—yes, that has happened)? This will point to their professionalism: are they treating you like you would like them to treat your clients?

How clear are they in their answers and questions? Their choice of words can often lead you to conclude whether they know their subject area or are merely name-dropping the buzzwords of the day. If you suspect they are buzzword-dropping, then simply ask them to explain their answer without using the said buzzword. Those who know can; those who cannot stumble.

How quickly are they answering some of your simpler questions? Did you have a rapport with the person? Was this someone you felt comfortable talking to? All these answers lead to your decision whether to invite this person through to the next stage of the interview process.

> **From the field**
>
> *Cutting to the chase*
>
> I have experienced candidates searching in real time and reading out the answer from Wikipedia. Though I applaud their ingenuity, this wasn't the skill set I was necessarily looking for. As a CTO, you have to be comfortable making tough decisions. In the pre-interview phone call, I will terminate the call, politely, after the first 10 minutes if the person is just not the right fit. I will give them feedback that they either don't know the basics or, more annoyingly, have not done their research on the role they are applying for. This is neither rude nor rash; you are being respectful of their time and yours, not wasting it chasing something that isn't going to happen.

5.1.4   *In-person interview*

After reviewing their résumé and getting them through the phone interview, now is the time to physically meet them (or video call, if remote). You will need to decide how you are going to structure this process, which will depend largely on the size of your team and the role that you are looking for them to fill. You have two primary options here:

- Single interview with you or a group
- Series of interviews with one or two people from your team

As noted earlier, if you are running a larger team with direct reports, the interviewee may not be reporting directly to you. You should decide at what point you want to insert yourself.

If you are going to sit in as a secondary in a single interview, it is important you remain a secondary. Resist the urge to take over; instead, give your manager the room to move and take charge of the interview. Alternatively, and probably better, is to tack yourself onto the end of the interview process as a simple 15- to 30-minute slot. By the time the candidate is seeing you, they will have been interviewed by a number of people, and at this point, your team still feels they are worthy enough to see you. Your job here is to get a feel for the candidate from a personality and work ethic point of view. You will focus on the positive aspects of working with your team and what a great move coming to the team will be for them. You should allow them to ask whatever questions they wish—this is their only time to ask the CTO before deciding to take the role (should one be offered).

Let's assume, though, that you are going to be the primary interviewer. How should the interview actually be conducted?

THE FETCH

If we go back to our overriding mantra, which is to treat all candidates as you would a client, you should go and greet them, bring them through the office space, and chat with them the whole way. You will most likely be doing all the talking: they will be shy and nervous, and, as we know, most technically inclined people are not known for their small talk. Ask simple things, like how their journey was, did they find the place okay—nothing that would trip anyone up.

The goal here is to make them feel comfortable and relaxed so you can get a proper read on their personality and ultimately decide if this is a person you want in your organization. Offer them refreshments (water, coffee) to further create a friendly bond. If you can, take them through the office environment in which you would have them operate, and note how they look around. Do they look excited, or have you just toured them through a cubicle farm where it looks like you are operating a software sweatshop and they have a face of fear, looking for the nearest exit? Do not underestimate the amount of information you can learn by this very simple act.

THE SEATING

The all-important question: how should you seat them? Gone are the days of power seating, of having them sit in a lower seat or too far from the person speaking. You should seat them as if you were talking with one of your team or a client. If you have a desk, don't put the desk between you and them—that instinctively acts as a barrier. Rarely do you want to remain behind your desk when you are meeting with someone. Show you are open and receptive by putting no obstacles between you both.

If you don't have a separate meeting table in your office, consider sitting at the corner of the desk. You want to make them feel relaxed and comfortable so they can make the best impression on you and your team.

For interviews that involve more than one person, seat the interview as you would seat a meeting. If that means some sit beside the candidate, so be it. The idea here is not to create any unnatural awkward situations and provide a real insight into how you operate normally. A good interviewee will be confident and be interviewing you as much as you are them, to determine whether this is the right fit.

INTERROGATION

The last thing you want to do in this process is to make it an interrogation. This is not you running down a list of prepared questions, in a cold, robotic manner. Instead, this should be a conversation, listening to the answers and steering the conversation to the topics you require insight into without the candidate realizing they are answering what you need to learn. This is also an opportunity not for you to show off but instead to listen. This is about them, not you. Always keep the following goals in mind of why you are spending your (and their) time on this interview:

- Can this candidate do the job I need them to do?
- Will this candidate fit in with the team dynamic?
- Can you sell this candidate on why they should be working with you and your team?

Forget about all the trendy articles you may have read on left-of-field questions, which the likes of Google and the other big boys are reported to use. Questions like "How many manhole covers are there in a given city?" don't really serve any purpose but to make you sound far more intelligent than you probably are. You may convince yourself that you are testing their lateral thinking, but in reality, you won't get as much from their answer as you think you will.

Your questions should be focused on what is relevant for your organization and the types of problems they will most likely face. The best ones have always focused on real issues the team has faced in the last year—problems that on the face of it may not have an obvious solution at first but, after a little thinking, turned out to be relatively straightforward. Had this person been there at the time, would they have contributed positively to the team's outcome?

As mentioned previously, the popular recruitment guru Lou Adler believes you should be interviewing the candidate about doing a specific task. So, you want to ask them questions that will allow you to determine whether they can perform that task. Ask them about a project they have done in the past that is similar to what you are looking for them to do for you. This will put them completely in their comfort zone and allow them to speak a lot more freely on the problems they encountered and the solutions they came up with to solve or circumvent the issue.

Along these same lines, if you have a specific project in mind, you could give a high-level outline of it and ask questions about how they would go about solving it. What solutions would they employ (if it is a developer or architect position), and why would they use that one? By all means, challenge their answer to see how confident they are. Did they push back and offer a good reason for their choice, or did they open up and confess they never thought of that idea?

Classic questioning to learn how they handle stress or confrontation will yield a lot of data points. For example, asking them to describe the last stressful situation they found themselves in that had to result in working late can give you a lot of data points. Who did they apportion blame to? Did they learn from it?

Depending on the position you are interviewing for, it is sometimes good to see whether the candidate is confident enough to point out an error. You don't want to surround yourself with "yes" people and be the smartest person in the room. You need to test this. You can do this in a subtle way that will allow them to offer an alternative without necessarily contradicting you or telling you flat out that you are wrong.

A good example that works well is mixing up the value proposition for two competing technologies or standards that you know the candidate knows. An example of this would be, in a comparison of JSON/XML, ask "Why is JSON harder and slower to parse than XML?" When it comes to trick questions, that is about the limit you want to go to.

The problem with trick or clever questions is that it could end up intimidating the candidate and putting them off from working for your team. They may think this is the way you operate all the time, and they won't be able to relax and do their best work. By the time you have them around the table, interviewing them in person, you are fairly confident you want this candidate on your team. If you are not, you should have removed them from the process much earlier.

You will want to find out why they are currently seeking a change in their career (assuming they are not a recent graduate). The reason for this is twofold:

- Are they someone who will speak poorly of their previous or current employer (red flag if they do—one day, this may be you and your team)?
- To make sure you can offer the sort of environment that will keep them happy and productive.

Make sure you leave plenty of time for them to ask you questions. The stronger, more confident candidates will be asking you questions throughout, so it is not uncommon for them to get to the end of the interview and say, "No, I have no further questions." Keep a note of the questions they ask throughout because it gives you a data point to reflect on.

Generally, though, most will hold their questions until the end. They will have been well briefed not to ask any salary or package-type questions—that is a major interview no-no. However, if they do, defer the question to a postinterview.

THE EXERCISE

If you are recruiting for a technical role—which, chances are, is very likely, given you are reading a CTO book—it is worthwhile to run through a live exercise with the candidate to get a feel for how they think and how they operate in a team. The best exercises are the ones that have cropped up in the past and for which you can explain the problem relatively easily and quickly without necessarily needing them to come up to speed with all your company vocabulary.

You don't want to make the exercise too complicated, either—something they could demonstrate on a whiteboard or walk you through their thinking as they come up with a potential solution. If you have a coding problem, then you are looking for them to walk through pseudo code, at a more algorithmic level.

Some organizations leave a candidate for an hour, with nothing but a basic machine, to produce a piece of code that will do something relatively trivial. The machine will have no tools installed, and part of the exercise is to see how well the candidate can self-start, install the necessary tools, and get themselves to a position of producing the problem. This approach is subtle because it highlights the candidates who can go and forage for themselves versus those that need a well-defined process to operate within. It depends on your organizational environment whether this is a suitable path. Be careful not to disparage too much—if the candidate asks for help, this is okay, too, because it shows they know their own limits and will seek assistance where necessary.

From the field

Tollbooth

One of the best exercises I saw presented was to have the candidate architect a back-end system that would operate the automatic tollbooth seen in most highways. The genius of this was that it was something everyone was acutely familiar with, but it forced the candidate to think about latency, efficiency, user experience (not waiting seconds for the toll to go up or stay down), and when to indicate that the user was nearly out of credits. To this day, every time I come to one of these, I am reminded of this problem. By the way, that candidate was me, and, yes, I did get the role.

THE EXIT WALK

After you are finished with the interview, either you or someone in your team should escort them off the property, treating them as if they were a client. If you can, it is better you have someone who wasn't part of the interview process. This will give them the opportunity to ask the candidate how things went, as if it is part of polite conversation and just making small talk. The more astute candidates will know the interview never really ends until they leave the building. You will be surprised at the amount of insight you can garner from this very simple act.

From the field

Left or right?

One of the techniques I have used successfully in the past was how I routed the candidate from my office. If I took them out and handed them over to the escort on the left, then I wasn't feeling this candidate had an opportunity. On the other hand, if I handed them off to the right, then I was signaling my support for this one. This gave the escort the cues they needed to tailor their exit walk questions accordingly, including upselling more if we really wanted this candidate to get a good feel for the environment.

5.1.5   *Video interview*

If, for whatever reason, the person can't make it on-site, then the next best thing is a video interview. This should be used only as a last resort. Nothing beats meeting someone in the flesh, and although a video interview can offer a lot more than just a phone interview, you still lose a lot of information. Even if the position is remote, if you can pay for someone to visit your offices or meet them in a public place (even a Starbucks), you should.

SETUP

The first thing is making sure you choose the technology platform wisely. What works for calling friends and family doesn't necessarily translate to present the candidate sufficiently to allow you to assess them. Classic favorites, including Google Meet, Microsoft Teams, Zoom, Apple FaceTime, and Skype, all offer multiplatform capabilities, so if the candidate is on a PC, Mac, or even a mobile phone, there should be minimal problems.

Commercial solutions include GoTo Meeting and WebEx and even the interview-focused BlueJeans, which all offer chat, screen sharing, and collaboration tools as well as being able to record the whole session. How you decide to use these tools depends largely on the type of interview you want to conduct. You may, for example, share some code and have them go over it while you watch.

Give the candidate plenty of notice of the technology you are using, and offer to have someone in your team do a quick test with them before the interview. Make sure they have sufficient bandwidth to properly conduct at least a one-hour interview. The last thing you want is for the candidate to start stressing because they are not being heard or can't hear you or your team.

A video interview is a two-way street—make sure the interviewee can see you and your interviewers. Nothing is more impersonal and unnerving than a one-way session. If you have technical problems that don't allow you to broadcast your video, either reschedule the interview or ask that the interviewee turn off their camera and resort to a voice-only session. Remember to treat each interviewee as you would a client, even with a video call.

THE INTERVIEW

Just because this is a video interview, it does not null and void all the observational items identified in the early section on interviewing in person. This time, however, a certain latitude has to be given due to the medium. If the video quality is poor (e.g., very pixelated at times) or the lighting is not Hollywood grade, don't put any negativity to that.

That said, how the candidate sets up the video session speaks a lot to their character:

- Do they look like they just woke up and never bothered dressing up?
- Did they take the time to find a quiet place, or are there people walking behind them?
- How do they sit for the interview? Did they make sure they were always onscreen?
- When you are talking, do they look like they are engaged, or are they doing something else at the same time, like searching for the answer (it does happen)?

How you judge these answers is up to you, but you can read a lot of untold information from the video if you look for the clues.

One thing you will notice is the perceived intensity of the candidate. When you are talking to someone in person, they will (should) look you in the eye for most of it, looking around as they move their head in natural speech. Video interviews have a tendency to make the candidate look extremely intense because they will always be looking at the screen, even though they may not be actually looking you in the eye. Forgive them for the killer intense stare.

The interview itself should still follow the scorecard you have developed, but be sure to allow a little more time. When technology is in the middle of things, communication tends to slow down a little. So, speak a little slower (and more clearly) than you would normally do in a face-to-face situation.

JOINT EXERCISES

It is not possible for you to have the full experience of the whiteboard sessions you might have done had the person been there physically. Therefore, you need to figure out an alternative way to reach the same objective using the collaboration features of the video platform.

Chances are, this is a technical role, so you may have an opportunity to jointly look through some code and have them make comments or changes to it while you watch. The whiteboard sessions you design should be a way to allow them to demonstrate their thinking, not the full-blown syntactically correct solution. If you can scale these down to use a shared text editor, this will yield the same results. For noncoding roles, follow the same procedure you would if they were in the same room: have them walk through solutions, allowing them to draw on paper, and then show you by holding it up to the camera. Let them know in advance if they should have pen and paper available, though most will, because they will be taking notes.

Solutions such as Google Docs or Visual Code's Live Coding feature let you jointly edit a document in real time, and this is a good way to be able to highlight an area and have them speak to it.

5.2   *Scoring candidates*

Interviewing a stream of candidates takes a lot of effort and energy. As much as you think you will remember the qualities of each, it is common to get candidates confused with one another or forget their qualities (good or bad) and how you felt about the candidate at the time. You are doing you and the candidate a disservice if you do not have a process to capture everything you need at the time, in a way that not only reminds you of their qualities but allows you to effectively score them against one another.

In this section, I present a scorecard methodology that will allow you to capture the essence of the interviewee and grade them against a simple scale to give you the data required to make an informed decision and ensure everyone is rated on a level playing field.

5.2.1   *Defining your criteria*

To recognize success, you must first know what success looks like. As part of defining the role, you will have developed a list of qualities that you feel are important for any candidate to have. These will be a mixture of soft (personality, speaking, presentation, etc.) and hard skills (language knowledge, coding ability, etc.).

A number of interviewers struggle with this area and end up being too general. The best way to think of this is to imagine the person, a few weeks into the role, performing the tasks you set for them. Now think of the skills required to be able to do the work. For example, if they are to sit with a client and determine their wants, then good speaking/listening skills are required. Or if you have them writing some queries to determine counts from a database, then you expect SQL skills.

These criteria should not read like a series of questions that you will ask them in an interview. Instead, these are the results that you are looking for from your conversation with them, which may come through in a number of questions or answers to other questions they have given you. To stop you from turning these into questions, I favor keeping them to a list of objective style points, such as the following:

- Soft skills
  - General appearance
  - General articulation
  - Meeting etiquette/professionalism
- Hard skills
  - Software development lifecycle
  - Design patterns
  - Coding knowledge (of a specific language)

Not all roles will have the same criteria, and you should take your time to come up with a list of between 10 and 20 items. For each of these items, you will rate the candidate between 1 and 10—the higher the number, the better the score.

Now comes the tricky part: scaling the criteria. For each of the items you have listed, you should set out what you have to discover from them to get into a specific range. Let's look at an example. Say you are looking for specific AWS skills. You may rate them as follows:

- 0

  No previous experience of AWS
- 1–3

  Used only a handful of services, such as S3 or EC2
- 4–6

  Has configured/set up their own account, used IAM to create multiple users
- 7–10

  Created subnets within a VPC with security groups and NAT gateways, as well as experience with role-based IAM accounts

Getting a 10 means this candidate has answered every question you had about AWS and has more than enough knowledge to be successful in their role. It doesn't mean they know everything there is about AWS—that isn't the purpose of this exercise. The purpose is to find out whether they know everything that will allow them to work in your environment.

Once you have developed this, communicate it with everyone who will be interacting with the candidate to ensure everyone understands the criteria and qualities they should look for. Not everyone will be able to rate the candidate in every area—that is okay. The more data you can collect, the better.

5.2.2   *Marking the candidate*

As you are interviewing the candidate, you can have your scorecard with you, discreetly jotting down notes, but it is acceptable to fill it in immediately after the interview, while it is still fresh. The key is not to leave it too long when you are trying to remember. An example scorecard is shown in table 5.1.

Table 5.1   Candidate scorecard

Criteria	Score/10	Notes
General appearance		
General articulation		
AWS knowledge		

As you can see, it has a very simple layout—nothing terribly complicated. The Notes column should be only a quick few words detailing why you gave the score you did—what led you to that conclusion? The purpose of this is to remind yourself when it comes to comparing the candidate with everyone else's score.

This scoring mechanism is meant as a data-led framework to make the decision of who to hire a little easier. It doesn't mean the highest-scoring candidate should automatically be offered a role, because there could be other factors not captured in the scorecard that as a group you've collectively discovered. As you debate each candidate's strengths and weaknesses, everyone has their score to reflect on. Interesting conversations happen when interviewers disagree with others' scores by a large margin. This gives people the opportunity to talk through and maybe reevaluate their scores. The success of this mechanism is predicated on the following:

- Accurately identifying the criteria that are important for this role
- Setting the score range of each criterion
- Communicating the scoring to each person interviewing
- Filling in the scorecard as soon as possible and not leaving it too long

The point is, you now have a common framework to talk through, taking personal bias out of the decision-making process, focusing on the qualities that will make this a successful hire.

The more roles you hire, the tighter and more efficient your scoring will become. You and your team will become familiar with what really works and what doesn't, and how you probed the candidate to reach the conclusion you did. Like anything else, practice makes perfect.

5.3 **Saying no**

One area of the whole recruiting process that is often poorly executed is the process of communicating with the candidates who were not successful. The reason for this is simple—we don't like delivering bad news. In this section, we are going to go over how you handle this important part so, even in rejection, the candidate is still left with a positive experience.

The worst thing you can do is to ignore the unwanted candidates, effectively ghosting them (not answering their emails or returning calls), hoping they will soon realize they didn't get the role. This creates so much resentment and ill feeling toward not only you but the company as a whole. You have no clue where this person will end up or who they talk to. They may end up working for one of your clients. They may end up working for a competitor. Such behavior is cowardly and unacceptable and generally results in a whole host of unintended consequences.

Now that we have that out of the way, let us look at how best to do this. When it comes to those you didn't hire, they generally fall into one of two camps. First are those who are definitely not a fit, either culturally or technically with your company, and you will never see yourself hiring anyone in this group. The second group are those who could definitely have a role in your company—maybe not now, but sometime in the future. They have what it takes. Irrespective of which group they are in, they deserve respect and honesty.

5.3.1 *Definitely not*

There are a whole host of reasons someone is not the right fit for your team, and assuming your scorecard was properly thought through, it will be obvious that this person falls far short of what you need. Therefore, keep it simple and to the point. Thank them for their interest in you and say they were not successful in seeking a position.

The good candidates who truly want to learn from every experience will ask where they fell short. Do not be scared of this question. However, you do not want to give them the impression that this is a negotiation and if they say the right things they still have a chance.

The best way to answer this question is to be honest but at a high level. Note the areas where they didn't meet your expectations, which suggests this role may not be what they are looking for.

Sometimes the person will attempt to plead their case, saying they can improve and fix that. Now you are in a negotiation, which cements, even more, that this is not the person you are looking for. If this happens, do not address it, reaffirm they were not strong enough in a field of candidates, and thank them again for their interest in your company. Stay away from the soft-skill areas and focus on the hard skills. Soft skills are more subjective and can be harder to argue if the candidate pushes back.

You have given enough feedback for the candidate to reassess themselves to help them improve their chances with other opportunities. Do not give too many details. If, for example, their Java experience isn't strong enough, just leave it at that. Too much detail will open you to being challenged, and you may not have enough recollection to remember why that was the case. Keep it professional, and keep it short.

5.3.2   *Definitely maybe*

This group of candidates are the ones who didn't quite meet the threshold or were just beaten out by a stronger candidate. Any one of these candidates could be a potential hire, and the areas they fell short in could be trained to bring them up to the standard you need. Treat this group of people as your prevalidated future pool of candidates. You've spent all this time and energy selecting and interviewing them—do not let this go to waste.

You also have to be prepared for your primary choice of candidates to say no. It is not always a slam dunk that everyone will accept your offer. They may have secured a position elsewhere, the salary or package wasn't what they were expecting, or, in some cases, they didn't like what they saw and no longer wish to be considered (remember: they should be interviewing you as much as you are interviewing them).

If that happens, you will have to look to your second, third, or fourth choice, if they all meet the criteria. If they do not and are still in this category of "maybe," you have to decide whether they are strong enough to take a chance on, given the extra training they may require. If that is something you can't do at this point in time, you will have to start the interview process again. This happens.

Let's assume you have an accepted offer from your first choice. You will have to tell everyone else they didn't make it this time. Again, honesty is the best path forward. Let them know they were close, but there was a stronger candidate in a number of areas. However, ask them if it would be alright if you keep their details on file because, although you don't have a position now, you do not want to lose contact and would like to reach out in the future should things change.

If you have a LinkedIn profile, ask their permission to connect, so they feel the genuine sentiment in your statement. This is a common path, particularly for candidates who may have overstretched their skills and weren't quite ready for the senior role they were applying for, but one day, they will be.

Many times, you can use this pool of candidates to dip into very quickly, because the acquisition cost is next to zero—you have already marketed, sorted, and interviewed them. It is not uncommon to go out looking for one position, only to hire two at the same time, because onboarding and training for both can be done in one swoop. Naturally, this is a decision for which you have to make a case to your CEO and CFO.

5.4 Onboarding

Imagine arriving at your hotel to discover no one at the front desk, and when someone does arrive, they can't find a room for you. When they do, it hasn't been made up by housekeeping, so the bed has no fresh sheets and the previous guest's litter is still on the floor. You would be outraged, and rightly so. Yet this is how many companies welcome new recruits into their team. Like the hotel, they knew they were coming many days, or even weeks, in advance, so there really is no excuse not to be prepared.

In this section, we are going to go over an often overlooked part of the process: welcoming your new hire and getting them to a position of being able to contribute as part of your team. It requires a little thought, preparation, and execution. Large organizations that have a dedicated HR group will have this step down to a fine art but often stop at the high level and leave individual departments to complete the onboarding process themselves.

First impressions matter. The first few days of your hire will either reaffirm they made the right decision or make them question the decision to join you and your team. Chances are, they turned down other offers that may not be too late to reverse if they don't like what they experience.

5.4.1 Bringing them up to speed

Before you even think about ordering their laptop or assigning their seating, they will have to be trained in the ways of the company and clients. This seems a trivial thing but is more than just reading the public website. You are not looking to disclose every confidential piece of information; instead, you are looking to go into greater detail about what you do for your clients and how you do that. As part of this, you can highlight some of the challenges, especially if your department is charged with resolving some of those. Areas that should be covered include the following:

- In-depth review of either the service or product that you produce
- Overview of the major terms and vocabulary you all use and the context in which they are used
- Who are the top and oldest clients? Which ones have a particular place in the heart of the company (often the first few clients a company ever had)?
- Other departments within the company, particularly the ones that interact with yours the most
- Any specific unwritten policies your company or department has
- Quick overview of all major meetings they are likely to be part of

The vast majority of this should not take any more than a day, and depending on the size of your team, you can task various members of your team to cover these areas with them. Set this on the calendar for your team members—that way no one gets blindsided.

Finally, don't forget to show them where the restrooms, the kitchen, coffee, and so on are all located. Go meet them at reception and treat them to a tour, introducing various people as you go. This will relax them and take the edge off any first-day nerves.

The last thing you want to do is to have them go and sit at a desk, alone, to read a binder of company documents. Do not be fooled into thinking this brings them up to speed. If you are the new recruit, you might be getting up and walking out and making a call to your second choice. Make them feel welcome, and engage them from the first minute.

5.4.2   Your expectations

With the main overview completed, you must now turn your attention closer to home: how to work with you and your team. This is the most important part of the onboarding process—how can this person be successful in your team?

Do not leave it for them to figure out; tell them. Lay out how you like your team to interact and how they should communicate. Give them the framework for when they can come and ask for your assistance, or when they should bring something to your attention. Show them how best you like to be kept informed, whether that is coming into your office, video chat, chat message, or email. It may seem trivial, but every leader has their own style of management, and the successful ones remove all of the guesswork.

5.4.3   Getting to work

Finally, you will want to get to the stage of having them start producing some work. To succeed here, again, preparation is key. Make sure you have set up their company email and specific logins well in advance of their first day. You don't want to be in a position where everything they try to do, they are forced to keep telling you it is not working, because you haven't set up or granted them the necessary access. This wears down both you and them.

Give them some simple tasks that will let them get acquainted with the way you work and have some quick wins out of the gate. If this is a development role, for example, some simple copy changes in code, where they get to see the full lifecycle without too much stress, is a great way to introduce them.

Give yourself plenty of time to prepare for this section, because, as your team grows, you will be doing this more and you don't want to appear as headless chickens with no real plan and looking like you are making it up as you go along.

Summary

- Interviews are hard. They should be practiced and never be treated as routine or just a conversation.
- An interview is more than just the one hour you sit with the candidate; how they interact before and after can give you more insight than a list of precanned questions.
- Evaluating each candidate should take a methodical and repeatable approach so you can easily and equally compare candidates postinterview without any unintended bias.
- Making a decision on a candidate does not mean you should automatically dismiss everyone else; much can go wrong, and assume nothing until they turn up for their first day.

- How you say no to those who didn't make the mark says more about you than celebrating the successful candidates.
- Onboarding a new candidate takes effort, and even when they do show up for their first day, it doesn't mean they are coming back for the second. In our industry, good people never have a problem finding work. Do not let hubris convince you that you are their only option.

Checklist

How many of the following items can you lay claim to having covered?

- At least practiced a number of interview techniques before doing one for real
- Developed a clear interview strategy for bringing on new team members, with clear goals of what you are looking for
- Created a scorecard against which you can rate all candidates for their suitability for the role
- Trained any other team members who will also be part of the interview process
- Developed a process to decline unsuccessful interviewees in a way that keeps the door open for the future
- Created an itinerary for onboarding successful candidates to get them up to speed as quickly as possible without them feeling lost

Team management

So many phrases and clever one-liners involving teams and their power have adorned many a wall with an inspirational image behind them, such as the following:

- There is no "I" in team.
- Teamwork makes the dream work.
- In unity there is strength.
- None of us is as smart as all of us.
- TEAM: Together Everyone Achieves More.
- Teamwork is what makes common people capable of uncommon results.

As corny as some of them are, a lot of wisdom and truth here shouldn't be overlooked too quickly. A good team can achieve anything they set out to, and it is your job as the CTO to build and lead teams to achieve success for your clients and business. Plenty of management books written over the years have detailed picking and managing the ideal team, and you should look to add them to your library as you continue on your career. For the purposes of this book, however, we are going to focus on the goals and reasons you have to think in terms of teams to be successful. The reason is very simple—you can't do everything yourself.

For a team to be successful, you have to lay out what your wants are, what the responsibilities of the team are going to be, and the expected output. Choosing a team is not unlike evaluating a piece of software. You have expectations that a piece of software is going to do a specific job or set of jobs, so you are free to focus on the output and do something creative with it. Imagine if every time you opened up Microsoft Excel to review your budget, you had to manage the code base, tweaking and compiling it before you could see your numbers.

A team is an entity that should produce a given output, at a quality and level of reliability that you can depend on, because the output from that team will be the input to another process or system. A good team is one that can think for themselves, take on the responsibility that is required, and be given the latitude to make decisions on their own, in pursuit of achieving their very purpose.

Beware

The curse of the micromanager

A micromanager is someone who has to oversee every single aspect of the people underneath them, detailing exactly how something should be done, checking every step, and generally getting in the way. Most people do not recognize this quality in themselves, instead justifying it as their way of maintaining quality. I bump into many of these people as we consult with private equity firms, and, ultimately, if they can't get out of their own way, we have to let them go, because they are a bottleneck to scalability and always are a huge detriment to team morale.

6.1 Charter

As you look at each of your teams, create a list of your expectations and the requirements you expect from them—this is their charter. This statement justifies the existence of the team and how they will contribute to the overall success of the group.

The leader of the team should then come up with a plan to fulfill that charter, including any resources, budget, and tools they need to achieve their goal. That charter must be clear and concise and doesn't have to be terribly long (a series of bullet points, if need be) and must be available to everyone in your group. This way, everyone knows the part they play in your bigger engineering organization.

Finally, and most importantly, leave that leader to do their job and get on with executing the charter. As we will discuss later, although they will be held accountable, they are given the support and guidance to ensure they succeed.

> ### Visualize
> Like a general devising battle strategies, I use LEGO people, on a large sheet of paper, to help me visualize how I want my teams to be made up and the lines of responsibilities between each. I literally draw lines between each one and make notes. This visualization technique lets me see quickly if I have missed anything or have overprovisioned in a given area. A small tip, though: if you using the Star Wars LEGO set, remote Darth Vader—no one wants to be assigned to that role.

If you find yourself inheriting a department, you will most likely have established teams that probably won't have a formal charter. In these situations, you will have to take time to learn and discover what each team does and create a charter for them. The last thing you want to do is to start making changes before you truly get a sense of why things are the way they are. Once you construct and understand this charter, you can then look to make changes, based on your experience of what has worked, or if the company is changing direction and needs to refocus.

When a new member joins the team, they should know very early on what the role of their team as a collective is and what part of that they will make up. As a small litmus test, if you were to poll every member of a given team now about what their purpose is in one sentence, how many different responses would you get? If everyone gives you something completely different, then you don't have a team—you have a collection of people drawing a salary. A charter helps focus everyone.

6.1.1 Knowledge

For a team to be successful, they must first have a purpose. This is the goal of the charter. Next, they must have the resources to execute that charter. That is the responsibility of you and the team manager to come up with and negotiate.

As a team moves forward, they earn experience and create knowledge. This knowledge has to be captured in a way that new members can benefit from for them to be more effective in their role as a participant in the group.

Too often, a team is centered around the strength of an individual, with that person holding all the information, maybe through no fault of their own. So if that individual departs, the team takes a huge loss. A solid, strong team should and must tolerate the loss of any single member without adversely affecting the output of the team as a whole. For the knowledge of a team to be captured, maintained, and usable, they should have the following necessities:

- *Onboarding/training materials*—Like an onboarding process to a company, a team should have their own onboarding and training materials, specific to the goal of the team. For example, if this was a release team, then the training would be around any specific tools they are using (say Jenkins/SonarQube).
- *Knowledge base*—It is hard to find a company these days that doesn't have some sort of wiki or document store in place, though how well these are maintained or updated is another matter altogether. But a knowledge base doesn't have to be documents; it can also be videos, which sometimes are quicker to produce, depending on the area you are trying to capture.
- *Defined processes/structure*—For the team to function, it has to have structure. The structure should not be inferred or assumed but properly documented and communicated, so everyone is following the rules to a successful outcome. For a development team, this could be coding and formatting standards and how one should use version control when working on tickets.

Simply pulling together a group of people and telling them they are a team never works. They have to be given the tools and structure to be successful.

6.1.2 Sample charter

A charter doesn't need to be long, complicated, or intricate. It merely needs to convey, at a high level, the whole purpose of the team. The following is an example of a charter for a support team for an online product:

- *Purpose*—To provide end users with live support with everything associated with the online user experience, including helping out the account managers with any initial onboarding issues.
  - The team is responsible for any data changes that may need to happen but will not make any code changes to fix any bugs or add features. They are responsible for filing any bug/feature tickets for the development team.
- *Customer*—Any user of the product, including internal and external users
- *Resources*
  - Knowledge base of the internal data structures via an internal wiki
  - Read-only access to the production data stores
  - Elevated access to the production data stores for key individuals
- *Skill requirements*
  - Familiarity with the web, including online video/chat systems
  - Strong written and oral communications
  - SQL skills

- *Key metrics*
  - Time-to-close resolutions
  - Total interactions in a given period

6.2 Team structure

Let's get this out of the way right from the outset: there is no perfect structure for our team. What works for one team does not necessarily work for another. Many factors feed into the structural decision, including company culture, personalities of the members, temperaments, importance of the work, and whether there is client engagement.

The more traditional form of management, derived from the military world, is the hierarchical structure, where there is a leader or manager, who one or more members look to for direction and guidance. Another popular structure, especially in technology-heavy companies, is more of a flat structure, where each member is given more personal responsibility and expected to know what needs to be done without being told.

Although not common, it is not unusual, especially for larger engineering teams, to have different types of structures for internal teams. For example, the support team may work best with a single manager overseeing everyone, whereas the research team could be a little less formal.

Popular reality TV shows, such as *Survivor* in the United States or *The Apprentice* in the United Kingdom, play with different configurations and personalities to create conflict and drama, all in the name of entertainment. The conflict is real, though, if you do not give due thought and consideration to the structure that is going to work best for your group.

As you begin to ponder the structure, let's give thought to two data points that you can consider to be immovable. The first, which is pretty obvious: there is only one CTO (aka you), and that person is responsible for everything your group does, both good and bad. Your structure has to give you visibility and transparency so you are never blindsided. The second, which is more of a logistical limit born from years of management experience from all industries: any more than five to seven direct reports becomes impractical. A direct report is someone who looks to you for their direction, guidance, mentorship, and overall leadership. To be effective, and to ensure you are not spread too thin, a limit of seven is often cited.

If you are a young group, just starting out, you may not have seven people in your group, so this may not feel like a worry yet. Think for the future. Plan as if you are double the size you are now.

Exceptions

Larger teams

Of course, the figure seven is more of a guideline than a hard and fast rule. Where this is often broken is in support and testing teams. These teams can have large numbers of people at a similar level, all doing a similar task, with very little day-to-day management really required. Even then, the manager who is put in charge of a larger team should have the experience to be able to manage this larger team and will most likely not be from a technical background.

Knowing that you can't have teams any larger than seven to be effective, you have to look for a way to divide and conquer that makes sense for your group. Let's look at some of the ways you can organize your teams.

6.2.1 Product centric

If you produce one or more products, arranging your teams in product lines may make sense. Each product line would have its own set of subdepartments, such as development, testing, and support, each headed by separate managers reporting to a single manager, who then reports to you.

This is a common scenario for companies that have one or more well established products, with their own lifecycle and product requirements. To know whether this structure is a candidate for you, ask yourself whether any of the following conditions are true:

- Different technology stacks
- Nonoverlapping client bases
- Independent release cycles
- Uniquely challenging support issues
- Significant revenue disparities

This structure should run like a mini-ecosystem within the larger group, permitting each to independently serve its own user base without impacting the others. This model is also a good strategy if the longer-term goal is to merge or integrate the product with another line, because it permits you to continue to serve the client base while you plan for a migration behind the scenes.

6.2.2 Lifecycle centric

This is probably the most popular model used by companies that produce in-house software, where structure is arranged like a factory assembly line, with each department responsible for some part of the lifecycle of the product as it is maintained and built. For example, you could have a development team, a testing team, a release team, a DevOps/infrastructure team, and, finally, a support team. Each of these teams is headed by a manager who would then report directly to you.

This model works smoothly when the SDLC (Software Development Life Cycle) is well defined and adhered to in your organization. Chances are, when you first start out, you will have team members serving many different roles at once. The time will come, however, when you will evolve to require dedicated resources with deeper skills to fully service each area. At that time, you will carve them out into a separate team with their own range of responsibilities.

6.2.3 Customer/vertical centric

Your industry may center around a number of large clients, or verticals, each with its own set of unique requirements and disciplines, but all using the same underlying platform. Say you are based on the Salesforce platform but have wildly different configurations, depending on the client or market space. If your offering is applicable to health care, financial, and education markets, it may make sense to arrange your teams in these spaces, so they can gain experience on each of the segments' unique qualities, making your teams more valuable to you and your end user.

6.2.4 *Hybrid approach*

Finally, there is the hybrid approach—a little bit of everything working at once. This happens often, especially for large organizations that have a lot of historical products in the works. Trying to shoehorn everyone into a common hierarchy will cause more problems than it attempts to solve, because you have to be agile enough to adapt to a complex and changing environment.

If you are going through a reimagination project with evolving legacy products, the hybrid approach is a good way to manage short-term production. Teams will flex—what works one day may not make the same sense in a year's time. Be adaptable and keep an eye on your structure. Once a year is often enough to ask yourself whether things are structured in a way that is serving the business optimally.

6.3 *Titles*

One of the most important things you are going to have to get a handle on is how you will design your team around a structure that allows people to evolve, grow, and know what is expected from them. One facet of that is the humble title—what are you going to call your team?

Do not underestimate the importance of a title. No matter who may profess that a title doesn't matter to them, they really do care, even if their bravado won't let them admit it. A title is a badge of honor, an achievement, and a status check on how well an individual's career has progressed. It is also a way to communicate to the outside world, family included, on the type of person they are.

> *"He's not just a visor, he's a "s-u-p-e-r" visor."*
>
> —*Mrs. Brown's Boys*, BBC TV

Unfortunately, there is no universal standard, or scale, for us to effectively compare the abilities of personnel across different companies. Titles such as "Senior" can mean a wide range of different skills and attributes from company to company. A Senior in one company may be classed as a Junior or Associate in another company. Later in this chapter, we are going to put together a matrix that will help you define the various roles of each title. But for the time being, let's just assume you need them.

6.3.1 *What is in the title?*

A title embodies a number of attributes that are both inferred and implied. When someone describes themselves with a title, we automatically assume a profile, whether right or wrong. For example, when you are introduced to someone with the title of CEO, you infer they are the boss and that they have seniority.

A good, well-chosen title will communicate and embody the following qualities:

- Responsibilities
- Experience
- Salary
- Seniority
- Industry recognition

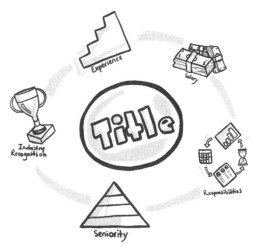

A title instills a level of confidence in the listener. Think of the titles we hear outside of our industry that instantly make us feel at ease. For example, do you feel more comfortable when fastening your seatbelt in the plane where the pilot introduces themselves as the "Captain" as opposed to the "Junior Pilot"? We don't want to hear of any "Juniors," because that implies lack of experience, lack of seniority, and lack of responsibility, as we trundle down the runway ready to be launched into the air.

> **Sense of security**
>
> I recently had to have neck surgery, and when I learned my surgeon was the "Chief Surgeon" of the hospital, I knew I was in safe hands. It may have been an irrational sense of safety, but the title conveyed a comfort to me (given this was my first ever surgery, I clung to whatever hope I could).

Although the assignment of a title within your own team may not mean life or death, it can mean a lot to an external customer who is interacting with your group. For example, that customer may not be happy to be dealing with a "Junior" because they may feel they deserve more, given the amount of money they spend.

Your company may not give you much flexibility with your choice of titles—they may be linked closely with the remuneration package of the employee. Even in these situations where you think your hands are tied, there is still plenty of wiggle room, and I detail this later in the chapter.

6.3.2 *Ladder to improvement*

Larger, established companies may already have a defined sequence of titles and what each level means. However, for smaller companies, these may not have been created yet. That said, even if they have, you as the leader of the Engineering Group will have to define what your expectations are for each of the levels. Let's take a look in table 6.1 at a fairly common and standard title ladder in the technology space.

Table 6.1 Title ladder: technology

Title	Experience	Notes
Junior	0–2 years	Typically entry level; recent graduate starting position
Associate	2+ years	Has industry experience but is still learning their trade
Senior	5+ years	Knows their trade very well, to great depth
Lead/Manager	5+ years	Ready to take on the responsibility of managing the output of others
Architect	10+ years	Has a deep knowledge in a number of disciplines within their sphere and responsible for thinking broader
Divisional Manager/ Vice President	10+ years	Responsible for more than one team that is focused in a defined area; usually involved with budgets
Fellow	15+ years	Special title, like a lifetime achievement, or a university tenure, to recognize long-term continued efforts

Each of these titles should ideally be tied to some sort of discipline, for example, "Senior Developer" or "Support Manager." The title serves as a marker within the disciplines of your group. There are always exceptions to the rule, and the titles will always be contextual to the circumstances of your company. Some organizations usually have a theme. For example, at IBM, everyone, it would appear, is a "Vice President" of something! Others use "Director" as a title of seniority, which is confusing, because the United Kingdom uses "Managing Director" instead of "Chief Executive Officer" (the "Director" title in the United Kingdom has a legal ramification because they are legally listed as a steward of the company with the company registration). Do not confuse the experience with the title—operating at a Junior level for five years does not make someone a Senior.

6.3.3 *Common mistakes with titles*

Some companies have created some serious problems for themselves through the simple act of misaligning titles to people. For the vast majority of decisions we make as a leader, we have some way to undo them. That said, once a title has been assigned to a person, removing that, or reassigning it, can be seen as a demotion, may have to involve HR, and will have demoralizing effects. Some common mistakes in granting titles follow:

- *Too rapid a promotion*—Promotions should come few and far between and should never be done as a result of a single win or event.
- *Title in lieu of salary increase*—When you need to reward someone, but you don't have the budget, it is tempting to change their title. All this does is give them a reason to start looking around for roles with a similar title for the money they should be paid. You can't pay a Senior the same salary you pay a Junior.

- *Rewarding longevity with a title*—Just because someone has been with the company for 20 years does not automatically make them a Senior if they have not met the criteria. This is closely linked to steadily increasing someone's salary, just because they have turned up on time. Both outcomes create major issues and are one of the most common problems new CTOs find themselves inheriting.
- *Being too clever with titles*—As tempting as it is, stick to titles that are recognized in the industry. This will allow you to not only recruit more easily but also allow your own existing team to feel a sense of belonging to a large community and be understandable by clients.

From the field

Chief Knowledge Officer

I once had this lofty title at a well-funded Silicon Valley startup, some 20 years ago. This startup had a lot of alumni of the early Java world, and we gave ourselves edgy and trendy titles . . . except they meant nothing to the outside world. In reality, I was playing the role of Evangelist, which is way more meaningful to others than the title we thought was clever. In the end, our titles proved too contrary—we kept getting overlooked because our potential customers could never figure out who they should be speaking to.

6.4 Team reporting

Now that you have your teams formed and they know what their roles are, the question focuses on finding a way to work with these teams. Because you are not going to be a micromanager and your teams will have autonomy, you need to find a way to coordinate their activity and keep informed of their progress and any issues they may be facing. This is where you need to find a good mechanism for working with your team leaders, so at any point in time, you have a good handle on the overall state of play of your department (good or bad).

Inspire

Lifting others up

It is not uncommon for some of your team managers to be lacking in managerial skills, or have had no formal training, if you are inheriting existing teams. They have learned on the job and have probably largely modeled their style on their only real frame of reference: their own boss. That is now you. How you manage will be seen as a guide for others to follow, hopefully. Keep this in mind, especially when times are tough or stressful, because everything you do will be remembered and copied as they manage their teams. I always ask myself, would I be happy working for me? For the record, there have been times throughout my career, I would have to answer NO to that one.

6.4.1   Define autonomy

Although you want your teams to be independent, at certain times, you will need to be involved and weigh in on decisions, just like you have to be answerable to the CEO. Just like the CEO will have outlined some things for which you need to seek their approval (or even the board's), you have to set a similar framework for your teams. Each team may have slightly different rules of engagement, depending on their overall role in your group and the experience of the manager, but everyone should have to adhere to a common set of rules.

You can break this down into three buckets: things they should be able to handle internally, issues that require you to be aware of, and, finally, decisions that you have to weigh in on and make a final decision. Some examples of topics you may consider are shown in table 6.2.

Table 6.2   Rules of engagement

No reporting required	Keeping you informed	Decision required
Interviewing potential candidates	Any problem or issue concerning a client	Final interview of top candidates under review
Internal processes pertinent to the team execution	Any production problem	HR consultation or termination considerations
Team one-on-one meetings; PTO management	Security concerns or issues	Purchase or licensing of tools
Project execution	Changes in how the team interacts with other teams	Change of technology or tools
	Any problems with individual team members	
	Timelines; updates	

It is important to give your team leads the right framework and find that balance of the level of detail required.

From the field

Client visibility

I have always said that I should be made aware of any problem related to client disaffection or security breaches or concerns, no matter the time of day. Even then, I made sure all my team had my cell phone, because if I did not acknowledge I read their email or message, they were to call me. I never wanted to be in a position where my CEO was asking me about something that I had no idea about. It is always better that you tell your management of problems before they are made aware through some means outside of your control.

ART OF THE "NO-UPDATE UPDATE"

A good tip taught to me many years ago by Kelley Powell (CEO/author), who at the time was Head of Client Operations at Royall & Co, was the importance of the "no-update update" for situations that had a lot of visibility. Have you ever been in a situation where you are waiting for an update from someone, and as time goes on, with no communication, you wonder whether they have forgotten about you? We've all been there, getting more and more frustrated and annoyed that nothing has happened.

Powell always insisted on updates, even if it was that there was no resolution yet, but things were still being worked on. She favored every 30 or 60 minutes (depending on the severity of the issue at hand) that she wanted to be updated, via email or text.

> **From the field**
>
> I have adopted this rule as my own and have insisted on this methodology from my direct reports. I also give the courtesy to those waiting on me, that I will keep them informed. As silly as it is, I ask that on the top and bottom of the hour that I am kept updated. That way it is easy for people to keep an eye on the clock and not have to remember when the last update was. It doesn't need to be time consuming or detailed—just a quick note to say things are still being worked on.

6.4.2 Reporting metrics

Although this will largely depend on the types of teams you have, it is rare that you can't come up with a set of metrics against which to let your team leads measure and report themselves. These should be metrics that make sense and not there just for the sake of producing some meaningless graphs. A good metric is one that lets you see progress holistically and feed into your overall report that you compile to inform your management team.

The advantage of raw data is that it takes the emotional ambiguity away from measuring the success of a given team. Though, a word of caution: one should resist the urge to have teams compete with one another, because you will most likely be comparing apples to oranges—an unfair comparison. Keep each team in their own metric swim lane and compare them only against their historical (or projected) selves. Examples of common metrics that most teams can use at least one of include these:

- Open/closed tickets
- Support interactions
- Release metrics (quantity and time it takes)
- Performance/load metrics
- Technical debt paydown
- Goal/sprint progress

The metrics should be relatively easy to collect for the team leads and shouldn't be a project in and of itself each time they collect them for you. A good metric will most likely come out of the core tool the team uses (e.g., JIRA, SonarQube, or Jenkins).

With the metrics decided, you need to decide what makes sense for you in terms of the frequency with which you would like to see an update. A weekly update is not unusual, or even once every two weeks. Anything longer than that, then too much can happen without you getting a real line of sight to head off any potential problems before they arise.

6.4.3   *Accountability*

A well-oiled machine is one where all the components are running in harmony, collectively producing the output required to make the engine successful. A team is no different; it needs to perform efficiently with predictability so your group as a whole works. For this to happen, team leads need to be held accountable for their output and take responsibility for their shortcomings or failures and celebrate their wins together.

Agreeing on metrics and goals will remove the emotion from any conversation and let you focus on the data that informs the success of the team. A team that has no goals will never know whether it is falling short or exceeding your expectations. That is unfair to the team and opens you up for subjective emotional rulings.

It may take a number of weeks before the right meaningful metrics are determined, especially if you are first taking over. Once those metrics are agreed on, measured, and assessed, you can start having meaningful conversations, within your meetings, either about how to improve the performance or to establish new benchmarks against which to measure.

Encourage openness and honesty at all levels. This does not mean that you are looking for the "fall guy" to which all blame is assigned when something goes wrong. You are a team of teams, and for a team to be successful, you need a good, solid communication channel based on trust and respect, so should the worst happen, no one feels scared or intimidated coming to you with bad news.

This is very bad

From the Earth to the Moon

This popular HBO series on how the United States got to the moon has an episode that is one of the best allegories for running an engineering team: "Spider." Everyone is working around the clock to meet aggressive deadlines, and they can't figure out why they keep crashing the lunar module, until one engineer sheepishly admits he dropped a rounding error. He goes to the lead, expecting to be fired or chewed out.

The lead Grumman engineer notes, "Did you hide this? Did you try to cover this up? No. It's bad. This is very bad. But go home, get some sleep, and let's get this resolved." Now imagine he had taken the other path: shouting and cursing. Will the next person feel compelled to speak up should they make an error? We may have never gotten to the moon, in that case.

Accountability does not mean all errors or issues are excused and life continues. Accountability means taking responsibility for the error, getting to the root of the problem, and putting in the necessary practices, processes, and even tools to prevent them from being repeated. If nothing changes or is repeated time and time again, then accountability means removing those people responsible from that position and putting in people who can make a difference.

That is your responsibility as the leader of your group of teams. It is not good enough to point the finger and blame a weak manager. They are your manager—it is your decision to keep them in the role and your responsibility to give them the mentorship and guidance to make sure they have all opportunities for success.

Their failure is your failure, which casts a shadow on all your houses. The CEO will be watching and managing you, and if they feel you can no longer manage your team, they will replace you. This is especially true if your company is part of a private equity portfolio. Private equity doesn't have the time to tolerate too many mistakes, and they have a long list of seasoned, trained, well-respected executives to replace you within a heartbeat—and you will never see it coming.

Keeping your team accountable means holding them to the metrics and responsibilities they have agreed to undertake when they take on the role. It is setting up your teams for success. Their success is your success.

6.5   One-on-one meeting

Of all the meetings that start to creep into your calendar, the one that should never be postponed or canceled is the classic one-on-one. This, as the name suggests, is when you meet individually with one of your team leads on a regular basis, typically once a week or every second week. The ideal length for these meetings should be from 15 to 30 minutes, and they are designed to be check-ins on the well-being of the person in question.

These meetings should be held in the strictest confidence, and some even think of them like mini therapy sessions. This is a time for your direct report to highlight any area they may be struggling with and seek your assistance with resolving it. An example could be helping someone be more confident in talking to the team because their nerves hold them back from addressing the group as a whole.

This is also an opportunity for them to bring up any concerns they may have working with you. Maybe you have a style that is coming over in a manner you didn't mean, and they should feel comfortable enough bringing that to your attention. Chances are, others may be feeling the same.

Conversely, this is a meeting format that should not be used for discussing project updates, deadlines, or issues. There are other avenues to discuss those agenda items. See table 6.3.

Table 6.3   Meeting format

In-scope topics	Out-of-scope topics
Personal goals	Project updates
Areas for improvement	New tasks you want them to address
Concerns they have regarding their execution	Disciplinary talks
Analysis of a recent event	Gossip about other members
	Company updates

You are not expected to have all the answers. You are expected to listen, sympathize, and offer guidance where applicable. These types of meetings are invaluable for the team leads who find themselves in this new role and may be making some rookie mistakes—a few cautionary words in their ears can transform their management style.

This is an opportunity to make small corrective actions over a short space of time before something gets so big that you have to consider whether you made the right decision putting them in that role in the first place.

From the field

I have found these meetings to be invaluable as a way to subtly get people to start thinking about their own output and how they want to be known. For example, if I have witnessed something that I felt could have been done better, I may start by asking how they felt something went—did they get their message across? Did they feel the room understood exactly what they were asking? Then, instead of saying how you would do it, you suggest different ways they could have done the same thing and ask them whether it would yield different results.

Use these one-on-one meetings as a way to build up trust and offer mentorship and your wisdom, in a format that doesn't come over as patronizing or lecturing.

6.6   *Education and training*

We are fortunate to work in one of the most sophisticated, high-paced industries, which continually reinvents itself every few years. Keeping up with trends, tools, and processes is not a want but a necessity. As the leader of your group, it is up to you to keep your team educated and trained in the latest information so not only do they provide improved productivity, keeping your platform modern, but they also gain self-worth and self-esteem.

The good news is that the vast majority of people who work in our industry know they have to keep learning and run toward it. Although some are not looking to switch disciplines entirely, they do need to keep on top of the latest versions of the tools they use, language improvements, and so on.

In the old days, you would think of training as some sort of formal classroom-style process for which you would send your team away for a few days at a time, at great expense. You'd beg for a training budget from management, who could never see the benefit in keeping their workforce educated. Fortunately, those days are gone, with an abundance of online resources, including material from top-rated universities, all just a click away.

With that, your role is not only to make these materials accessible to your team but to build in the necessary time to allow them to take advantage of them properly. We are going to go through a number of options open to you.

Whatever path you take, make sure you keep on top of your training. Training and retaining existing employees is so much cheaper than terminating, with resultant training and onboarding new employees.

6.6.1 *Online libraries/resources*

Many different online resources, both free and for a free, are available. These come in many different forms and packages. Many technical publishers have special subscriptions that give you unlimited access to their back catalog of books for your team. Specialized sites (e.g., Khan Academy and Coursera) offer more formal online-class-style courses, with exercises and tests, all for free. Other sites, such as Udemy, offer a learning experience for a few dollars per course.

It is important that you and your team lead vet these courses to make sure they are going to be relevant for your team and worth their while. This sort of learning is ideal for people who like to learn at their own pace and by themselves.

6.6.2 *Platform/software certifications*

Many of the large players, such as Amazon, Microsoft, Cisco, and Oracle, offer certification opportunities for many of their products. The prices for these have dramatically fallen over the years, with many of the certifications costing only a few hundred dollars (compared to thousands a number of years ago).

The advantage of a certification is that it proves the person has completed the necessary training and been tested to prove they have a grasp of the subject at hand. This is very advantageous for not only their own personal résumé but also for you to know you have trained and certified people on your team. Nearly all certification programs offer online courses with testing and small exercises along the way, resulting in a final test at the end.

6.6.3 *Bootcamps*

Bootcamps, particularly coding ones, have become really popular in recent years because there has been a push to get more people into programming. They can take many different forms, from intense immersive sessions all crammed into a week, to those spread over a series of weeks, run either in the evening or over lunchtime. They are run as in-person, classroom-style setups, so you are learning from a teacher, networking, and learning from others.

The cost of these camps makes them accessible; they are designed to be paid by the individual to improve their career, so it should not present any significant budgetary hurdle for a company to send individuals to them.

6.6.4   *User groups*

A more subtle form of learning is to use local user groups. These are usually centered around a specific technology or language and meet once a month (in the evening with pizza and beer), where a guest speaker comes and talks about a new feature or process or dives into an existing area so others can better understand and use it.

A user group can be a great networking event and one you should always encouraged your teams to seek out and attend. It is always good to know your peers in the local area who work on the same technologies, so should they hit a problem, or need some advice, they can reach out and have a chat.

Most user groups are not financed and rely on the goodwill of local companies to donate speaker space and sponsor the food. If you are in a position to offer your own office space for a guest speaker, it is a great way for others to not only learn about your company and what you do but also to meet like-minded people within your area.

6.6.5   *Internal training*

Given the internal intelligence of your own team, why not structure sessions to share the knowledge? You can create an environment where specific subject matter experts take some time to create a small session to introduce or go deeper in their area of expertise.

If you don't want to be quite as formal, you can look to do what is called "brown bag lunches," where a topic is discussed at length over lunch—the idea being that everyone brings their own lunch and eats while they learn, though in these situations, it is always a goodwill gesture to buy lunch for everyone who attends.

6.6.6   *Conferences*

Conferences used to be very popular, before the COVID-19 pandemic, and it remains to be seen whether they will ever come back to the size they once were (think AWS re:Invent, when 30,000 people would descend on Las Vegas for a week). That said, many have gone online to great success, capturing the essence of what made them great, albeit without the networking aspect.

Conferences pack in a lot of sessions, of differing levels, to give delegates an easy way to sample a lot of things at once. Sending one or two members to a conference (particularly one that involves travel and accommodations) can be expensive and not something you can offer to everyone (someone has to mind the shop while they are gone). A good way to work this is to reward your top performers with this opportunity and have them come back and present one or two summary sessions to everyone else. You can also send people with a specific task to learn about a given technology or product and have them come back and educate everyone on what they learned.

6.6.7   *University/college courses*

Some people want to take a significant leap in their career and look to obtain a degree in a given subject. This is a big commitment both in time and financially, sometimes costing many thousands of dollars over a number of years.

Depending on the type of degree, you may consider sponsoring all or part of the education, allowing time to be taken during the working day to go to classes. If you see value for your organization, you can structure an agreement where your company will help, on the assumption that when the person graduates, they must stay with your team for a designated number of years. Failing that, they will owe you the investment you made in them. Be thoughtful when establishing a policy around this offering so as not to inadvertently create discontent with those who do not receive this benefit. They can see and support why the specific employee is participating.

6.7   *Communication*

Ask any happy team member what makes them happy, and somewhere in that list, the word *transparent* will come out: the feeling and comfort of knowing what is going on around them, to be included. Transparency does not automatically mean you have to tell everyone everything the moment you learn it. You will learn confidential information from the other C levels that is maybe not yet ready to be shared or has not been thought through enough to be relayed without causing undue stress and anxiety.

As the leader of your group, you are there as their conduit to the business, distilling down and contextualizing information that is meaningful for them. Justin Marquardt, Partner at the private equity firm New Harbor Capital, puts it succinctly: "Crucially, they [CTOs] are strong communicators, effectively articulating both to their team, other senior leaders and the board how that roadmap aligns with the company's strategic initiatives, including an ability to elevate from the specifics of the underlying technology to convey how the various initiatives interrelate with core business goals."

Transparency is being respectful and thoughtful enough to take the time to communicate information in a forthcoming way. In this section, we are going to cover how you should communicate and the types and frequency of meetings that you should consider.

6.7.1   *Email*

One of the most popular ways of distributing information is still email. Although chat systems are increasingly found everywhere (Slack, Mattermost, Cliq, Teams, etc.), these should be treated as real-time communications and not as a historical record that you expect people to read and catch up with. These systems are transient and for the moment in time. Do not use them as a way to broadcast critical information that you wish everyone to read. Stay with email.

You should create an email alias for your whole group (engineering@xxx.com) that includes everyone currently in your group. This way you don't have to worry about leaving anyone out, and part of the on-/offboarding process is keeping this list updated. The following topics are good candidates for a group-wide email:

- *Hires/additions to the group*—A quick introduction of the person joining, with a brief summary of their accomplishments, the role they will be playing, and when they will be joining. It's always better to send this email before the person arrives so people are more welcoming to a new face.
- *Terminations/resignations*—Let the group know when someone is leaving, including the date. Invite others to share in your best wishes for their future. Even with terminations, wish them the best. Phrases like, "We've agreed mutually that our journey together has come to its conclusion," are all you need to say, without getting into any details that may be sensitive. If they are leaving for a better role, celebrate the fact you all had a part in making their career step.
- *Company announcements*—For any broad company announcements that have been shared, it sometimes requires a follow-up communication from you that will help contextualize what this means to your group specifically.
- *Group announcements*—Major milestones, major successes, and recognizing exceptional team members are all good candidates for talking to the group. Also, any failures or missteps should be highlighted, without finger-pointing, as well as the remedies you are implementing to prevent such in the future.
- *Industry trends that may impact the company*—These should be used cautiously and not simply for sharing links every time you find something interesting (use a Slack public channel for those). These are major shifts or changes that will have a near- to long-term effect on the way your group operates.

Resist the urge to use the distribution list for informal topics; you want to set a precedent that when receiving this email, recipients will know that it is not noise but important enough for people to pay attention to.

WRITING STYLE

If we are honest with ourselves, we all have written that email or text that we wish we would never have sent. Either the tone was interpreted in a manner contrary to our intention, the humor failed to land, or we offended someone (intentionally or not). Such communications have no place and do nothing for your legacy.

> **Find your style**
>
> The best piece of advice I ever got from my now-deceased mentor, Jeremy Geelan (journalist, BBC producer, and publisher), was to write as if it was going to be published and live forever. Before pressing Send, upon rereading, would you be happy for this to be reprinted? It is a simple but effective litmus test, because every time I am sending an email I hear his voice asking me this—and many times I have reviewed and edited the tone.

Tips for writing a good professional email for a wider distribution include these:

- Use your natural voice; don't try to be too formal.
- Do not use any profanity, innuendos, or slurs.
- No personal attacks no matter what.
- Be honest: no conjecture, no hyperbole.
- Keep it professional. Keep it on point. Keep it honest.

It is worth remembering that email never gets deleted. Increasingly, companies keep copies of every single email that is sent and received in a special audit vault that can never be manipulated. This could be for regulatory reasons, or if a company is feeling particularly legally cautious. Services such as G Suite and Office 365 make it trivial to set up this vault. So even if you think you have deleted the email, as soon as it leaves your outbox, it is probably too late to take it back. It has been preserved forever, and because the company owns that email, it may be used for or against you.

6.7.2 Meetings

Meetings are an important part of keeping the wheels of industry turning. Even if you use video conferencing, it is vital you have that personal connection with not only your team leads but all the members of your group. In this section, we are going to go through some of the common types of meetings you'll want to use.

ENGINEERING MEETING

This is a meeting for you to communicate to your group as a whole how things are going. The engineering meeting is one that is scheduled either weekly or biweekly and should last no more than 30 minutes. Topics include celebrating major releases, customer acquisitions or losses, process improvements, and structural changes. The format should be fairly steady, so people get used to what to expect.

Keeping it to 30 minutes allows your team to avoid getting fatigued and feel that each meeting is worthy of their time to come together.

TOWN HALL MEETING

A town hall meeting is a special meeting that should be reserved for a specific topic and scheduled only as and when the need arises. The format of this meeting consists of someone taking the lead to present on a given subject at hand followed by an open Q&A with the participants.

This type of meeting is particularly useful for when you are proposing a new initiative, change in product direction, or something from the company that needs to be distilled down for your group. This is also a good type of meeting to have if you want to invite another leader from elsewhere in the company to let them explain what it is their group does or what impact a decision they have made recently will have on your group.

TEAM MEETINGS

Regular meetings with your team leaders will not only keep you informed but will ensure the other team leaders are kept updated on others' progress. These should be held once a week and focus on the high-level issues affecting each team without getting derailed into discussing specific details. If this happens, which is common, table it and invite those concerned to either hang back after the meeting or schedule another one with just the necessary parties.

Keep these to 60 minutes at most, and give each team lead the same amount of time to report on their group's status. Create an agenda that clearly states the order of play and the time you are going to give to each while leaving room at the end for any other business.

AD HOC MEETINGS

Too many people default the meeting length to 60 minutes; this is a mistake, and you will slowly get your time sucked away as your group and company grows in size. Instead, set the default to be either 15 or 30 minutes, asking people to set a specific one- or two-agenda-item list, which allows everyone to know what to expect.

A meeting is one of the most disruptive devices in the corporate world, so be respectful of the time you ask for people to come around a table (virtual or not).

INTERACTIVE MEETING RULES

Running an interactive meeting is more than just bringing people together and having them talk. This is a business exchange, not a social event. Rules will make everyone focus on the task at hand to get the desired outcome much quicker. Some suggestions can include these:

- The agenda should be distributed in advance, including any reading materials.
- Have only the people who will contribute; do not include people for simply keeping them in the know.
- No interruptions are permitted; cell phones are off the table.
- No catering—the meeting should not be long enough you need snacks.
- Laptops are used only for presentations; it is too easy to become a distraction while checking emails or messages.

A meeting should be focused, productive, and convenient. Today it is easy to record meetings that are online, but that is sometimes overkill. I tend to save meetings where users are demonstrating something that would be useful to a wider audience. Minutes should be taken at a minimum, which means taking note of any action items people have agreed to do.

> ### Further reading
>
> *Meetings Suck, Cameron Herold*
>
> I would highly recommend buying Herold's book on how to make meetings far more productive. He goes into the logistics of running meetings, frequency, and setting agendas that people will actually adhere to. I interviewed him on the MacLaurin Group's *Demystifying Technology* podcast, where we spoke at length about how meetings can be made more efficient.
>
> ISBN-10 : 1619614146
>
> https://www.amazon.com/Meetings-Suck-Elements-Business-Valuable/dp/1619614146/

6.7.3 Feedback

It is important you are accessible to anyone in your group to answer any queries, without them feeling they have to necessarily follow the hierarchy. It completely depends on your communication preference on how best you wish to interact, but be cautious with simply throwing your door open, in the classic "my door is always open" manner—people will use it.

Instead, invite anyone to reach out, and if you feel it needs more time, ask them to schedule 15 minutes on your calendar so you can give them the attention and respect they deserve. Simply dismissing someone or listening to someone while you still type at your keyboard is the worst thing you can do. Yet, you don't want continual interruptions. That is why it is important to set your expectations clearly and be up-front.

> ### Manage expectations
>
> I would always welcome people to walk with me and talk, or, if it was important, to set time on my calendar. I would never let myself get sucked into a conversation on the spot. I would quickly ascertain whether the situation required more than a one-sentence answer, and, if so, I would then ask them to find time on my calendar. That way, I knew I could give them the time they deserve and never be that person who was always running out on them or checking messages while talking.

You want to make sure you are genuinely accessible and welcoming. It isn't something you say because it sounds good, but you never follow through with it. Make your words have actions. People will understand if you let them know you are busy and the topic is important enough to wait so that you can give your full attention and focus. This allows the employee to feel important rather than dismissed.

Summary

- Creating a charter for each team that lists precisely what their responsibility is keeps everyone informed and aligned.

- There are many ways to arrange teams, be it skill based, product based, or process based. Each one has its role and should be evaluated against your needs.

- You are building not only a team but a career path for people to evolve and grow. Taking time to map this out will show you value your team's development.

- Defining a structure for the titles is more than just fancy-sounding titles—these are badges that are worn outside of your organization and others will rate and judge subconsciously.

- Establishing a process for how you want your team leads to report, complete with the level of detail and cadence expected, will make sure people will not let you down.

- Encouraging and promoting individual one-on-one meetings gives you an opportunity to work with people on their softer skills.

- Having an ongoing training program is important to not only keep your team relevant but to allow people to explore new disciplines that may be useful at a later date.

- As the leader, deciding on your communication style is important, but more openness and transparency will make people trust you more and have more confidence in your decisions.

Checklist

How many of the following items can you lay claim to having covered?

- Created a charter that details the reason a given team exists and the metrics for them being successful

- Clearly defined how each team is structured and aligns with the business

- Thought through each title in your team and what it means both internally and externally

- Laid out how you wish your team leads to periodically report their progress to you

- Scheduled regular one-on-one meetings with your team leads

- Expressed to your team the support you give for continual learning and improving

- Scheduled meetings in your calendar with a clear objective and outcome, so people know their time is not being wasted

Annual reviews

7

Owning and running a car requires annual inspections and servicing to keep it running optimally and for you to get a heads-up on any potential issues before they become too problematic to resolve. Managing your team requires the same inspections: a yearly check-in to make sure everyone is happy with progress and to track where they want and need to go. It is an opportunity to make any corrections and for people to understand the areas they are excelling in, the areas in which they need improvement, and any new opportunities you or they would like to explore.

You may already be doing reviews or some version of them. Most people dread that time of year, because it creates a huge administrative overhead, depending on the number in the team, and can result in a very superficial/rushed experience with no value coming out of it, except to tick a box for HR. Often annual reviews are tied to a time of the year when a company determines compensation adjustments and bonuses. This has the benefit of having everything done at the same time, but it also means everything is done at the same time!

In this section, we are going to go over how you can structure annual reviews to be beneficial to you and team members alike, so they are something to be looked forward to, not dreaded, and relatively quick to perform. I'll introduce a skill matrix that will break this whole process down into a more data-led engagement instead of one that is led by the gut or emotions.

The task of terminating an employee (for any one of a number of reasons) takes careful execution, and we will go over the ways you can do this so everyone comes out with no bitter taste.

Some organizations do more frequent reviews, such as quarterly or every six months. It shouldn't be too frequent, and as long as your team has regular check-ins with their managers (or you), then anything more than annual is too much overhead.

Finally, we will look at remote working, and how this can affect the review process.

7.1   *Skill matrix*

You may have seen, or been subject to, the classic review questionnaire, which goes something like this: "List three areas that the employee is exceeding in, and identify three areas that need more attention." It's a very popular format, but it really helps no one develop in their career because it is too vague. Not only is it hard (and tedious) for the manager to fill in, especially if they have a large number to do, it is also difficult for the employee to truly interpret. It also assumes the employee needs improvement—a presumption that can be argued, but managers have been known to say, "But I have to find something; otherwise, HR comes after me."

Let's also consider the team member who is seeking a promotion. This format gives them very little information on how to achieve that promotion. Their review is seen through the lens of their current role, with very few indications or advice on what they need to do to gain the next level in their career. How many times have we heard, in our own careers, "Just work a little harder, and you will be promoted"? That helps no one and leaves a bittersweet taste because promotion seems to be the result of working harder (in other words, putting in more hours for no extra pay), not smarter.

This is why the skills matrix exists—a system that not only rates how well people are doing in their current role but clearly lays out what they need to do to achieve the next level, all without having to write long reams of text or contriving feedback for the sake of feedback.

Interview

Using the matrix

As you will see, a well-created skills matrix is not only for annual reviews but can also make your interviewing process easier because you will have something solid to rate each candidate against. You can form your questions/exercises around each area so you can rate where on the range you believe they sit at the time of the interview.

7.1.1 Basic matrix structure

The matrix is a grid of competencies, aligned against an axis of areas versus seniority. Each role you have within your department should have its own separate skills matrix, specifically tailored for the key attributes that you require for that role to be successful.

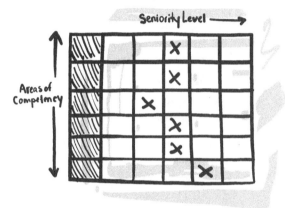

The left-hand side is a list of areas that are important to each person in the role, irrespective of their seniority. Here is an example list from a matrix for a developer/engineer:

- *Core discipline knowledge*—Technical information pertaining to their discipline/area
- *Business knowledge*—Knowledge of not only the company products but the marketplace and trends
- *Communication*—General communication, including emails/chats, talking, and presentations
- *Planning and work*—Managing tasks, identifying, scheduling, and execution
- *Output and ownership*—Quality of output/end result and how they manage the support of that output
- *Problem-solving and innovation*—Ability to solve problems and innovate where necessary
- *Mentoring and leadership*—Interacting and knowledge sharing with others

These area should be tailored specifically to your organization but should be broad enough that they cover both hard (technical knowledge) and soft (interpersonal) skills. For example, if your group regularly interacts with end clients, then how they present both the company and themselves externally is important.

Spend time determining these competence areas that are important to your group but also align with the core values of the company. Solidifying these core areas will make the next phase easier. Do not be too abstract, because you need to explain and describe these to your group.

For each role in your team, you need to identify a progression or seniority level. This will be different for each role, and depending on the size of your organization, it may be tied to a specific pay grade. Some roles may not have as many rungs on the ladder to climb as others. That is okay, but determining that up front removes all ambiguity going forward. These will be the titles/labels you associate with each person—think of it like the title that would be printed on their business card. An example range for a typical developer role could be as follows:

1 Associate, Junior/Graduate
2 Associate
3 Associate, Senior
4 Lead
5 Manager
6 Director
7 Fellow

The goal here is to show a career growth path, illustrating the levels that your organization recognizes at both a compensation and responsibility metric.

At this point, the x-axis (the competencies) and the y-axis (the seniority levels) are defined. This is everything required to complete the skills matrix.

7.1.2 Filling out the grid

For each x/y position, we define the expectations required for each role against a given competency. Craft one or two sentences that describe, without being overly detailed, what success looks like in each area. A good description is one that allows you to easily talk through it and for you to give concrete examples of where things are succeeding or failing for someone. Although you may be looking at well over 30 descriptions to be filled out, it is an exercise that will repay you with every review and interview you do from here on in.

Table 7.1 shows examples of what a typical matrix could look like for a developer with at least three levels of seniority to strive for.

Table 7.1 Basic matrix structure—Developer

Competency	Junior Associate	Associate	Senior Associate
Core discipline	Basic understanding	Shares discipline knowledge with others	Follows industry trends, knows advanced techniques/patterns
Business knowledge	Understanding of what business does at a high level	Knows at least one area of the business at a high level	Knows all the major units of the business at a high level

Table 7.1 Basic matrix structure—Developer *(continued)*

Competency	Junior Associate	Associate	Senior Associate
Communication	Clearly articulates their own status	Within the team, clearly communicates their technical detail and status	Clearly translates technical detail/status to nontechnical people
Planning and work	Clearly articulated to fine detail by lead	Clearly articulated by lead but must further define the finer details	Basic task provided by lead but must further define details through research and questions
Output/ownership	Verified by seniors	Verified by senior, but at a high level	Output trusted to be high quality; designs are reviewed by leads
Problem solving	Offers solutions narrow in their scope	Proposes solutions for a wider scope	Proactive in identifying and solving problems
Mentoring/ leadership	Accepts direction and guidance from others	Mentored by seniors; may mentor juniors	Mentors associates and juniors in their discipline

Over time, the definitions will evolve, as you see how your team grows and matures. One of the key goals is to be crisp and clear enough so the reasoning why someone is at the level they are is not subjective but that they are demonstrably performing at the expectation level.

7.1.3 *Logistics*

Once you have the rough timing of when you are going to be running the annual review, then make sure you set a date and give the person being reviewed at least a week's notice. This gives them time to prepare. As part of the preparation, give them a copy of the matrix for their role, and ask them to self-assess where they believe they are currently operating. As part of this, guide them to think of examples for times they are operating at a higher level.

As their manager, you will do the same, referring to the previous years' matrix if available, to see how they are evolving. Look at it as a whole, and do not let one particular incident (successful or otherwise) influence you into thinking they deserve a promotion/demotion.

For each discipline, rate in which seniority column they are consistently operating. If they are falling behind in a given area, note down examples of situations that have led you to that conclusion. If someone is close but not quite hitting the mark for a promotion, it is perfectly acceptable to communicate what they need to do and set a date for, say, six months to reevaluate so you are not having them wait another year for a chance at a promotion.

When the review meeting arrives, the first thing to do is to review their self-assessment against your assessment. Lay them on top of each other and note the differences—this is where you focus the conversation from there on in. By focusing on specific areas, explaining the reasoning, it is much easier to determine the corrective plan that is needed to succeed in the area in question. Be prepared for the following outcomes:

- *No improvement*—It is perfectly acceptable that a person stays consistent, performing at the level you and they are happy with. Some do not want extra responsibility, depending on where they are in life. For these, any pay raises should be related only to inflation.
- *Overconfidence*—Most people have a tendency to be overconfident in their ability and will most likely rate themselves one or two levels above where they are, citing a given example of where they truly excelled. One swallow does not make a summer, as they say, and it is important to continue to level the conversation back down to being consistent. Sometimes you may lose someone who believes strongly that they deserve more. In my experience, you are never going to truly satisfy them, and it is best to let them continue their career elsewhere.
- *Underperforming*—If someone is underperforming in a number of areas, this can point to a number of things, including being overstressed or overworked, or, in some instances, just losing interest in the role they are in. In these situations, probe to discover whether there is a reason they have slipped, and look to work together to address it. Do not immediately demote them, but review the situation in six months' time to see whether a realignment is required to them put in a role that will give them success and enjoyment.
- *Outperforming*—For someone who is outperforming their current role, consistently across the board, then promotion is definitely in the cards. However, be careful not to jump too many levels at once; my advice is not to skip over any levels at all. No matter how well they are doing, they will be lacking the experience in the levels they are jumping that may prove key for consistency at their new promoted level.

The circumstance in which you promote someone is up to how important you believe each of the competencies is to the role. For example, someone may be excelling in six of out eight competencies, but that might be enough to promote them. Remember, the skills matrix is a guideline, not a hard-and-fast rule book.

When promotions are being awarded, celebrate these with communication out to the group as a whole, citing the reasons for the promotion. This cements your transparency and commitment to data-led decisions that show no favoritism or bias.

7.2   *Handling failure*

Failure in our technology world isn't a case of if but when. Failures come in many different forms and at all the wrong times. System failures, software crashes, hardware breaking, power loss, natural disasters, wrong buttons pressed, buttons forgotten to be pressed—with all these traps ready to spring, it is a wonder things work as well as they do.

In this section, we are going to focus on the failures that resulted from human error and the best procedures for handling these in a controlled and structured manner. Most errors can be attributed to someone having not anticipated the failure. For example, power loss can frequently happen, but you would expect your IT Manager to have the necessary procedures in place to have backup power in place—or maybe you decided not to fund it. Either way, a human is responsible for the break in business continuity.

7.2.1   Initial reaction

When it has been established that a human error has occurred, the first thing you should never do is to start blaming that person for the problem, especially outside of your group. No matter the issue, at the end of the day, their failure/mistake is yours to own. The well-known phrase popularized by the 33rd US President, Harry S. Truman, "The buck stops here," is more than just a snappy saying. It embodies a manager taking the responsibility for failures in their organization. Many managers claim that they hold themselves up to this standard, but few actually do.

Being quick to blame others and dismiss an issue as someone's lack of focus or incompetence says more about your leadership than the individual in question. So, the top things you should never do follow:

- Shouting and using expletives or body language that suggests intimidation
- Using threats or direct insults
- Carrying out instant terminations

No matter how stressed you are, how angry you become, or how disappointed, no justification can excuse any of these reactions.

Determining the root of the issue is paramount before you continue, or at least enough of a reason to stop it from continuing while you investigate further. Your role is to come up with a plan to prevent such a thing from happening again, and if you can't truly prevent it, then determine how can you minimize the "blast radius" should it happen again.

7.2.2   Investigation

As you are going through the reason for the problem, you determine whether it falls into one of the two following camps:

- Mistake/incompetence
- Lack of foresight/planning

A popular framework for helping get to the root of the problem is the "five whys" iterative narrowing approach, devised by the founder of Toyota. It doesn't always work, because sometimes there are many reasons for something to fail, but what it does do is to start the questioning at a high level and, at each answer, try to narrow it down.

If this was a genuine mistake, then you have to determine whether this is a training issue. Was the person in question properly trained in the first place? If they were, was this a basic error, or was this a rather sophisticated edge case that no amount of training would have prepared them for? How did the error happen in the first place—was the individual distracted or stressed and, as a result, did something they shouldn't have? Were steps missed?

Determining the answers to these questions will give you a broader picture of where the system fell down and the steps you can take to prevent failure. Are there things you can put in place, in terms of software guard rails, for checks and balances? Or is this just a case of retraining or additional reviews to make sure everyone is made aware?

From the field

Wrong window

I worked with a client where pandemonium broke loose one morning when all the alarms went off, alerting us to something big in production. Attempts to log on to the servers (these were early days when you still SSHed into servers) yielded nothing— it was as if they had disappeared. They had! The System Manager had accidentally "deleted" a cluster of web servers in production. He had too many terminal windows open, and he thought he was working in the dev environment and was cleaning up resources no longer being used. After this, a number of safeguards were put in place, but the most obvious one was having any terminal window open to a production server be rendered in a horribly obnoxious color so it stood out.

Record the incident and why it occurred. Document the steps for rectification.

If this employee turns out to be a repeat offender, then maybe you have the wrong person in the role, especially if others in the team are coping with the same tasks with no problems. A change in personnel may be required if this skill is core to their role and they are failing to live up to it. Termination should not be seen as a punishment or retribution but instead a recognition that this person is not qualified for the role they were hired for. Although upsetting and inconvenient, use this particular incident as a part of your interview process so you may gauge how others would cope in the future.

On the other hand, when the issue could have been prevented by better planning, the conversation takes a different tone. Although no one can plan for every eventuality, you should expect some basic things from your team that has been put in a role of responsibility. Examples can include the following:

- A security breach because the person responsible for security didn't install or update the firewall

- Data loss because the person in charge of databases didn't properly test and confirm backups
- Loss of service because the person missed an email for a problem in payment
- Hardware failure because the person responsible for the hardware never had an upgrade or continuity plan

We are always wise after the event, and what feels obvious in a postmortem is not always clear or important prior to the event. It is amazing how many basic, simple things could have been done to prevent a catastrophe, yet they kept being pushed down the priority list.

Because you are the one in charge, you have to ask yourself whether this was a result of you not authorizing or making a decision that had been on your desk for a number of months. If the Security Manager failed to install the firewall because you didn't authorize the purchase order, then they are not at fault.

Again, document the event and consult the person in charge, and if issues begin to repeat, you may have the wrong person in the role, which can be either resolved by better training or, as a last resort, replacing them with someone who can perform the role.

7.2.3 Learning

No matter the failure, there is always something to learn from it. A CTO who has never experienced failure hasn't yet led. Recording and documenting the issues is an important data-gathering exercise that will let you analyze the issues holistically. A list of potential issues you could document follows:

- *Does a problem keep coming up repeatedly?*—This suggests the processes you are putting in place to prevent the problem aren't working.
- *Are problems isolated to a handful of clients?*—For organizations that are very client centric, it could be something unique about a given client that makes it hard to replicate with others.
- *Is there any seasonality to the problem?*—If a problem happens at the same time consistently, figure out what the external factor is: for example, does the switch to daylight savings cause downtime?
- *Are the same actors involved?*—If the same people keep popping up, then maybe there is a lack of knowledge that requires more training or changing out these employees.
- *What is the impact of the problem/failure?*—Rating the severity of the problem will allow you to determine how much effort you want to deploy to resolve it; sometimes problems are just easier to live with, especially if they are short term or rare.

By documenting your group's failures, you get a better sense of how well your organization is running. No one is going to get it perfect, but learning from failure will make you more reactive and experienced to react to future problems.

7.3   Termination

Probably the thorniest and most troublesome area for any would-be leader, which goes against all human instinct to be a pleaser, is terminating a member of your team. It is an area in which many ask for assistance, hoping there is a back door or trick to remove all the potential ugliness associated with the removal of a resource. You may find yourself having to terminate someone for a number of reasons:

- Downsizing the department
- Skills no longer required
- Poor performance

We will go through each of these scenarios and how to prepare and execute to have a successful outcome for you and the person in question alike. As has been noted a number of times prior, any decision to either add to your team or remove someone should never be taken lightly or in haste. These are people's livelihoods you control, and a level of respect is required when making big decisions that will affect a person's ability to provide for themselves and their family.

> **From the field**
>
> My attitude is that this shouldn't be a problem area and should be treated like any other aspect of running your group—a purely data-led decision, devoid of any emotion or personal bias. If, on the other hand, you are looking to terminate someone because you just don't like them, I would bet the problem is more with you than them, and you are allowing your emotions to spill into your professional decisions. If this situation arises, you need to seek counsel with your HR department and your CEO for their input.

Although it probably does not need saying, when it comes to terminating someone's employment, you should never take this action in isolation. You should always get the support of your CEO/CFO and, if you have one, the HR department should be involved at every step. If you can't convince them that you are making the right decision, you are probably being a bit impulsive and need to have a rethink.

7.3.1   Downsizing the department

Not everything works out as we think it may. We are in an industry that continually reinvents itself, trying out new things and exploring new areas. Sometimes it works better than others, and sometimes, there comes a time when a company has to cut its losses and disband an initiative or group. It could be the market has shifted, or a competitor has beaten you to the punch. Inevitably, when this happens, you may find yourself overstaffed with no other place available for these employees to be moved. Due to no fault of theirs, you no longer have a role for them.

The first thing to do in this instance is to make sure you exhaust all avenues and ensure there is no opportunity for you to use these resources elsewhere. As we know from previous chapters, recruiting and training is expensive, so if you don't have to go through this process, then all the better. Explore all of your options, including retraining them for another role or seeing if there is an opening in another department in the company.

If you have been open and honest with your communication, it will be no surprise to the people involved that this was coming and how hard a decision it was to make. You, your CEO, and the HR department will have come up with a timetable for finally pulling the plug on the initiative, and this is the time all spending must come to an end. Communicate this to the group as a whole, explaining in as much detail as you are permitted about what was achieved and why it is no longer a viable option.

Most likely, depending on their tenure and the governing state, there will be a compensation or redundancy package that has to be offered. This is something your CFO/HR department will advise on and is beyond the scope of this book.

Sit down with each individual, thank them for their efforts and contributions, and assure them it was nothing that they had done that resulted in this. Depending on your organization's ability, it is good practice to help the individuals find new roles, which may include references, calling around, and offering career advice.

It is not unheard of for another company to hire more than one (or all) of the people you are letting go. In this situation, they get a team that is used to working together and has a collective knowledge base. If you see value in the group as a whole, start asking your network whether they would be interested in at least talking to the people.

Dot-com boom
Commoditization of software

Unfortunately, in the 1990s, departments and sometimes entire companies disbanding was very common. The early internet days saw a lot of different competing technologies attempting to solve the same problem, with no standardization. Once standardization started to appear, some of these components became part of larger open source frameworks, freezing out companies and groups that had a business centered around them. Examples included web servers, messaging servers, and utility libraries. This resulted in a very active job market—companies would literally let go of large groups of engineers at once, who would then be scooped by the next dot-com who thought they had all the answers.

7.3.2 *Skills no longer required*

Another common reason related to a group disbanding is when their skills are no longer required in the department. This is common when you have finally replaced legacy systems and that skill set for the platform/language is no longer needed.

The methodology is the same here, but, in this case, no one should be surprised at the result of this, because the group as a whole would have been working actively to replace this area. While this is happening, it is imperative you communicate regularly with the people whose primary skill set will no longer be needed upon successful completion. This gives them the opportunity to retrain as the project evolves, so when the new replacement is ready, they are able to make the switch.

Not everyone wants to retrain; some are more than happy in doing what they do. Unfortunately, you will have to let these people go to explore new horizons. This conversation should be relatively straightforward with no surprising shocks for the person in question. Again, thank them for their contribution and give them as much help as possible in finding their new role.

The key with this area is to give people plenty of runways for them to make their own plans when they know the project is coming to a completion. You have to be careful, though, because you don't want everyone finding new roles before your task is complete. So, if you think you are going to run this risk, then be open and offer a stay-on bonus to make sure you have coverage until the project is complete. Treat those employees as you would want to be treated yourself.

7.3.3   *Poor performance*

You may encounter a situation in which the person simply does not have the skills required to perform the role you need them to do. The determination of this falls into one of two camps:

- Death by a thousand cuts
- The "event"

DEATH BY A THOUSAND CUTS

This is a well-known phrase in combat that comes from the notion that no single cut or wound caused the fatal blow, but instead, it was a sum of all the smaller inflictions that overwhelmed the body. In our less violent and combative environment, this is when the person is failing to come up to standard on a number of fronts at the same time.

These can be hard to spot at first, especially for new hires who interviewed really well, but now that they have been in the role for a period of time, they may have exaggerated or overestimated their ability.

Once you, or your manager, have an inkling that someone isn't performing to the level required, you need to isolate the areas underdelivering and detail what needs to be done to come up to standard. At this point, involve HR or your CEO/CFO (depending on company size). Let them know that you are putting someone under review, and again, if you can convince them, then you are on the right path.

Sitting down and discussing this with the person, citing specific examples, is paramount. After all, you do not want to really lose this person and have to start again with the recruiting and onboarding process. Create a list of the things you need to see improved and by when. This should not be seen or sold as a trap or set of tripwires. This process should be something that shows you are wanting to set them up for success and will offer whatever assistance is required to aid in that goal.

If the person continues to come up short, then upon the date agreed, you have the conversation detailing where things haven't improved and then let them know there is no longer a role for them with the group. This should not be a surprise or be seen as an emotional response by the person in question. With everything documented and communicated, you have laid out your expectations and shown clearly where they are not achieving them.

Structured demotion

It is worth noting that an alternative that I have seen work well in various situations is the structured demotion. If someone is supposed to be operating at a senior level but is really coming in at a junior level, then you can adjust expectations and set them at the level at which they can achieve success. This may involve an adjustment in compensation, but it works well for both parties. I have seen this happen when someone is given a chance to lead engineers but realizes they don't really like that and just want to code.

THE "EVENT"

When something catastrophic has occurred as a result of negligence or incompetence, it can result in a huge fallout for you and the company. Negligence is when something that could have been prevented or mitigated wasn't. Usually, it is a core attribute to an employee's role and their top responsibility. Some examples follow:

- A Data Security Officer who failed to maintain the basic defenses of the system they were hired to oversee
- An IT Manager who managed to lose core data because they didn't think hard disks would ever fail, so, therefore, backups were unnecessary
- A Support Manager who ignored a key client's problem, resulting in the client moving their business

Think carefully before you act. Never terminate someone out of frustration, anger, or revenge, or even for being seen as doing something. Take your time to do the investigation and learn as much as you can as to what led to the event happening. Was this a failure in the system, or a failure in the person not doing something they should have? Could this have been easily avoided? Is the right person in the role?

If your conclusion is that this person doesn't have what it takes, then you take it to your CEO/CFO and HR department, and again, if they agree, then you can plan when you are going to remove them from the team.

Another area where this can come up—which applies to everyone in your company—is poor conduct. Being rude or abusive, using drugs or alcohol, theft, dishonesty, and sexual/racist overtones are all examples that would be enough to have someone immediately fired from most organizations. Should this situation arise, HR needs to be involved as quickly as possible.

7.3.4 Logistics

You need to do the following things when you are letting someone go from your group:

- *Notice period*—Are you going to have the person work a notice period? Depending on the situation, there may be some knowledge transfer required. If you do not need that, then, most of the time, it is advisable to not have the person be physically present for their notice period.

- *Timing*—The age-old question is, "When do you have the conversation"? It is better to have it first thing in the morning and never the last working day of the week. No matter the reason, it is always better to give the person the ability to do something about their next opportunity the next working day, instead of forcing them to wait until Monday rolls around.

- *Communication*—Decide clearly on the points and reasons you are letting the person go because these will be communicated to the person in question. Next, decide on the messaging for the rest of the group to alert them to this. In most situations, simply expressing a skill mismatch and wishing them the best for the future is good enough to cover most situations without getting into too much detail.

- *Delivery*—Never terminate someone without someone else with you. Usually, this will be an HR representative, but failing that, it could be the CFO or even the CEO. If it's one of your managers that is terminating someone, you and HR should be in the room with your manager, because they can help with other logistical questions. You want a witness that all the necessary steps have been taken and the talking points communicated and understood. Say as little as needed while keeping on message.

- *Remove access*—Finally, you need to execute your offboarding procedure to remove all access.

7.3.5   The exit interview

Some people favor the exit interview. This is the last opportunity for an employee to express feedback before they leave the company. Others believe no good ever comes from this process, except to serve as a final venting opportunity for the employee to get something off their chest. Although some companies perform this step, many do not keep the notes and disregard the vast majority of what is communicated—they use it as an opportunity for the ex-employee to think they have lodged a complaint or blow off some steam.

If you are running your group well, nothing new can be learned in an exit interview that shouldn't already be known if you have been regularly meeting with your team and properly conducted one-on-one meetings. You want to foster an environment where people feel they can express their views and feelings without repercussions. You want to know the problems bubbling under the surface before they become something bigger.

7.4   Remote working

Remote working or work from home (WFH) is a popular way for people to juggle the demands of the office and home life by performing their duties away from the office. The technology world led the way in pioneering this working environment once seen as a perk. When bandwidth became faster, it paved the way for greater integration to remote teams via simple-to-use video conferencing. WFH truly took a front seat in 2020, when the global pandemic COVID-19 erupted, forcing workforces all over the world to abandon their offices and quarantine in their own homes. For most of 2020, companies wrestled with the mass switch from a few employees working from home on an occasional basis, to everyone using a variety of chat and video software to stay within their teams.

Not everyone embraces the WFH ethic. There are those who enjoy the physical separation of going into an office, performing their professional duties, then returning home, to switch off and continue their family life. There are those who enjoy the flexibility, especially workers with young families, to see their children grow up while maintaining an active career. This is a policy that is usually set at the company level, but depending on your group, technology teams lend themselves more to a WFH, or at least a hybrid approach, than others.

Managing a remote workforce comes with its own set of challenges and rewards. In this section, we are going to go over how to successfully make sure you still continue to deliver for the needs of the business, whether you decide to have a permanent WFH workforce or a mix of those in the office and at home.

7.4.1 Setup

For WFH to be successful, you have to make sure your team has the necessary resources, including a good, reliable internet line, office furniture, and, of course, a laptop that is powerful enough to do all their work. It is not uncommon for companies to help out when it comes to setting up, purchasing furniture, and cofunding a faster internet line.

Two of the most important items a company should at least purchase—and the payback will be instant—is a high-quality webcam and a headset, including the training on how to use them effectively. Choosing the right video platform that includes screen sharing, guest access, and recording is crucial, especially if you can link it into your backend IT system, so there is a single-sign-on environment. Good examples include Google Meet, Microsoft Teams, Zoom, and Ring, which offer solid offerings with intuitive and easy-to-use interfaces. The goal is to remove as much friction as possible for your remote team to be accessible at the click of a link.

These steps would be taken for those who are going to be coming into the office, including setting up any conference rooms with the necessary resources to be able to join others into a meeting quickly. The good news is that none of this is expensive.

Another key component to an integrated WFH force is a chat system that everyone is logged into. This chat is a virtual way to bring everyone together in one place and has quickly come to replace email as the primary communication channel. However, you should encourage people to use the status feature, indicating when they are away from their desks. Do not assume that just because people are out of the office they are chained to their home desks—you don't expect your office team to be at their desks the whole day. Let the software help communicate when people are up and about. Slack, Mattermost, Cliq, and Teams are all great examples of powerful, integrated chat systems.

If you can bring any of your team into a (virtual) meeting as quickly as you would have them huddle around a whiteboard, then you have the foundation to make WFH work.

7.4.2   *Managing expectations*

Managing a remote workforce should be no different than managing one that is physically in the office with you; you have to trust your team to get on with the work as directed, and if they do not, then it is no different from someone coming into the office every day and failing to deliver.

What a remote workforce does do, however, is force you and your immediate managers to be firm in their expectations and to be diligent in periodically checking in with your remote team. This does not equate to hounding them every 15 minutes for an update. Because you've lost that visible clue that they may be struggling with a problem or assignment, however, you have to consciously reach out and ask. Depending on the type of work they are performing, once or twice a day via chat isn't unreasonable.

Embrace video conferencing, and encourage anyone who may be nervous or intimidated by seeing themselves to use it regularly. The more natural and regular it becomes, the more people will use it. A video call is not a performance—it doesn't need to be perfect or rehearsed. If people need help, then instead of trying to work with someone over chat or email, jump on a video call and make it more personal. A video allows both parties to see the body language, which can accelerate a resolution.

When managing your remote team, lay out your expectations. Establish core hours, for example, during which you expect your team to be available online as if they were in the office. Determine how best you wish people to communicate that they are not at their desk, for example, breaks, lunchtimes, or anything else that pulls them away. This way, no one treats your remote team like a call center that is instantly available to any query at any time.

Working remotely does not necessarily mean flexible hours (where you choose your own hours). It can be a healthy mix, but this comes down to how much interaction you require your team to have in real time. It is perfectly okay to expect your WFH people to be aligned with what would have been office hours. If you can support flexible time, then that should be a completely separate discussion and agreement that is outside of the WFH plan.

7.4.3 *Preventing abuse*

Both manager and employee have to work a little extra to make sure remote working is successful. This does not mean putting in extra hours—it means making the extra effort to make sure both parties set out the expectations as outlined previously. However, as a manager, you need to make extra allowances to ensure you do not subconsciously harbor prejudice against your remote workforce or have higher expectations for them.

The UK government conducted an extensive study, ranging from 2011 to 2020, on the effects of remote work (http://mng.bz/PoQg). Some of their observations, which follow, were enlightening:

- People who worked remotely were 50% less likely to be promoted.
- Homeworkers were more likely to work into the evening.
- Remote workers had a lower absence rate due to sickness than office workers: 0.9% versus 2.2%.
- Bonuses were 38% less likely for to remote workers than those in the office.

What this pointed to was a distinct "out of sight, out of mind" mentality. People who were not visibly around were more likely to be overlooked for promotions and bonuses, yet ironically, were expected (and did) work longer hours than their office counterparts.

This disparity will most likely decrease in a post-COVID-19 remote workforce, given the sheer number of companies adopting this setup as the norm, but it is important you keep an eye on this as your organization grows. Put in the necessary checks to make sure your remote workforce is treated as fairly as your in-office teams.

> **Idea**
>
> *Virtual team events*
>
> One of the real problems that a remote workforce can have is the feeling of being separated from the social aspect that comes with being on a team. A good way to address this is to host virtual team events, via video conferencing, that have nothing to do with work. I have seen happy hours work very well, where people all lift up a drink and just talk about anything and everything. We have hosted online gaming and quizzes successfully, too, using a variety of online tools, including Jackbox.tv and YouTube. Thirty minutes every few weeks at the end of the work week can yield dividends when it comes to team building.

Summary

- Annual reviews of your employees need not be a huge time drain and something that is done to satisfy HR. With preparation and thoughtfulness, they can be something to look forward to for all parties.
- Things will go wrong, and how you get in front of them, communicating with the necessary stakeholders, will define your leadership.

- When the time comes to terminate someone, taking all the necessary steps possible to make sure the decision is not an irrational response but a data-led, thoughtful reasoned decision will earn you more respect.
- Managing a remote team is not dissimilar to managing a physical team, but you need to be aware of some extra steps to truly benefit from this new, emerging style of team.

Checklist

How many of the following items can you lay claim to having covered?

- Clear understanding of what each level and role is within your organization
- Ratable matrix with which to place your team members' ability in a data-led manner
- Have a mechanism to perform annual reviews that leaves the employee a clear path to improvement
- Have a mechanism for analyzing, reporting, and learning from mistakes and failures
- Procedure for terminating an employee's contract based on data
- Policy for effectively working remotely with clear expectations for people to be successful

Technology decisions

Making decisions on the technology that will power a company is one of the most important responsibilities a CTO will take on in their role. Although we like to think we are in a fast-paced industry, always changing, always evolving, the reality is that production systems can last decades without any significant change. This is quite a sobering thought—the system you are developing now could still be running when you are looking to retire. How can this be, you ask yourself? The reasons a production system can last for so long can include the following:

- The technology stack does not lend itself to incremental updates easily.

153

- The technology leadership over the years don't wish (or know how) to touch the sacred cow.
- The leadership has no experience of anything but the current technology.
- It becomes so critical that replacing or upgrading it is too high a risk or cost.
- Hubris—it was built perfectly, so how can you improve on perfection?

Assuming at some point you will be moving on to another role, you will leave behind what you are designing and building today for someone else to manage. For your own reputation at the very least, it is prudent that you leave a system that the next person can build upon and celebrate your genius for taking the path you did. The last thing you want is for the next person to dismantle everything you did and start again—a situation that can arise in a change of leadership.

From the field

The 40-year-old systems

I get involved in a lot of modernization projects, postacquisition, when the new owners want to spend the money to bring the platform into the modern-day stack. Older systems suffer from high running costs, lack of security, and limited scalability. The oldest I have seen so far is 46 years old (running IBM's RPG via green screen terminals), though more commonly, you'll find 30- to 40-year-old systems running Cobol. I also see a lot of 30-year-old systems built using a 4GL GUI language, such as Visual Basic, Gupta, and Delphi. They all have one thing in common: no matter their age, they are key to the success of the company. If they weren't powering what they are, the business would not survive.

When you are picking a technology, you should be thinking about the following factors:

- How will it age?
- What happens if it becomes obsolete or no longer supported?
- What dependencies does it need to function? How will those dependencies age?
- Will there still be people wishing to work with the technology in the future?

Examples are the earlier Visual Basic apps that were built in the mid 1990s, using third-party libraries that are long gone support-wise and stuck on Windows 95/XP, which can't be ported to a modern Windows platform. Microsoft gave up trying to be backward compatible and, instead, shipped a complete Windows XP virtual machine with its Windows 10 platform to give at least some sort of path forward for these legacy apps.

There are examples of technology becoming obsolete and forcing companies into taking corrective action. There was a time in the web environment when browser plugins were all the rage. You could add rich "desktop-like" experiences to a web page through the likes of Adobe/Macromedia Flash, Microsoft's Silverlight, or Sun's Java Applets. With the advent of HTML 5, coupled with the dramatic improvements of in-page JavaScript, these plugins showed their age (and security concerns) and in a matter of a few years were removed completely from future browser editions.

The moral of the tale is that it isn't just your own in-house software stack you have to be concerned about but also all those third-party systems you rely on. Keeping software updated is paramount, and it is something we will go into in more detail in chapter 13, on housekeeping.

8.1 Avoid lock-in

Whether it is a vendor, language, or framework, you want to avoid any decision that will lock you into that particular choice without any easy recourse to take corrective action. You want the ability to change something in your environment without necessarily having to take on a full rewrite. Easier said than done, and many a well-intentioned CTO/Architect has failed at some point in their career. The problem is that it is hard and sometimes more expensive to take a path that gives you more future options. Think of it more like an insurance policy: should something happen, you have the necessary provision to cash in your policy and save yourself greater heartache.

> ### From the field
>
> *In a flash*
>
> I recently had a client whose SAN (storage area network) administration software was neglected by years of upgrades, and when it came to making a small change, they were all locked out—the SAN administration software was built with Macromedia's defunct Flash. We had to hunt around for an old laptop that had not been on the network for a long time and, therefore, was denied autoupdates. Once we got in, the SAN upgrade took the admin console from Flash to HTML5.

Java is a good example of a core language that provides plenty of choices. Java was developed to handle the myriad of specific processor languages that support embedded development. By creating an abstracted virtual machine, developers could write in a standard portable language, with the JVM (Java Virtual Machine) providing the glue between the underlying hardware/operating system and the developed code. Java offers a number of high-performance JVMs (Oracle, IBM, OpenJDK, Amazon), without requiring you to change a single line of Java code. Whether you deploy Java on Linux, Windows, Amazon, Google, or Microsoft, the code is the same. You have control over your operating system, your virtual machine, and your environment, all without having to disrupt your development team.

If you are going down the path of a solution that incurs license costs, you should plan for what happens when that cost increases—will that dramatically impact your budget? Organizations often regret purchasing Oracle/SQL Server database licenses only to see prices increase over the years, with reduced flexibility (e.g., the inability to move into the cloud), all while realizing they aren't using anything specific to the vendor.

Avoid choosing platforms or software that offers no alternative. If you go down this path, you are at the mercy of a vendor's feature set and pricing; this includes back-office environments such as Office 365, Google Workspace, and Salesforce. For some applications, this may be an acceptable trade-off, especially for large vendors who traditionally do not make large, disruptive price changes.

The goal is to give yourself a number of "outs," as if you are playing a hand of poker. A good poker player will never chase a single card, hoping to make a hand out of nothing. They want to know they have a number of hands at their disposal as the cards unfold on the table. Enterprise planning is the same. You don't know what is around the corner, whether the business decides to pivot and go a different direction or an entire subindustry finds itself fighting for survival because of a change. It is your responsibility as a CTO to react accordingly. It is infinitely better to manage and fund small, incremental upgrades or updates than huge, wholesale rewrites.

8.2   Build vs. buy

When it comes to classic technology debates, such as tabs versus spaces, the one that has many technologists tossing and turning at night is the build-versus-buy dilemma. This decision has far-reaching consequences beyond the engineering department and

is often challenged at the board level. This tug of war plays out between management and the technologists, with management believing that buying will get them a solution "overnight," whereas the technologists have the "not invented here" syndrome and believe they can do better for cheaper. The truth lies somewhere in between.

Enterprise software is not Microsoft Word; no off-the-shelf software will run the business. If there were such a thing, the business wouldn't need a CTO. The average restaurant doesn't need custom software—they can use many online services designed for managing a modern-day restaurant, including automatic integrations such as DoorDash and Uber Eats.

However, if you are McDonald's, running franchises all over the world, then a custom solution is required (and a CTO to run the custom solution).

Conversely, it makes no sense to reinvent the wheel. Finding the right place to innovate and build, while using off-the-shelf tools/services or open source libraries, is what creates truly flexible solutions.

Determining where your IPR (intellectual property rights) or secret sauce lies is where you focus your "build" strategy. This is the part of the enterprise that is unique to you, the piece that sets you apart from the competition. It could be code you develop or how you integrate components to form a larger solution. Anything outside of this is a distraction: solving problems that have already been solved. Irrespective of your particular leaning, it is important to do your due diligence and evaluate both sides of the equation with the same thoroughness and vigor.

8.2.1 Buy

When evaluating whether to buy the basis of your solution, you need to factor in the following considerations:

- Setup/license costs, including any annual or usage fees
- Professional services to aid in setup
- If self-hosted:
  - Hardware costs and additional licenses to support the software
  - IT costs to maintain the hardware and software (backups, security updates, etc.)
- Time to configure and customize the software
- Whether the data be easily and periodically exported

Do not underestimate the time it takes to properly research, shortlist, and evaluate each solution. Be wary of professional sales pitches from the various companies; just like with software development, where the whiteboard is the only platform where everything works flawlessly, their solution will always be the best, fastest, and quickest to configure before signing the contract. This part of the process can take months and be a huge time sink and distraction for the team involved.

To make this process more streamlined, list out the requirements you need the software to meet. Construct this list, marking each item as either must-have or nice-to-have. This will give you a punch list to evaluate each of the platforms against, and once you get down to two candidates, it will give you focus to do some proof of concepts (see table 8.1).

Table 8.1 Advantages and disadvantages of buying

Advantages	Disadvantages
<ul><li>Proven/tested platform</li><li>Reduced time to market</li><li>Professional support network</li><li>If SaaS platform, then no scalability, security patching, or software updates to worry about</li></ul>	<ul><li>Don't own the IPR of the full solution stack</li><li>Vendor lock-in</li><li>Inflexible/limited feature set</li><li>Can be harder to recruit for</li><li>Bug fixes/feature releases constrained by vendor's schedule</li><li>Competitors have access to the same tools</li></ul>

A word of caution: if you find a solution that works exactly as you want, with minimal configuration and complications, and it gets you into production quicker, presume this same thing can be done by a competitor to get to the same place. This is an indication that you may not have as much IPR in your technology as you may like.

From the field

The big purchase

Depending on the size of commitment you are making with a vendor, you can look to them to prove their solution will work for you, making their engineers go through the effort of building some proof of concepts. This is all part of the technical sale, and large software vendors have teams of people dedicated to this role to help with both pre- and post-sale—not dissimilar to an auto dealership allowing you to take a car for a test drive or for the full weekend.

8.2.2   Build

Building is when you decide to dedicate development resources to custom build a solution that is specific to the company's requirements. This solution may take longer but will definitely do everything the business wants. Building is a big commitment, especially for an organization that doesn't have the resources readily at hand; it is more of a natural path for a company that has a development infrastructure already set up (see table 8.2).

Table 8.2   Advantages and disadvantages of building

Advantages	Disadvantages
▪ Complete control over product feature set ▪ Control over the environment ▪ Recruitment is more mainstream ▪ Own the complete IPR to the solution ▪ Quicker to react to bugs and feature requests	▪ Product management, including design, architecture, implementation, and delivery ▪ Longer time to build ▪ Greater effort to plan and resource ▪ Not as tested; specific ▪ Support has to be provided in-house

A good mix is to "buy" where you can and "build" for true flexibility and customization. As we will note later in the chapter when cloud solutions are discussed, building doesn't mean you have to build everything. You can use and integrate many commodity components. For example, sending email can use a third-party service, or if you need to provide detailed analytics, then it is better to offload that to a BI (business intelligence) solution, with you importing the raw data.

A word of caution in this world, too: be wary of "low/no code" solutions. These are the modern-day versions of Visual Basic, allowing nondevelopers to develop solutions through point-and-click or drag-and-drop environments without any real coding. These tools lull you into thinking you have 80% of your work completed in a short space of time, but you can then spend way more time trying to close the last 20% because the tool makes it hard. Worse case—you make compromises to justify the tool not providing the flexibility needed. Will your competitor compromise, too, or will they leap-frog you with a richer feature list?

8.2.3   Considerations

The side of the debate you fall on is largely influenced by the type of environment you have gained experience in. The following points illustrate that it is a wrong assumption that all CTOs want to automatically build:

- *Buy supporters*—These CTOS have little or no experience running a development team and believe that what you lose in capability and flexibility is more than made up for in platform stability.
- *Build supporters*—These CTOs have experience in running development teams and know how to use them to get things built to do a specific job. They generally get annoyed at the inflexibility of bigger solutions.

Successful CTOs know how to use the best from both worlds, ruling nothing out, looking at each requirement in its own right.

> **From the field**
>
> *Creating enterprises*
>
> When architecting large enterprises, I start out by making the assumption that I will be building everything. I make no decisions, but this is my basis as I look to break down each of the problem spaces into manageable pieces. As I get to know the requirements of each area, this is when the mist will begin to clear and potential "buy"' candidates will present themselves, including commodity pieces that can be used.

Like everything in the world, nothing is binary—there is always some fuzziness that serves to complicate. Specifically, platforms that look like they span both worlds of buy and build create a lot of gray area. A good example of this is the Salesforce platform, with a whole ecosystem of prebuilt components that satisfy most organizations, but it also offers a complete environment in which to develop significant code.

A good rule of thumb when evaluating these solutions harks back to the vendor lock-in points made earlier: if you can't lift your code and drop it on another platform and just run it, you are locked in, at the mercy of the vendor to provide everything for you to be successful. If they experience downtime, or degradation in performance, there is nothing you can do but wait it out.

8.2.4   Checklist

To properly evaluate both sides, you need to be methodical and be able to defend your decisions to the CEO or /CFO whose support you will need to succeed. You have to decide what is important to the business at the end of this. What are the success criteria you need to meet for this to be a successful initiative? This is where compiling your own checklist can help you come to a build-versus-buy conclusion. An example checklist for a project could look like table 8.3.

Table 8.3   Build vs. buy evaluation

Area	Build ...... Buy
Need to react quickly to client's changes and feature requests.	.. | ....
Don't want to manage any infrastructure.	...........................|...
Would be advantageous to use the existing development team.	............|.................
The IPR of the solution is not important; not core to the business.	.........................|....
Data needs to be directly accessible by other systems.	...........|.....................
The solution will be managed by nonengineering folks in the business.	........................|.....
Time to get solution to market.	............................|.....

If the overall checklist is tending toward a "buy" solution, then this is where you focus your investigation and solution. Again, be data driven, not gut driven.

One thing that is worth noting is that if you go down the "buy" path, then the moat around your organization is drastically reduced. This may not be relevant for organizations whose IPR is not the technology. *Moat* is a term investment groups use to determine how hard it is for competitors to copy what you are doing. If you are buying third-party tools, then nothing is stopping your competitor from doing the same thing.

8.3   *Cloud vs. on-prem*

For a lot of modern-day organizations, the thought of running and managing their own physical servers never even enters the discussions. Other organizations may still have a large investment in hardware, making it is hard to justify switching over to the economics of the cloud. In this section, we are going to go through the pros and cons of the cloud and look at how to use existing hardware and to avoid some of the problems that people have discovered when using the cloud. Let's define what we mean by *cloud* and *on-prem*:

- *Cloud*—An environment where CPU, memory, network, and storage are consumed and charged on a per-usage basis, sometimes down to the second. These setups can be packaged in server-like configuration or on a per-service basis, with no consideration for the underlying physical hardware.
- *On-prem*—On-premises is where the underlying hardware (CPU, memory, network, and storage) is owned and managed by the company.

Think of the cloud and how you should be treating it not unlike how you look at electricity. We are conditioned to simply plug into the wall and draw as much power as needed, and at the end of the month, we get a bill for the amount we use. Economics dictates that this is way more efficient and convenient than managing our own power plant. Over the years, we have designed and evolved all our devices to be able to quickly and easily harness this power by standardizing a three-pin plug. For cloud applications, we call this evolution "cloud native"—an app that is specifically designed to harness these on-demand resources, permitting scaling up and down on demand, automatically. Sometimes, though, you'll have applications for which running your own hardware makes more sense, as described here:

- *Cloud supporters*—Applications that have peaks and troughs in load, either hourly, daily, or seasonally
- *On-prem supporters*—Intensive computing requirements, where the CPU is running 90%-plus most of the time, such as for complex data or graphics modeling (or bitcoin mining!)

8.3.1 Cloud

In this section, we will go over many of the weaknesses and strengths of using the cloud to power your enterprise.

CLOUD RESISTANCE

The cloud has grown up a lot in the last 20 years, with all the criticisms used to resist going to the cloud having been addressed. Yet you will still encounter excuses being used by companies that are steadfastly refusing to even entertain the cloud. Let's go over some of the arguments that may help you, should you find yourself in the same situation:

- *"The cloud is not secure."* There was a time this was hard to dispute, but given the great advancements in monitoring, network isolation, encryption management, container runtimes, and fine-grained access models, the pendulum has swung in the opposite direction. You would be hard pressed to make on-prem as secure without a lot of cost and work. That is not to say that cloud equals security; effort still has to be made to implement all the necessary (and logical) security mechanisms. A good cloud architect does this effortlessly, and it is integral to their cloud design.
- *"My data will be held hostage."* This one has no real basis in any form of reality, yet it still persists. With a cloud solution, all your data is held within the confines of your cloud vendor, with access available through the tools and APIs from the cloud vendor. Data sits in a variety of data stores, whether it is file-like storage services or database structures. Data is no more inaccessible than it would be sitting on a local SAN. If there is a large amount of data, then, yes, it will cost network charges to download that data. That is far from a hostage situation.

  This fear originates from the irrational fear of missing a monthly cloud bill. Let me address that one now: you have to go many (many) weeks before the larger cloud vendors will start arbitrarily deleting your data without warning.
- *"It's too expensive."* Yes, it can be, if you treat your cloud vendor like a data center. After a period of time, the economics of running your hardware will become more attractive (assuming, of course, you factor in all the costs—more on that later). A properly designed cloud-native application will have significant savings, year over year, especially as cloud costs continue to fall.

The cloud, like anything else, requires the necessary skills to truly make it effective. It is not the panacea for all problems.

TOP 10 CLOUD WARNING SIGNS

There are those who proudly boast they are running in the cloud, but after a little discussion, it transpires that although they may not have any off-cloud hardware, their use of the cloud gets them none of the real benefits and, in most cases, probably costs them more. If you are wondering whether you are using the cloud properly, see if any of the following checklist points applies:

- *Your cloud bill is the same every month.* If your cloud bill is roughly the same each month, particularly if you are a seasonal business with periods of high and low usage, then this points toward not using the elastic nature of the cloud—paying what you need for when you need it.

- *You require downtime when releasing new updates.* If the engineering team schedules downtime with each and every release, this suggests they are using servers in a static mode, where software has to be updated on each server. Modern cloud practices encourage replacing servers with each release (think containers, like Docker) and switching over traffic when satisfied all is well, along with deleting older servers.

- *You're unable to scale up (or down) to cope with load.* As Warren Buffet said, "You can't produce a baby in one month by getting nine women pregnant." In the cloud, though, you can, and if you can't introduce another mother to cope with the load, then your application is not cloud ready.

- *You're running out of disk space.* If you hear reports of servers running out of disk space, then this points to servers running in a static manner that requires manual maintenance. A good cloud application uses the effectively infinite, pay-as-you-go storage.

- *You lose data.* No one wants to hear (or report) loss of data, and it shouldn't really happen in a good cloud environment (outside of intentional user deletion). This suggests single points of failure, with no real elasticity or redundancy to the infrastructure.

- *You assume servers are immune to failure.* With the absence of hardware in your new virtual world, it is easy to assume hardware failures won't affect you. Although rare, they still occur, and if such a failure takes down a piece of your architecture and causes a major disruption, your cloud setup may be too tightly coupled, with no redundancy.

- *You're running your own XYZ, such as a load balancer.* Modern cloud providers offer a rich array of services that remove the need for you to manage individual servers yourself. For example, load balancing, logging, caching, and configuration are all software layers that traditionally you would have run on servers and managed yourself. If you have pieces of your architecture like this, ask why, because it may show a lack of knowledge or understanding of the available cloud facilities.

- *Your data center security practices in a cloud world.* How you secure your traditional hardware-based servers is not the same as in the cloud. If you have manually configured firewalls on each server, or have no real network separation, you may be missing out on a whole layer of security on offer from the cloud provider.
- *Your disaster recovery (DR) still revolves around hot swaps.* If you are still talking about DR as something you switch over to in the event of the day you hope never arrives, complete with a lot of redundant duplicate servers just waiting for said day, you are definitely not cloud enabled. With a well-architected cloud, DR comes as part of the equation free of charge.
- *You have multiple services on a single server.* Hardware is expensive, so it is common to run multiple services on a single server (think the classic Linux Apache MySQL PHP stack). The same economic constraints do not exist in the cloud. In a cloud world, each server should be as light as possible, making it easy to replace, maintain, and scale.

If you treat the cloud like a data center, thinking of it in terms of servers, with no elasticity for when loads change, then the cloud will fail for you in terms of flexibility and cost. Many cloud installations can cost far more than the equivalent hardware setup would have been, simply because of a fundamental misconception of what the cloud really is.

PRIVATE CLOUD

Most associate the cloud with the public cloud, but a common strategy, especially attractive for organizations that have large investments in existing hardware, is the private cloud. Provisioning hardware with a cloud OS that lets it be managed in a per-usage model can unlock the potential of your hardware and give it extra life. Both commercial and open source solutions are available, depending on the level of management you are seeking. This path is recommended only when you have the resources to manage this private cloud pool. Although the net gain is more stability and reliability (because you can easily move resources away from failing hardware), you still have the overhead of hardware to manage.

This leads naturally into the hybrid cloud, where you use a mixture of private and public cloud. When the resources of the private cloud are exhausted, the public cloud can come in and augment the shortfall, all transparently.

CREATING SUCCESS

The cloud, for those more used to traditional hardware installations, can be daunting and foreign, but it doesn't have to be. All the skills and experience you have gained can be transported to the cloud; all you are doing is reframing the question. The people who have successfully transitioned to cloud frequently asked themselves the same question: "This is how I would have solved this in a hardware setup; so, how can I do the same thing in the cloud?" Let's look at the three mantras that will lead to a successful cloud installation:

- *Security is not a given.* Security still has to be thought through, architected, and designed into every part of your solution. Do not assume any level of security just because you have deployed the service. Misconfiguration will get you every time, so test thoroughly.

- *Failure will happen.* A large appeal of the cloud is to not have to worry about hardware and the subsequent failure that will happen as a result. The cloud is not an error-free environment; things will and do go wrong. Plan, build, and practice for failure. A well-architected cloud can make these errors completely seamless and not disrupt the overall production, without any significant extra cost.

- *It's easier to get into trouble.* The cloud makes it really easy to create and consume resources. It also makes it really easy to destroy resources. Be careful of that. The notion of a "production" environment is just that—a constructional notion. The cloud provider assumes you know what you are doing and will happily oblige your request to remove the production database.

The cloud removes a lot of problems that you would have to manage in a traditional hardware foundation. However, do not assume the job got easier. All that has happened is that your problems moved to a different area.

From the field

Honey production

One of the analogies I use when describing the difference between legacy apps and cloud apps is that of the humble bee. Mother Nature has mastered the art of honey production by not relying on the success of any single bee; bees have failure built in. The death of a single bee does not cause any problems in the production line. This is how a good cloud-native application is designed—failure is part of its DNA. On the other end of the scale, most software enterprises are designed as if there is a single, huge, genetically engineered bee, producing honey consistently. However, should that "bee" die, then all production is halted. We have too many genetically engineered bees in our world.

8.3.2 On-prem

On-premises is a blanket term used to describe the provisioning and management of physical hardware to run your organization's needs. It does not necessarily mean the hardware is located within your office environment—it can be in a dedicated data center. In this section, we are going to cover the considerations for either creating a new on-prem installation or, more likely, maintaining an existing installation.

In the "old days," maintaining your own hardware for a multitude of servers was the only way a company could power their needs. It was a hard thing to properly estimate—companies either bought too much hardware that was never used or, at the other extreme, didn't buy enough, which led to high periods of stressing the hardware (and staff, who hoped things didn't crash). Servers have to be bought, delivered, provisioned, and installed—this can take weeks. Scaling on demand is not something you can do quickly. Of course, this is all assuming you can convince your CFO that you need to make the large capital outlay in the first place.

Today, such issues can be alleviated to an extent by pooling your hardware into a private cloud that can then be carved up as and when needed. For example, if you need extra servers to power an online promotion that will cause a spike, you could turn off some internal servers and use that extra space in the private cloud to create more frontline servers. However, you still have a limited resource to draw from (you only have so much hardware).

HOSTING

When it comes to physical hosting, you have two primary options:

- *Office building*—The hardware is located somewhere in the same building as the workforce, either in its own dedicated room, cupboard, or even under some developer's desk (though not recommended, it's not unheard of).
- *Remote data center*—The hardware is hosted in a specific data center, usually in racks, with other servers.

A server is like a plant that needs sunlight and water to survive, except here, we need power, cooling, and a network connection. Although modern-day hardware doesn't generate anywhere near the same level of heat the older systems did, it still generates enough that a cooling solution is required to keep it operating within normal limits. You will notice this if you host in a cupboard with no A/C duct—a wall of heat will hit whoever opens the door!

Power is another underestimated requirement. We just assume we simply plug into the wall and let the power company do the rest. Although that is true, you have to make sure you don't overload the circuit and the power is clean (free from spikes that may cause damage) and uninterrupted, should said power company fail to deliver a supply.

> **From the field**
>
> *Clean environment*
>
> I recall, back in my early career, fresh out of university, sitting quietly, getting on with my work, with the servers all humming away in the room next door. Then, suddenly everyone was in an uproar—people were running around, shouting, and asking lots of questions. The servers had gone down all at the same time—completely unheard of. As silence fell, the only thing that could be heard in the sea of voices was the rhythmic roar of a vacuum cleaner moving back and forth over the floor by a very enthusiastic cleaner. A new lady had been assigned to us and, in her innocence, had unplugged the server to plug in her vacuum. To this day, I never take power for granted.

Finally, the network, the true life blood of any server—without this, the server has limited use. The network is more than just plugging in a RJ45 cable and hoping traffic makes it there. We need to make sure only secure traffic gets there, and, again, should the connection to the internet go down, we'd better have a backup strategy. A number of elaborate multiserver setups exist, all relying on a single six-stranded wire to the outside world.

The good news is that a dedicated data center will take care of all of this (and charge you accordingly for it). Data centers usually charge on two primary metrics: the physical space used inside a rack (measured in rack units, or U's; one U is 1.75 inches) and bandwidth (the amount of network connection you need provisioned). Most data centers build the cost of power into the price, assuming standard power supplies. Servers come in long, flat configurations, so they can be tightly packed, vertically, in a rack. This is why the term "pizza box" is used to describe servers that look like this. "Pizza box" (or rack-ready) servers are usually a little more expensive than the boxy containers.

A data center will also have the necessary network hardware, creating your own private network, with automatic redundancy to the internet. All you have to do is plug in the network cable.

For self-hosting in the office, however, you'll need to architect some of the considerations. You'll require routers, network hubs, and optional firewall devices, which themselves need cooling and backup power.

PROVISIONING/MAINTENANCE

When it comes to installing hardware, irrespective of where it is going to end up physically, you need to first define the configuration (CPU, memory, disk) before placing the order, aiming for a machine that has some upgrade capability. Upon arrival, it needs to have an operating system installed on it. You then must remove all unnecessary software, install the security protocols, and allocate its space on the network. All this takes time.

If you are self-hosting, consider allocating a special room that is lockable (you don't want anyone in the company wandering in), is well ventilated, and has dedicated power. Plan your space well, laying out the hardware in a logical way, with cabling clearly labeled and clamped.

Come up with a system for keeping a hardware inventory, whether as crude as writing on the boxes with black marker or sticking printed barcodes on them—it is important to keep track of all hardware. The key metrics include the following:

- *Purchase/installation date*—On what date was this hardware purchased, and when was it given power?
- *Purchase source*—Where was the hardware purchased (including full contact details)?
- *Configuration*—What is the configuration of the hardware? Provide enough detail so you don't have to dismantle the unit to discover what is inside. This includes any free slots for future upgrade potential.
- *Time to failure*—The manufacturer will have guidance on the expected life of the unit. Anything that has moving parts, such as fans and hard disks, is expected to fail in only a few years.
- *Access details*—Does this machine have a console? If so, which network is installed, and where is the username/password stored?

Keeping all this data will allow you to easily manage your hardware and have a line of sight when you need to perform any preventative measures, such as replacing specific units. Note that it is so much easier to document these metrics at the time of installation, when you have all the data at your fingertips, than it is years later, as you try to remember when something was installed.

> **From the field**
>
> *Part of the furniture*
>
> I have seen many horrific self-hosting setups, but I think the one that truly had me reaching for my heart was one where the main server (yes, the only one) was situated underneath one of the developer's desks and was regularly used as a footstool. It was plugged into the same power strip that was used for other appliances with no marking that this machine should not be unplugged. Needless to say, this situation was quickly rectified.

When running your own servers (including those in the cloud), you incur a level of maintenance. Software updates that are part of the operating system is something we are used to doing and should, of course, be part of regular maintenance. An area that is often overlooked is the software that power the hardware. For example, if you have a SAN (storage area network), router, or server blade chassis, these have software consoles as well that need to be regularly kept up to date.

Hardware is harder to maintain. It is difficult to justify replacing a component that has yet to fail, but it is a wise habit to get into—or, at least, source the component, so when failure comes, you can quickly replace it. Hardware goes out of date very quickly and is not as backward compatible as we like to think. This leaves organizations having to resort to looking on eBay for spare parts on the secondary market.

By keeping detailed records, you have a clear idea of the future budgetary requirements of maintaining your hardware infrastructure. This way, there are no surprises when you go asking the CFO to authorize the funds for replacement.

8.4   *Disaster recover*

Let us define what *disaster recovery* (DR) is. Assuming the absence of your enterprise (for whatever reason) is going to be significantly detrimental to your clients, DR is creating a plan for when (not if) that happens to have a backup to continue the enterprise's operation. This usually implies failing over to a geographically different location from the primary, so things like fire, flood, or theft can be accounted for.

> **From the field**
>
> *Godzilla attacks*
>
> Back at the start of my career, when I first heard of disaster recovery as a term, my mind instantly went to Godzilla, striding through a city, wrecked buildings in his wake. I wondered just how often this happened that we needed to have a plan for it—I was a boy from the country, not yet used to life in the city. After I realized I was overthinking, I tempered my expectations down to more "mundane" disasters such as fire, flood,

> **(continued)**
>
> or theft, and even then, the most likely cause of a disaster event will be a power, network, or hardware failure (a far cry from my Godzilla event, yet to this day, it is still the first thing that comes to mind when I hear "disaster recovery," as I crack a wee smile).

It is fair to note here that for a well-architected and -implemented cloud-native app, disaster recovery comes free of charge because it is built in and not explicitly called out as an event. That does not mean just because you are running in the cloud that you are disaster ready. This section assumes you are dealing with a non-cloud-native application.

As CTO of your organization, responsible for all the technology in your company, it is your role to keep operations running, through thick and thin. To be clear, DR is not a straightforward or easy-to-achieve operation. Most organizations have a poor (read "nonexistent") DR strategy, and the ones that think they have a good one have never truly tested it, with it serving as no more than a placebo, a safety net that isn't tethered to anything.

In this section, we are going to outline the considerations and questions you need to answer to properly formulate a DR plan for your organization. The three foundational areas that will drive your strategy follow:

- What is the downtime tolerance?
- When in recovery mode, do you need full or partial service?
- Will you be failing forward (a new primary), or will you eventually come back?

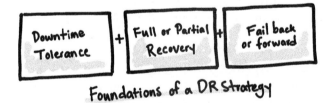

Foundations of a DR Strategy

For the sake of discussion, let's assume two zones: the active one and the backup one, ready to take over. DR does not need to be restricted to just a single backup zone—there can be multiple zones ready to take over. Remember, if using only a single zone, as soon as you are in a failed state (running in the backup zone), you no longer have a backup for the backup.

8.4.1   *Downtime tolerance*

It is very easy for your CEO to demand a zero-downtime strategy. Although possible, this is hugely expensive and extremely complicated, especially if your enterprise has a number of points within it that can't be made to be run as multiple instances. The prime example here is the humble database: most organizations have not designed their tables in a way to make real-time redundancy easy (if you are relying on database-generated, autoincremented, primary keys instead of GUID, then you have a struggle on your hands). Older systems, or enterprises that were poorly architected, just do not lend themselves to having a duplicate system ready to take over.

When you are running two geographically different enterprise zones, you have the following two primary concerns that will dictate the complexity (and cost) of your DR solution:

- Keeping data synchronized across both zones
- Switching traffic (users) over to use a new active zone

Keeping data synchronized across two geographically different zones takes time—and we mean literal time. Data takes time to travel through networks, and even a small latency of 50–100 ms can make a huge difference when it comes to keeping databases synchronized with each other. Assuming the network remains up and uncongested, you will be limited by the time it takes to transfer the data between locations. When choosing your DR locations, keep note of any special peering arrangements between data centers (think of it as if they are directly connected to each other to avoid any general internet routing congestion).

Although modern-day databases (such as SQL Server and Oracle) have strong synchronization features (which usually come at a much higher license cost), they are still limited by the speed of the physical network to move bytes back and forth.

Therefore, depending on your enterprise design and network configuration, you may not be able to offer a zero downtime for the enterprise. Once that lofty goal is off the table, attention focuses on what is tolerable to your clients: minutes, hours, or days? This is a decision that only you and your CEO can come up with, after you have presented the economics of the consequences of the acceptable downtime.

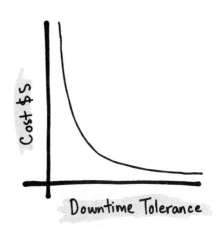

Two configurations are often talked about in DR circles: the hot and the cold standby. Hot is the most expensive, because it assumes very little downtime, and servers are always up and running, continually being synchronized, ready to take over as soon as traffic starts coming to them. Hot standby consumes power and network bandwidth and is also running out the clock on your backup hardware lifetime.

Conversely, a cold standby is one where the bare minimum of machines is kept running, and when a failover event is initiated, the machines are turned on and started up as and when needed. This is the cheapest solution but also the slowest, because you have to wait for machines to boot up and synchronize data. For some situations, a cold standby is more than acceptable and a cheap way to offer some level of DR.

8.4.2   Full or partial service

Another level in your DR control panel is determining, in the event of a disaster, whether you need to run a full service. Can you make do with a partial service? Consider something going wrong—ask yourself which services you offer could be temporarily unavailable or made to be offered in a read-only mode.

For example, imagine you are in charge of Twitter, and you have been really squeezed on budget. A partial service could allow people to view previously published tweets, but they are temporarily restricted from writing and publishing new tweets. Or if you are an ecommerce site, let customers view and add items to a shopping cart, but they can't complete the purchase through the checkout. It is rare to not be able to identify areas of an enterprise that can operate in a reduced capacity for a period of time.

If you are in a partial-service mode, consider the things you may lose for a period of time that, again, are acceptable but not visible to the end user—things like logging, reporting, and any scheduled administrative tasks.

Failing over to a fully serviced solution is far more complex, especially because you may be in a situation where you need to determine where things were left, so the new system can take over. Will there be things that will be reprocessed and duplicated, because the backup zone was not aware that something was already done, or completely lost altogether? An example here is email alerts being generated from the system—did it fail in the middle of sending a batch of emails so we now have to fathom which emails went out successfully, or is it acceptable that some users get duplicate emails?

Depending on the system for which you are attempting to create a DR solution, you may be struggling to provide a truly clean solution, without a lot of hands-on manual database and file manipulation.

From the field

Price is not directly related to quality

When I first work with a client, I love hearing about their DR strategy, assuming they have one. Like a proud parent, they light up as they describe how much money is being spent to safeguard client data and operations. I had one client that had put too much faith in one three-letter company, and the sheer licensing money for software and hardware they were spending each year was well over six figures. Expectations were high, and management assumed that, due to the price, it was rock solid. Everyone slept at night. After a bit of questioning, all was not what it seemed, and long story short, within a few weeks, we reduced the spend to only four figures for a configuration that actually worked using AWS. The issue was a common one—they had put too much faith in their outsourced solution, assuming the three-letter company was doing way more than they really were. DR is hard and is not something that can be outsourced without getting involved.

A word of caution on the partial solution: you have to build in the possibility that your partial solution needs to become a full solution. If you have a power outage at your primary zone, you are going to assume the power company will get you back up eventually. However, if you experience fire, flood, or theft, then your partial solution may have to be primary, full-service backup. Think of it like a light bulb: you never want it to go out and leave you in darkness, but most likely, you can tolerate the light dimming for a time.

8.4.3 Fail forward vs. bounce back

Let's assume you have failed over to your backup zone, either in a full or partial configuration. What is going to be the strategy when the primary zone comes back online again? If you find yourself wondering about this situation, then be warned. This is a very telling sign, usually meaning that a DR event has never happened (or been practiced) and the thinking as to what happens after Godzilla has come through and the rebuilding needs to happen hasn't been considered. Yet, it is a very real situation.

Depending on the DR configuration and hardware, and assuming it is a like-for-like configuration, consider just letting the backup zone now become your primary zone. Why incur another switch back when it's not required? Your focus now becomes resolving all the issues with the original failed primary zone to make it a new ready-to-use backup zone. This process is called a fail-forward configuration—no turning back.

If, however, you don't have a like-for-like setup, then you have no choice but to bounce back to the primary zone upon resolution—a common situation when you are running in a partial-service mode. The good news, however, is that you do not need to bounce back immediately. You can plan your second outage and come back in an orderly fashion, at a time that is convenient, usually over the weekend or late at night.

8.4.4 Managing the event

So far we've talked about the various configurations your DR strategy can take, taking each part of the ecosystem and evaluating it in its own right for what works for your organization. What hasn't been spoken about yet is the logistics of switching over from one zone to another. Like the rainy day fund we all have, the hardest part is identifying whether it's raining enough to be able to dip in and spend from it. Switching over to a DR zone is not an insignificant event and isn't something you want to do lightly.

Some events are easier to give the go-for-DR approval (think the NASA Apollo launch when thinking of the switch) than others. For example, complete hardware failure, fire, flood, or theft are events that are not quick things to recover from, so switching makes complete sense.

Other events, however, are not quite as clear cut. Take a power supply that keeps going in and out, just enough that the UPS (uninterrupted power supply) struggles to keep most of the key servers going, or a network outage, where the upstream provider assures you they are on it, and it will be back online "very soon"—define "soon"! Creating a switching strategy will take away all the ambiguity and hesitance in knowing when to "flip" the metaphorical switch, including all the different criteria, such as which services are affected and the time they are down, to trigger the event.

Now that you know what triggers the event, the next important thing to detail is the logistics of the switch. At a high level, they include the following:

- Make sure all contacts, networks, and passwords are stored in a secure place that is immediately accessible.
- Determine which services need to be started up (if in a cold standby mode) and populated with the most up-to-date data.
- Identify all the network addresses that need to be updated, which can include both public and private DNS resolution. DNS changes will take time to propagate, depending on the time-to-live of the zone records, so build this into your plan.
- Identify all the roles, configurations, and tests that need to be done and by whom, to validate the recovery zone.
- If working in a bounce-back configuration, come up with the reverse plan to bring back the primary zone once the issue has been resolved.

Once these issues are worked out, make sure it is communicated and put in a place that is readily known. Nothing is worse when trying to switch over than for people to be scrambling to determine the console password for the DR zone.

It is vital that this procedure is tested relatively frequently, during off hours, to make sure all the documentation and processes are in place and easily understood. Enterprises evolve, changes are made, systems are added, and systems are removed. The DR has to evolve and should always represent the current state, because disasters are rarely telegraphed in advance.

From the field

Unintended consequences

It is not uncommon for a company to provide a virtual private network (VPN) for employees to be able to interact with servers that are located inside the office. What happens, though, when you switch over to a new zone, with different access points? Well, one portfolio company I worked with knows only too well the DR version of sawing the branch you are sitting on. They managed to lock themselves out of the failover DR zone because all firewall rules were written with the primary zone in mind. The silver lining: the security worked really well!

It is recommended that a DR should be regularly checked, at least once a week, to ensure all the data is still flowing where it needs to go should you need to bring up the zone. Approximately once a quarter, or every six months, you should practice a full switchover to allow people to become familiar with the processes to the point where it isn't seen as a big event, and, like the old adage goes, practice does make perfect.

8.4.5 Cloud and DR

Although we have assumed that the enterprise you are looking to create a DR strategy for is not a cloud-native application, that doesn't mean you can't use the cloud as part of your solution. Using the cloud as an on-demand, temporary data center is more than acceptable and can work out to be quite cost effective.

The cloud, as a hot or cold standby, makes an ideal candidate because you can stream data to it and incur the cost only of the data you are storing. Creating the necessary infrastructure is a little easier to get a more like-for-like configuration, because you pay only for what you need, as and when you need it. The cloud does make it easier to test various configurations and strategies on a small budget.

8.5 Data management

Data is the lifeblood of our industry. It flows in and out of our organization, generating more data about data, reproducing into other data, all needing to be sorted, translated, stored, and processed. Data is more than files on a hard disk or rows in a table. It has meaning, context, and value. Conversely, it can be wasteful, distracting, and worthless, all at the same time. The trick is trying to know the difference.

In the old days, storing data was an prohibitively expensive logistical challenge. In today's cloud infinite-storage paradigm, storing data has never been easier or cheaper (and the cost continues to fall every year). The two questions that come from that are (a) should you store everything, and (b) how should you organize it to make it accessible?

Managing and securing data effectively is not an easy task. Security is a separate chapter later in the book, so some of those concepts we will touch upon only lightly here. CTOs are the ultimate stewards of a company's data, and in my experience, not enough manage it as well as they could, largely because they don't know the true value of this asset or are unaware of some of the tools and techniques available to them.

In this section, we are going to cover the different types of storage mechanisms available, the types of data you may be responsible for, and, finally, the security, compliance, and ownership issues you will be addressing. Along the way, we will address some of the buzzwords associated with data, because the marketplace is swarming with vendors and solutions to help you better unlock the insights associated within data.

8.5.1 Storage

When we think of data, we naturally think of it in files, with folders as the next logical structure. This is how the average C-level executive broadly thinks of their data, with most of them thinking in terms of an Excel spreadsheet. This is natural for them, given most of their financial backgrounds. Executives will talk of databases freely, but again, in their minds, they are just thinking bigger Excel sheets. As a CTO, part of your job is to help them contextualize the value of their most prized asset in more than just a spreadsheet. Another part of your job is to think and plan long term where data is going to reside so it can be better used by the business.

As stated earlier, data storage has never been so cheap, and there is no excuse for not keeping data around. But what does that really mean? And should you really keep everything? First off, let's look at the following broad types of storage we can pour data into:

- *Files/folders*—To this day, a file—a self-contained collection of data, named and residing on a physical medium—is still the most universally understood way of holding data. With many different popular formats, like JSON, XML, CSV, and TXT, for example, it is extremely versatile with nearly every data tool able to open and operate with a file. Files can be easily copied, encrypted, moved, and shared. There is no limit to the type of data you can store in a file.
- *Relational stores (SQL databases)*—Data that has common attributes (columns) and relates to one another (rows) fits neatly into what we call tables. Tables can be linked to other tables, with a collection of tables known as a database. Tables can be queried using a pseudo language (SQL) that describes our question of the data, to either return, change, or create new data in a table. This is very popular mechanism for storing large volumes of similarly structured data.
- *NoSQL stores*—NoSQL, or document, stores take the building blocks of the relational store but step away from the similarly structured restriction. A NoSQL store stores only the data you have and not the placeholders for the data you don't have. A collection is a group of documents, and a document can be radically different from another.
- *Data lake*—A data lake is a place to store large volumes of files, of differing structure and size, for either backup or future analysis. It is commonly used as a staging area for data coming into an organization where there isn't a permanent home yet assigned for it.
- *Data warehouse*—A warehouse is a specially designed database that is primarily used for analytics and business intelligence. Its purpose is housing large datasets arranged in a way to make it easy to draw out reports and year-over-year analysis.

Prior to the cloud, running and managing all of these types of storages would have been prohibitively expensive, with decisions being made at each stage to trim the data down to only what was required for that day. Should the business evolve and decide they needed richer data, then that was only for that time going forward, and historical data was lost.

Files and relationship databases are common. Whether it is SQL Server, Postgres, MySQL, or Oracle, every organization has their own flavor of database. That said, many organize their databases poorly, for example, using a single database to serve multiple areas (e.g., driving the customer-facing website while also providing reports on the health of the business). Instead, databases should be split up into the areas of business they serve, with processes to replicate the data to where it needs to go. That way, when the CFO asks to run a huge report to figure out the end-of-quarter sales, they don't take the website down in doing so.

NoSQL databases (like MongoDB, CouchDB, DynamoDB, and Elasticsearch) are becoming increasingly popular, particularly during the early development of projects, when the structure of data is probably not yet well known. Their performance has increased over the years to the point where, with the right semistructure, they can perform as well as their relational counterparts. Be careful with this one—some teams swing too far, building everything on a NoSQL architecture. When this happens, there tends to be a lot more data inconsistency (e.g., some documents will store the same type of data, in different formats, such as "2" (string) versus 2 (integer), because some process isn't adhering to the data standard). NoSQL does not enforce any data integrity or structure.

A data lake (Apache Hadoop, Amazon S3) is really just one big storage space for files to reside in. However, it is more than just a big file storage. A data lake has tools and mechanisms that let you transverse over all the files, picking out the data elements as you need them. For example, it is a great place to put log files from your production system. You don't have to worry about the format too much, because that can evolve over time. A data lake will give you the mechanism to easily crawl over the log files, looking for a given keyword or string, for example, should the need arise (this is called map/reduce).

Finally, a data warehouse (Amazon Redshift, SQL Server) is where data that is destined for reporting goes. It is specifically designed to arrange data in a way that makes it extremely fast to transverse to get at the types of reports the business needs. Data in a warehouse is usually aggregated, anonymized, and designed around answering the questions the business wants to ask. A warehouse is only of use when a significant amount of data has been amassed. A traditional relational database can answer most of the questions asked of the data, but there will come a time when it struggles to do what needs to be done.

From the field

A little knowledge is dangerous

I have seen many howlers of database configurations in my time, including one made by someone who didn't believe in table joins. The one that stands out, however, was when my team was brought in to help with a very poorly performing database that was taking down the whole site. Digging in, we could see a lot of disk I/O going on, pointing toward the database and doing a lot of writes on the disk, which was odd because there wasn't that much data being stored. Turns out, one of the techs had read an article that to speed up a table, you should put indexes on the tables. Eager to help, they took their newfound knowledge and created an index for every column on every table. The database was drowning in its own metadata, storing more data about the data than the data itself. Needless to say, information can be dangerous if in the wrong hands!

In our cloud-enabled world, all of these services can be consumed without the overhead of running and managing the logistical servers (and licenses) underneath. The vast majority of teams we work with have all benefited from moving their data storage over to the cloud, where it is scalable on-demand, so running out of storage is a thing of the past and their data is more secure, thanks to the multitude of tools available to them as standard.

At the very least, your organization needs to have some sort of data lake as part of your storage solution. Think of this like your data attic: you know, the place that has all the things you can't bring yourself to throw out, because one day, you just might need them. A data lake is where you put all that data that doesn't have a permanent home, so one day, should someone ask for it, you at least know you have it. Although it might take you a little time to find it in the attic, it will be there.

8.5.2   *Data types*

Not all the data in your organization is equal. Although that seems obvious, a surprisingly large number of companies do not realize this simple fact and, as a result, get themselves all tied up in a whole manner of issues. It is important to get a handle on the major types of data you are responsible for.

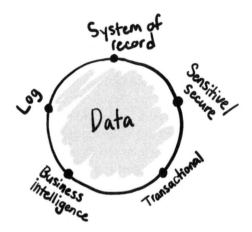

Although not a definitive list, the following are good places to start bucketing your data:

- *System of record*—Data that is considered core to your company, usually in a database of some sort. Data in this category is thought of as the "truth" for a given entity.
- *Sensitive/secure*—Data that requires additional security falls into this category. Examples include Social Security numbers, driver's license numbers, bank information, and credit card details.
- *Transactional*—Data that is generated in pursuit or delivery of the core product; often referred to as operational data.
- *Business intelligence*—Data that is used for powering the reporting analytics; usually a copy of the transactional data, in an aggregated/anonymized version.
- *Log*—Data that is produced by the various systems and software that power the enterprise. This data is used for forensic bug/fault tracking and auditing as well as performance analysis.

For each classification, you need to come up with rules that make sense for your enterprise. Again, there is no need to get too detailed initially, but you should at least be viewing each bucket through the following lenses:

- *Ownership*—Who actually owns the data in this bucket? Your first instinct is to assume you own it. Ownership means you are free to do with it as you wish (sell it, delete it, or even make it public if you want). As you think of the data, you probably will identify buckets that are really your clients'/users' data that you are merely stewarding. Data can be rented for a limited period of use (such as mailing lists or datasets for analysis). Determining the true ownership will allow you create the rules around what and where you are permitted to use this data.

- *Retention*—How long will you hold this data? This includes both in operational stores but also backups (if the ownership permits you to even do so). Included with this concept is the aging policy: how long will data stay in a given place before it is moved to a longer-term (cheaper?) storage? What are the business triggers that delete all the data, including backups (e.g., a client leaving you)?

- *Visibility*—Who gets to see this data, both internally and externally, and what restrictions are you going to place on securing this visibility (encryption, access lists, etc.)? When data moves, or ages, from one classification to another (e.g., going from operational to business analytics), this area will define the rules on how this data changes (e.g., you may anonymize user data) so it can take on the new rules of that bucket.

- *Compliance*—Is this the type of data that falls under special compliance or regulatory considerations? If that is the case, you will have additional audit and security processes to comply with, which may be different for the different geographic regions you are operating within. Personal, health, and financial are examples of data that would need special handling.

Data is one of the most valuable assets a company manages and owns. The more data you have, the more data is generated. Getting a firm handle on the data that is flowing through your company will ensure you are taking all the necessary steps to avoid being blindsided, either ethically or legally.

It is worth taking special note about data that falls under compliance monitoring. No matter the type of compliance you need to adhere to (PII, HIPAA, PCI, etc.), they all, at their heart, have the same goal in mind: to be secure and respectful of how you handle this data. Historically, no matter the type of data, if you have to manage it securely, follow all the best practices. Although some of this is over the top for some types of data, it ensures you have instilled a sense of responsibility in the team, so when an audit comes, it is not the dramatic event it can be for some. Designing data security and audits into your architecture from the start not only makes sense but also buys you insurance for any change in direction for the future.

8.6 Microservices vs. monolithic

Primarily two large design principles exist when it comes to enterprise development: monolithic and the more modern microservices. Many enterprises are a hybrid of the two. In this section, we are going to go over the primary differences and why microservices have captured the heart of the industry as the way to design and maintain a modern architecture.

Monolithic is the elder statesman of the two, with the enterprise (or large parts of it) built and deployed as a single entity. Generally, the code base is a single unit, compiled in a manner that suggests no one else is using it, with little code reuse and tightly coupled.

Consider the checklist in table 8.4. If you answer yes to three or more characteristics, you are most likely managing a monolithic architecture.

Table 8.4   Microservices vs. monolithic checklist

Single code base, with no internal libraries.	Yes / No
Single database that drives all systems.	Yes / No
An outage causes everything to stop delivering.	Yes / No
Single-server architecture.	Yes / No
Upgrading software requires a planned outage.	Yes / No

Microservices is the art of splitting up the enterprise into discrete "mini" applications that are narrow in scope, performing a specific action or role. They interact, or advertise their services, via an API, service bus, or message queue. A strong microservice is an independent entity, with its own data store, execution environment (powered by a language/library that makes sense for that role), and release cycle that doesn't impact any other part of the system.

The main appeal of microservices is to reduce the risk and allow components to use the best tools available for the task at hand. They became very popular when the technology caught up with the theory, allowing remote API calls to be made in a fast enough time to be near code-like in performance.

From your chair as CTO, microservices permits you to break up your enterprise into a series of smaller independent units. These units will update on their own schedule, and given that there are large parts of your enterprise that will rarely change, you can rest knowing that they will not suffer from any unintended consequence as a result of the update.

Monolithic, on the other hand, is what a lot of legacy enterprises have currently, making it very risky to make changes because the risk of unintended consequences is very high. Upgrading even a small library, though seemingly innocent, could have ripple effects because the code is very tightly coupled.

A common trap with microservices is that if they are not tightly controlled and managed, they can evolve into a series of mini monolithic apps. This is a result of giving them too much responsibility over time, and although the original architect started out with all good intentions, and may even still convince themselves they have a microservices architecture, it is in name only.

Microservices give you the ability to future-proof or delay a technology decision on a given area. By defining a strong, consistent API, you can evolve the implementation of that service over a period of time, as and when the need arises. Say, for example, you have a need to store and retrieve files from all over the enterprise—you could define a file microservice (File MS).

This File MS would have one simple API that accepts a file for storage, and another that retrieves the file. Now, initially, this implementation may simply store the file in a local directory (that is backed up). As the service grows, it may store the file in a network SAN with greater capacity. If the service is proving really popular, then you can look to have the implementation use a cloud provider, such as Amazon S3 service.

The microservice has abstracted away and removed the logistics of file storage and given the rest of your enterprise a consistent manner (or API) to manage files. A microservice is like a code library but at a much higher granularity. This power gives units of your enterprise the framework to evolve at a pace that makes sense for the business.

Monolithic has its place, but if you find you're needing to bring down large chunks of your enterprise for upgrades and updates, you're doing your company a disservice. Unfortunately, for some legacy applications, you may be forced to manage this world, because the underlying technology does not lend itself to this modern, connected architecture. That said, as part of any modernization effort, the ability to break out components into separate units is key to a path out of the mess.

Sometimes a monolithic design is completely acceptable and encouraged, especially if you find yourself in a proof-of-concept phase (or at a startup) where the real value isn't how you are going to do something but the fact that it works and the business thinks there is indeed value in going further with the idea.

Another side effect of a microservice environment is that you can arrange your teams around specific units, where each one is responsible for developing, maintaining, and managing the unit. This is a common strategy in much larger organizations, where they see the users of their API as their customers.

If that sounds familiar, then you are right—this is precisely how all the modern cloud providers operate. AWS is just a series of microservices, all exposing their functionality through APIs that we can then consume on a pay-as-you-go basis.

The vast majority of AWS grew out of the need to power Amazon's main ecommerce sites. They built such a strong library of microservices that they started to sell the functionality independently to external developers—aka you and me. Although you may not be the next AWS, a strong microservice environment will allow you to lean in closer to your clients by giving them access to your APIs in a way that lets them build their own ecosystem around the services you provide.

8.7 Open source

Open source is code that has been contributed to the community, for the greater good, that is available for anyone to at least view and potentially incorporate for their own use, with some restrictions depending on the license type. It is these restrictions that we are going to explain here, because a number of companies don't really know the subtle differences and have found themselves in some legal difficulty when it comes to selling or interacting with specific clients or organizations.

Open source is a great pool of commodity software, letting you accelerate the development of any software project by reusing software components. Some examples of popular open source software include complete operating systems (Linux being one of the most popular), database servers (MySQL, Postgres), and desktop applications (Firefox, Open Office), as well as software libraries (JQuery, Gson). Given the popularity of open source, there is always something at all levels to use.

8.7.1   License types

Just because you have access to the source code, through whatever means on the web, does not necessarily mean you can take it and claim ownership. Although I can play "Let It Be" (I can't, incidentally) on a piano doesn't mean I can start selling renditions of it without paying royalties to McCartney's/Lennon's estates. Source code is the same. Source code can be copyrighted like any written word, and if made available under open source, it usually comes in the form of a license that dictates precisely what you are allowed and not allowed to do with it. The open source world offers two broad categories of license:

- Copyleft
- Permissive

Copyleft-style licenses are generally not considered business friendly. This style of license (with a general public license [GPL] being the most popular) states that any software utilizing a GPL must itself be released under a GPL, including all modifications. In other words, if your secret-sauce algorithm is using GPL software, then you would be legally obligated to make your source code available to anyone who asked, including your competitors.

Permissive licenses, on the other hand (such as BSD, MIT, or Apache), do not have the same restrictions because they permit commercial software to use open source software, or extend open source products, and declare the work as proprietary or closed source, which is, therefore, much more friendly to business use.

Some permissive licenses state that you have to declare your usage of the library in the end product through a public, available notice. You can see this on a number of devices, if you look at their "About" section (e.g., for Android phones, you can see all the open source libraries in use).

Each of these licenses has explicit language around the copyright, patent protection, and derivative works that are subtle enough in their differences that they matter only if you make significant modifications and create works based on the original source.

Although GPL is a very hard copyleft license, a lesser version of it is known as the lesser general public license (LGPL). This license type states that you don't have to release your code as open source if you dynamically link to the software instead of statically. This is a lot more business friendly than GPL.

This is by no means an exhaustive look at the differences between each one, so if you find yourself needing to venture further into this field, you should do your own research.

NOTE It is worth noting another type of license called *public domain*. This is the most free license there is, stating no ownership, no copyright, and absolutely no restrictions on use. It isn't seen that often, though code samples in books are often released under this type.

8.7.2 Usage guidelines

Utilizing open source should be encouraged, especially if you are a Java, JavaScript, or Python shop, because there is a world or experience and utilities available through the likes of GitHub and SourceForge. Before you let your development team off the leash, it is wise to provide the following guidelines on how to incorporate open source:

- Create a list of acceptable licenses your team can use—most likely Apache/MIT/BSD-style licenses.
- Libraries should be used as a whole—code should never be lifted and incorporated as if developed independently. Stealing is not acceptable.
- Provide a centralized place where all external third-party libraries are registered (e.g., a shared spreadsheet), with the following information:
  - Library name
  - URL website
  - License type
  - Component it is used in

Setting down and communicating guidelines will give your team the confidence that you support, respect, and encourage the use of open source.

8.7.3 Publishing open source

Another way to use open source software is by contributing your work for others to use. You may want to contribute your work to the world at large for the following reasons:

- Give something back to the community after years of utilizing other people's work.
- Make your software more robust by having others help debug it.
- Establish a standard in a given niche, and accelerate development by inviting others to help contribute.

Many large corporations release open source code (under a variety of different licenses), including Google, Oracle, Microsoft, IBM, Netflix, Amazon, to name some of the large contributors. Microsoft owns GitHub, for example—one of the largest properties that host open source projects.

Should you decide to open source a library that you or your team have developed, it is important to recognize that you are not just tossing the library into the wild. An open source project must be maintained and updated. No one wants to contribute to a library that has not been updated in years. A successful open source publication is one where the team treats it the same as an internal library and keeps fixing bugs and adding features.

Before you publish a single line of code on your newly created company GitHub account, it has to be clear to your CEO (and legal team) what you are aiming to do and why you are doing it. Be very deliberate about the code you are releasing and the way you are going to be packaging it. Make sure you are not releasing any specific company IPR or trade secrets, and, of course, make sure it is yours to open source in the first place.

> ### Code contribution
>
> I have personally published many projects, both small and large, to open source and had great feedback and contribution along the way. I have also contributed to other open source projects by fixing bugs and adding new features. The goal for me personally is the feeling of giving back. Throughout my years of coding, I have used many open source libraries and, for me, I want to at least put something back in.

Good candidates for open sourcing are small libraries that your team has developed along the way to creating something larger. One of the great benefits of this, particularly if you bump up against a similar library, is that it validates on some level that you are heading in the right direction.

8.7.4   *Using code from the web*

No matter how good your development team is, there will be a point where they will reach for the browser and search for a solution to the problem they are working on. Whether trying to figure out why a given library is behaving the way it is or how to do something in a given language, they will eventually be looking at some code in a browser. The answer to all their problems is sitting there, waiting to be selected—CTRL+C and then CTRL+V into their IDE or editor. Problem solved.

Wait one minute: just because it is read on StackOverflow.com or found in a blog post or article doesn't mean it is free to be taken and incorporated into the solution. Remember, any code that is produced by your team will be considered your company's asset and intellectual property. You have to believe code produced by your team has been created in good faith, free of any copyright material, and not copied. This is potentially a legal minefield, but with some commonsense considerations, you can provide the guidance that will make sure your team is working in the right spirit.

On the whole, "copying" code from developer help forums is okay. As a simple rule, anything more than 5 or 10 lines should be rewritten, using the algorithm only for inspiration (merely renaming variable names is not acceptable). Most of the time, code in those forums is demonstrating how a given library or API should be used and isn't proprietary.

Code blocks from open source libraries can be copied if the license of that library permits it, and if it does, it should be treated as if you incorporated the library as whole (registering the usage of it).

Code validation

Code can be and is checked

Depending on the type of deal, a technical due diligence may look to confirm the legal ownership of the source code, especially if the value of the company is the source code that has been produced. You can find many tools available to look for such plagiarism (ask any computer science professor). I have seen a deal go south quickly when it was discovered that large chunks of code a company was passing off as their own were actually lifted from open source projects. This finding cast doubt on the validity and legality of everything else the team was producing. In contrast, if I am doing due diligence on a development team, and they say they don't use any open source, I am instantly suspicious and will dig deeper than I normally would have.

8.8   *Languages and frameworks*

Choosing a language and subsequent framework is another important decision a CTO can make. This decision will have far-reaching consequences, potentially longer than even your tenure at the company. A lot of the time, the choice of language has been made for you, because you have inherited a technology stack from your predecessor.

The business, by and large, does not care which language is powering the enterprise, as long as it is solving the problem and keeping the clients happy. That said, switching a language (or even a framework) is not a trivial matter. Not only is there an existing investment in the existing development team, which would require retraining, you need to consider all the deployment processes and support knowledge that has gone into supporting the business. Switching a language would entail rewrites of large areas of the enterprise, without much real justification.

How do language choices happen in the first place? In many owner- or founder-led companies, the language choice comes largely from the first language the founder or original "CTO" knew. They used it for everything, contorting it into shapes it was never designed for. There was no real choice or decision—it was just a case of no other choice.

A framework is a set of libraries or standards written on top of a language to mitigate some of the repeated mundane tasks (e.g., handling security for a logged-in user or managing the creation of files). An example would be the Java Enterprise Standard, or Spring, sitting on top of Java, or ReactJS for JavaScript and Express.js for Node.js. A framework is much broader in scope than a language and, as such, can be much more restrictive than a language. Developers who specialize in a framework, while understanding the underlying language, may have difficulty moving to a different framework in the same language. Framework expertise is as important as language expertise.

Languages and frameworks go in and out of fashion. With frameworks sitting on top of a language, it is more common for a framework to fall completely out of favor, while another takes its place. This can be troublesome if a company has invested heavily in a framework for a lot of the plumbing, only for it to be obsolete in a few years.

Instead, the company is faced with supporting both the framework and the solution built on top of the framework.

Languages go out of vogue, too, though on a much longer curve. Languages that suffer this are ones that are tied to a specific company, with one independent standard body governing them. You should avoid these types of languages if at all possible. If the primary company gets bought or goes bust, then the language is left to die on the vine. Examples of this include the likes of Gupta, PowerBuilder, Delphi, and countless others that sprang up around the turn of this century.

When deciding on a language, it is important to think long into the future, with a good figure to aim for being five years. You are about to invest a large effort in this language, hiring developers, creating knowledge, defining deployment processes, and coding standards, all while hoping the language will evolve to provide a richer environment.

8.8.1 Legacy language

If you are faced with a language or framework that has gone into life-support mode, one of your first tasks will be to replace it. We will go over deciding what you are going to replace it with in the next section. Replacing a language should not be done just because you are unfamiliar with it. Instead, you should be looking at the overall landscape and making the decision on a number of factors, including how strong the recruitment market is for that technology. If your development team is aging, and there is no sign of any young blood coming in to bolster and take up the mantle, you are looking at a language that is dying out.

Replacing a language requires significant effort and resources. One of the best ways to tackle this, as discussed previously, is to attempt to split out the areas that can be easily refactored as a microservice. This will give you the opportunity to carve out chunks of the enterprise without being forced to do a complete rewrite.

8.8.2 Choosing the next one

The good (and bad) news is that there is no right answer as to which language you should use. Our industry is always coming up with the latest and greatest technology, which always seems to cast a darker shadow than need be on the existing technologies. Buyer's remorse is something you will experience, but as long as you have done your research, then no matter what decision you come to, it will be right for the time. With that, let me present a series of questions you can rate any language/framework against:

- *Who is behind it?* The driving force behind the language is important, especially if it is a single company. How much of their revenue is based on the success of this language? If the business landscape changes, how will it survive, if at all? Languages that are built around an independent standards committee are usually better long-term candidates.
- *How long has it been around?* Maturity is a big factor. You are not here to be a champion for the language but to provide a solution and stability for your clients.

Typically anything less than two years old should be avoided, allowing others to work out all the kinks and give it a chance to prove it has legs to grow and expand.

- *How active is the community?* When a developer has a question, they reach for their search engine for an answer. However, a new language will have limited support. You want to see how active the online community is for a given technology: how many search results are there, are there active user groups, is there an active and vibrant open source community, and how many books have been published on it?

- *Is it being taught at university?* A good indication of longevity is to look at what the universities are teaching. They have to think long term, because the students they are churning out need to be still relevant in the coming years up to and after graduation. Typically, languages that are tied to a single company are not taught at university.

- *How many job listings are there?* Finally, if you had to hire a sizable team tomorrow, could you? Look around at the various recruitment sites, call up some agencies, and get a pulse check on not only who else is looking for people but also how many people are looking for the role. Being too early in the lifecycle may mean you are paying too much of a premium for a small pool of experts.

Making the right decision is sometimes hard; however, if you make the wrong one, that will present itself very quickly. Take the time and choose wisely. Do not get seduced into choosing the technology that a proof of concept was made in, because that doesn't generally scale too well when you need to productionalize it.

Summary

- Decisions on technology can have long-lasting consequences.
- It is important to pick a solution that does not lock you in to a given vendor.
- It is not always obvious when you should build versus buy.
- Vendors will attempt to seduce you into believing their solution is the answer to all your problems.
- Cloud computing has reached a maturity, which, if used properly, can yield great flexibility and cost savings.
- On-prem hosting has its place, depending on your specific requirements, but that space is getting smaller.
- Disaster recovery (off the cloud) is much harder and requires more experience than most businesses realize.
- Understand strategies for failing forward and back should a disaster event happen.
- Data is the one of the most important assets you have—look at the different buckets on how to categorize it.
- Categorizing data allows you to define ownership, aging, and security.
- Microservices are a different way to break down your enterprise into manageable mini sections.

- Monolithic architecture still has a place, especially in proof-of-concept projects.
- Open source is a great way to take advantage of community code; however, the license can have a major impact on your company.
- Contributing back to the open source community comes in a number of different forms, especially if you try to create a new standard around a commodity.
- Languages and frameworks can impact hiring and future growth, so it is important your stack is future proof.

Checklist

How many of the following items can you lay claim to having covered?

- Not being reliant on a single vendor for a pivotal piece of your enterprise
- Created the necessary comparison matrix for your build-versus-buy decision
- Have not fallen foul of any of the 10 cloud warning signs
- If running your own hardware, have it in a dedicated data center or at least an isolated environment within your office
- Created a disaster recovery strategy, including how you are going to fail forward or back
- Practiced your disaster recovery plan in the last 12 months
- Mapped all of your data, which includes security, visibility, and retention policies
- Are familiar with the open source license types and educated your team on the differences
- Got a clear core small list of languages/frameworks, including standards to maintain quality production

Development 9

This chapter covers

- Managing projects and communicating progress (good or bad) to the business
- Evolving development practices to cope with a growing team
- Governing quality and testing to achieve successful releases
- Avoiding client lock-in solutions

Many CTOs come from an engineering background, steeped with building and producing code. They have evolved and risen through the development ranks, taking on larger projects and more responsibility. Every developer has their own way of doing things—their own mark they like to leave on something. That is what makes a development life so appealing: the creative freedom to do what is needed. When it comes to building a team or growing an enterprise, one has to step outside of that world and think more broadly, think more as a collective and less as an individual. What was clever and cool one day is a pain to maintain and adapt for someone else.

This chapter focuses on the areas that a CTO, who is evolving their career from developer to officer, needs to consider seriously, sooner rather than later, because this will set the right foundations for success moving forward. As with many of the topics we touch on in this book, each area is its own discipline in its own right. As a CTO, you don't need to master them all, but you do need an appreciation and understanding of them all and how they all have a role to play in your group. From getting your hands around properly communicating project planning for the business to rely on you and your team for timely products, right through to managing releases in a professional and predictable manner, it all needs to be systemized or, as we like to refer to it, productionalized.

Simple things, like laying down some coding standards for everyone to follow, make code more readable and, therefore, maintainable. Small steps can have a big impact. We will also go over the need to properly create a repeatable build process, so the business can rely on getting out updates without them becoming logistical nightmares.

This chapter is all about creating a professional, repeatable, and reliable development process, one where you can bring on new resources and make them productive in hours or days instead of weeks as they wrestle with the idiosyncrasies of an antiquated coding process.

From the field

Development environment running production

A well-crafted and polished website can mask a world of chaos, bandages, and shortcuts. One particular due diligence I was involved with reminded me that the failure to make some simple decisions at the start can literally cost millions of dollars in the future. This SaaS company had a great product, but the CTO had not laid down any standards or enforced any formal release policy. The result was a Wild West of code and libraries, with no security to really speak of. The release process was down to a single person (the CTO). By not productionalizing the team's output, this CTO created so much technical debt, the company price ended up being devalued to allow for the repairs. The CTO was simply not equipped with the right knowledge to grow the team beyond their own development skills.

9.1   *Project planning*

One of the hardest things you will have to do as a CTO is to communicate timelines to the business. Whether it is a large initiative or project or a small task, everyone needs to know the team's availability so they may then continue with their tasks that rely on that delivery. Technologists are infamous for their inability to stick to a deadline. Conversely, we are very good at giving dates and then completely missing them. The reason for this is we are eternal optimists, believing things are never as complicated as they actually are. Generally, we are right; however, what we don't allow for is all the external forces that come in to disrupt a perfectly good deadline (like pesky clients getting in the way of a perfectly achievable deadline!).

Predicting, therefore, is hard. With external events, discoveries, and scope creep, it can feel like an impossible task at times. Yet it doesn't need to be like that. A little careful planning and tempering your optimistic communication style to the business can make even the most demanding of CEOs patient as you and your team continue working.

9.1.1 Project manager

There are two types of organizations: the ones that have a good project manager, and the ones that do not. The reasons for not having a dedicated project manager can range from not having the budget for them (reasonable) to not needing one because the CTO knows how to project-manage (not reasonable). It doesn't matter the reason for not having one—as soon as the engineering group is more than around five people, a dedicated project manager is a must. With fewer than that, most groups can coordinate effectively among themselves.

For the sake of discussion, let's assume scrum masters have the same goals as a project manager. Although subtle differences can be argued, the spirit of their role is very similar. A project manager is there to help you execute your vision by helping manage and report on the status of all the resources, predicating and continually updating timelines based on day-to-day events. Contrary to popular belief, a project manager is not a task master or there to hold people accountable—that is the role of the leads. If a deadline is at risk of slipping, they will be able to tell you that very quickly and the reasons for the slippage, allowing you an opportunity to take corrective action if feasible. They will run various periodic meetings and keep a close eye on any ticketing system to maintain a near real-time pulse on the output of the group. The real good ones encourage an open flow of information, good or bad news, to let them properly maintain a handle on the timeline.

People in these roles have an inherited organizational gene coupled with a practical outlook on life and a methodical process approach. Although we technologists kid ourselves into thinking there are more than 24 hours in the day, they know there really are only six hours in a typical working day (factoring in breaks, lunchtimes, restroom visits, daydreaming, and so on). They know when someone comes back from vacation it will take time to come up to speed, whereas we believe they can be productive the second we come back from a two-week vacation sitting on the beach, completely tuned out from the hustle and bustle of the workplace.

Project management is not a science but an art, taking an ever-changing landscape, filtering the noise, and continually adjusting the trajectory to aim at the target. Anyone who has enjoyed fly-ing a drone is probably in awe of the drone software, which corrects the flight path when a gust of wind comes in and blows it off course. How it maintains its position, adjusting the various propellers in real time, making it look effortless, is a joy to behold. A project manager is like the drone, analyzing all the inputs and projecting what will happen if that path is allowed to be traveled and feeding back this informa-tion to you as the CTO to take the corrective action. A project manager will help with the following:

- Getting a handle on the output of each resource
- Identifying milestones and deliverables
- Predicting and continually improving accuracy of deadlines
- Coordinating release cycles
- Managing handoffs between milestones and communications with internal/external teams
- Providing you with actionable items, based on data, to help improve your time management
- Reporting the state of all items, making sure nothing gets lost or falls off the radar

For organizations that don't have quite enough work for a full-time project manager, it is common for them to step into the business analyst role, which helps define the details of a given project from the business perspective. This is an area project manag-ers usually go into with some detail anyway, as they attempt to align milestones in a way that makes sense.

Getting into a constant cadence with your project manager—communicating daily, for example—is very important. You want them to be able to feel they can deliver bad news to you without you reacting unprofessionally or blaming them. They will remind you of the things that need to be done, building that into any plans accordingly, such as yearly maintenance that requires some of the team to be taken away for a period to perform upgrades. Building these occurrences into a plan, with a line of sight, allows the team to run like a well-oiled machine, compared to the reactionary nature of han-dling items as and when needed. This insight gives you all the information you need to help communicate any expectations to the CEO and board in a far more predict-able manner.

TICKET SYSTEM

Knowing what your team is working on at any one point in time, including what is scheduled for them, is crucial to running a group of any size. Technologists are gener-ally people who love getting things done—we love lists of tasks, coupled with the satis-faction of marking an item completed. Taking these two things together, you can see why ticket systems are the number-one method of managing tasks in technology, with the industry standard being Atlassian's Jira, which takes tickets to a whole new level.

Many alternatives exist, but they all work around the same principle: a ticket, with a unique identifier, is a unit of work that is assigned to a given person at a given time. A ticket has its own lifecycle, starting in an open state and finishing at a closed state, with many states in between. *Closed* can mean many things, like the task was completed, or it was purposely ignored because it was not relevant. *Open* means it needs to be looked at and actioned.

Tickets can be grouped into epics, stories, or projects (we will talk about the agile process later), and they can have subtickets as well. The meaning you assign to a ticket is up to you, but whatever it is, it should be communicated to the team so no one is in any doubt.

Consider having a ticket represent a unit of work that should take no more than a period of time (e.g., four hours) to complete. If a ticket is going to take more than that, it should be split into a series of smaller tickets. This technique has an added bonus of putting a stop to wasted efforts. If a person starts working on the ticket, and it looks like they aren't going to complete it at the halfway mark, that is their opportunity to stop and ask for assistance. Maybe they are overcomplicating the task, or the person who set the task didn't appreciate the complexity, and, therefore, it needs to be further split into a series of smaller tasks. You never want to be in a situation where a ticket takes multiple days or weeks to complete—this makes the role of project management so much harder. Whatever resolution you choose should work for your organization and be communicated. Getting your team into the discipline of managing their own tickets, reviewing priorities, and planning out their day will continue to pay dividends well into the future, because it gives everyone a line of sight into workloads and permits autonomy to manage their own to-do lists.

The other big advantage that a centralized ticket system offers is providing a language with which to talk about tasks. It gives me such joy to hear a team toss ticket numbers around, as they discuss various tasks ahead of them or if they need help with something. A ticket number lets anyone look up the task, see the background, read any comments, look at any code that may be associated with that ticket, and become far more knowledgeable about the task at hand, enabling them to offer more informed contributions.

A ticket system, if well maintained, can also serve as a living, breathing knowledge base, particularly if used as a client-support system. This requires anyone closing a ticket to give a little more detail on the steps to resolution, so others can learn from their wisdom.

Developers and engineers are not necessarily the best at keeping the basics of housekeeping tasks up to date. In this area, a project manager will also help maintain and monitor the ticket updates, with the best project managers showing the benefits to everyone, so it becomes second nature. This system will be the project manager's source for the vast majority of their reports and action points, so it is in their interest that this central resource is updated. I show later in this chapter how a ticket system can aid in the release schedule of projects as well.

9.1.2 *Defining projects*

At a high level, we can all agree on what a project is: it is a collection of tasks, grouped together, that, once completed, forms a desired outcome. Where we get into some interesting discussions is the scope of a project: how big should a task be before it is considered a project? A project can be a few days or years in scope. Irrespective of the length of time, a project should have a defined goal—the reason the project exists in the first place. The goal doesn't speak to how something is going to be accomplished, or even how long it should take to complete. It merely defines the success criteria, which, once met, marks the project as completed.

Write the outcomes of a project in terms that can be understood by those outside of the engineering group. This promotes transparency and communication, particularly with your CEO/CFO, who will want to understand where you and your team are spending time and money. An example of the same project with two different definitions follows:

- *Internal*—Upgrade the customer intake process, removing the reliance on Windows XP, and rewriting it with Java running on a serverless environment.
- *External*—Modernize the customer intake process, rewriting it for the cloud for greater flexibility and increased throughput.

Now that you have the outcome of the project defined, which is the easy bit, you have to figure out how you are going to do it, breaking it up into a series of smaller tasks that all contribute toward reaching the final goal. In the computing world, we have two primary styles we use to break down a project. The oldest methodology is waterfall, with the more modern approach called agile.

WATERFALL

This project model is where as much as possible is planned up front, before any work starts. The idea is that everything starts from the top of the waterfall and then flows down. This places a lot of emphasis on the analysis of the problem domain to identify all the issues and problems that need to be resolved. As part of the waterfall process, a lot of decisions are made on the design and structure. The goal of this process is to know as much as possible before committing any resources to the project.

Although you might spend a lot of time planning at the start of the project before any work is completed, you can more easily predict time and cost for a well-defined project. Another benefit of a well-defined waterfall project is that it is in a good position for putting out a call for external company bids.

The downsides of a waterfall include the up-front time it takes for the definition to be done, particularly if it is a large project—no work can be started until the definition is completed. Imagine a project that involves driving from Miami to San Francisco—the team can't start driving until the complete route is fully mapped out.

A much larger downside of the waterfall model is its inability to cope with change. Change can come in many different forms—technology or requirements are no longer relevant, or new feature requests are identified. Some larger projects might just ignore these issues and stay the course, given how hard it is to accommodate the new event. It is not uncommon for projects to be delivered that no longer fit the purpose they were designed to do, with outdated technology (it does appear more common in government/public-company-style projects where any change would take too many people to agree and cause too much interruption).

Waterfall projects generate a lot more up-front documentation, which can include wireframes or mockups, and is usually performed by a mixture of subject matter experts, business analysts, architects, and project managers.

AGILE

If the waterfall model involves knowing everything before you start, then the other end of the spectrum is agile—making it up as you go along. (This is a somewhat flippant statement—it may be that not all the problems are fully realized or solved before starting.) Agile, deriving from *agility*, is the ability to react to a changing environment, taking incremental steps, all in the pursuit of getting closer to the final outcome and being agile to navigate any change quickly and successfully. For example, going back to our project to drive to San Francisco: as an agile project, as soon as we know how we are getting out of Florida, we can let the team start by getting to the Floridian border, while the next phases are planned. In reality, agile is a set of guidelines and principles focused on continuous delivery of outcomes that have involved all stakeholders of the project, including the end client or user, to ensure a higher quality, because issues are identified and rectified much sooner.

A common misconception about agile is that it equals a lack of planning, which couldn't be further from the truth. A project in agile still requires planning, just not to the same detail as the waterfall approach. Instead, milestones (or *epics*, to use agile terminology) are identified, which are then turned into a series of tasks, ready for execution. These tasks are then arranged into small bursts of activity, or sprints. These usually take one or two weeks, and after that, a review is made on how well things went. Typically, the sprints are designed to deliver a piece of functionality, so others can interact with the end result, if possible.

Agile can be very process oriented, which can be intimidating to begin with. It is more of a set of guidelines than hard and fast rules that must be followed—a framework that attempts to enable a level of order and flow for what can be a nebulous challenge. Some organizations get themselves so wrapped up in the rules that they suck all enjoyment and flexibility from the project. Finding the right balance that works for your team will make the agile philosophy successful. The scrum process is one example of an agile methodology.

An agile project can make and incorporate changes much easier, because there is plenty of opportunity to see whether something is going to work way before too much time has been wasted on it. Flexibility is the key to making an agile framework succeed. Identify the areas that are natural to the way you currently work, and then slowly adapt more discipline over a period of time, warming up the team as you go along to the benefits and successes. For a more in-depth review of the agile and waterfall methods, visit: https://www.guru99.com/waterfall-vs-agile.html.

9.2   *Development standards*

Although it is tempting to let development teams do their own thing, with no standards or guidelines, it will create problems in the future as you grow. The last thing you want is large blocks of code, crucial to the success of the business, that are untouchable, brittle, and gnarly, with only a handful of people daring enough to make any change for fear of consequences. Every company has its "sacred code blocks" that, over the years, have taken on a mythology of their own—a perceived complexity—and as soon as anyone suggests rewriting them, there are long, deep intakes of breath followed by shaking of heads, as the elders of the team dissuade any attempts to modify, let alone rewrite them.

As noted many times in this book, your role as a technology leader is to not only solve the problems of the day but to lay down the foundation for the future. The systems being developed now need to be supported and expanded many years into the future, usually well beyond your tenure.

Standards help develop and foster a common narrative on how code should be structured, laid out, and written. Coding for scalability and readability takes effort, because many developers believe their code is untouchable and doesn't need any sort of review. Beware of these types, root them out quickly, and, if you can't get them to change, let them go.

With coding being more art than science, people can play in a huge field of ambiguity. What seems logical or natural to one developer will feel foreign and awkward to another. Developers have this bad habit that if they find something they don't understand, they just rewrite it—does the saying "Out of the frying pan, into the fire" sound familiar? Therefore, it is to everyone's benefit that code is developed in a way that can be easily read and understood, with common methods and patterns being deployed.

The good news is that this is not an uncommon problem. All the major languages have a number of different standards on how things should be constructed, so you don't need to reinvent the wheel. Basic standard adherence is relatively simple to enforce through third-party tools that plug into most IDEs. You can also look at tools that augment the code-build cycle that examine code before it is deployed. SonarQube is a common open source tool that covers all the popular languages, finding dangling variable declarations, null pointer traps, and logic cul-de-sacs (areas where you can't get out of), among many others.

Coding standards are more than just formatting code in a text file. They can define common design patterns—for example, how you should prepare to interact with the database or output logs. More importantly, though, they should provide guidance on how code should be structured, the density of functions, and class hierarchy, right down to naming conventions.

These things can evolve over time, bit by bit, building up your team's standard. Code reviews should be done regularly, and no one should feel their code is beyond reproach—including yours, if you are still contributing code with your CTO hat on.

Code should be readable, maintainable, and, above all, as error free as possible. Standards and code reviews help to make this a reality.

9.3   *Version control*

Version control (VC) is a library and time vault for all your digital assets rolled into one. Once solely used by large development teams, version control has woven itself into the very DNA of coding and is even making its way into other areas of the business with the likes of Google Docs, which never forgets any edits on basic Office-style documents.

VC has evolved a lot over the years, from the likes of CVS to SVN to Git (being the most popular, GitHub is one of the largest repositories of open source software). Yet, the guiding principle is the same: to enable parallel development by one or more developers, in a way that does not rely on developers having to contort their development environments to maintain different versions. Imagine being in the middle of a large development of a new version, and you need to fix a bug in the current production system. You need to have the source code that is running in production, absent of any new features, so you can reliably fix the bug and release the code without fear of any new work leaking out in the wild.

Some development teams have not embraced any sort of version control. They sometimes maintain directories of released versions, or maybe even the odd zip file. All the excuses for not jumping in—from they don't need it, to the language doesn't lend itself to checking in and out, to it would only slow them down—are completely invalid. What it comes down to is fear of the unknown.

From the field

Price of not having version control

Back at the start of my career, I had an engagement with the United Nations, in Rome, writing Java Servlets to process satellite photos of agricultural land in Africa. They had built all these Perl CGI scripts to allow academics to access the photos via the Mozilla browser. We were invited to trial the new Java Servlet standard to see how it would hold up under a real load. I was out there for months, and one specific week, I was working really hard to finish a new section before getting on a plane to go home for a few days. There were no coding standards or processes to speak of, let alone version control—not uncommon in shops 25-plus years ago. I had made my own backups as I went along, on a separate network directory (I thought I was being clever). I was doing a test, and, well, there was a part of the process that deleted temporary files (because disk space was a real premium in those days). However, in my rush, I got something wrong, and it deleted all the source files, both locally and from my backup network drive. I couldn't restore them—and I tried. I had deleted my entire week's work. I had no choice but to stay over the weekend and rewrite everything. There were so many lessons I learned that week that, to this day, I have never had a repeat occurrence of this issue.

At the highest level, version control is organized as a series of repositories. Although you can think of these as folders, that is doing them a disservice because they are much richer. They are more akin to components, or building blocks, that make up your enterprise. A repository is a living, breathing time capsule, a collection of parallel universes, that collates the effort, history, and evolution of a given piece of work.

Choosing the right granularity for a repository is more of an art than a science with no one solution that will fit everyone. Some things to consider when deciding on a repository follow:

- Does it have a defined function or role?
- Is there a different or narrow set of skills required to maintain the component?
- How does it relate to other components?
- How is this component or project released?

Try not to have too many repositories, and conversely, don't have a single one that encapsulates everything. Too many, and the overhead associated with them becomes too heavy, whereas having too few makes it harder to segregate and manage commits. This is your traditional Goldilocks not-too-hot-not-too-cold dilemma.

Like how files and folders do not dictate the content that should be in them, or how nested or granular you are with them, version control alone does not define any strategy—only a set of rules and tools to operate on them. The good news, though, is a number of popular versioning patterns are generally accepted and understood, allowing you to choose one that works best for both your team and enterprise. Here are just a couple of examples:

- *Gitflow*—Two main branches are used: master (all code here is deployable) and develop. For any development, you create a feature branch from develop that is then reviewed and merged back into develop. To create a release, you create a merge of master from develop and push that out. No code is committed directly to either the master or develop branch.
- *GitHub flow*—A simpler version of Gitflow, with only a main master branch. Any development is done by branching off into a feature branch, which, once reviewed and tested, is merged into the master, ready for deployment.

Within each pattern, you can define how the integration with your ticket system works, the naming convention of feature branches, the granularity or lifetime of a branch, the release cycle, and so on. These all should be something that makes sense to your environment, so you can build the necessary tooling and reporting to get the most out of your version control environment.

9.4   *Quality assurance (QA)*

Quality assurance (QA), or testing, like every other topic here, is itself a complete discipline. The goal of the QA process is very simple: is what you just developed or installed going to do what you expect it to do?

Testing is not easy—it's probably one of the hardest things to do in your group. Trying to anticipate every permutation or action a piece of software can go through is nearly impossible. Tests are like money—no matter how much you have, you could always do with a little more.

One thing we engineers do know, though, is we make very poor testers, especially of our own work. Therefore, it is always advised that someone or something else tests the code independently. For this reason, it is a good idea to have separate QA teams within engineering that are away from the source code, so they can test fixes and features as an end user would use them. You may find yourself needing to manage the following two types of testing:

- Manual testing
- Automated tests

9.4.1 Manual testing

As the name suggests, manual testing is when a human has to be involved in running one or more tests to sign off on the success criteria. Usually this is done when automated tests are too difficult or brittle to run for given scenarios.

It's common to have a specific QA team who knows the product extremely intimately, who has developed a suite of test plans that exercise the areas that, at the very least, are used the most. A good practice is building up a test plan and methodology so anyone can run the tests and to avoid having only one person who knows how to properly test the code.

Testing can be very time consuming, and depending on the area being tested, testing fatigue can set in. Take, for example, a given section that always passes, so the tester naturally skips it, assuming it will work. This is a dangerous situation because it is hard to spot.

The test team is a good place to rotate new developers through before they are let loose on code. Doing so not only familiarizes them with the product but also gives them an appreciation of the level of testing the group does, so they know they can't let just anything slip through.

> **From the field**
>
> *Testing the testers*
>
> I am aware of a few CTOs who, while rotating their new recruits through the QA team, purposely give them failing areas instead of real tests, to see if they pick up on them. This can be anything from outright failing functionality to areas that don't quite conform to the standard (be it a process or the look and feel). This practice may be sneaky at first blush, but it instills a level of detail and confidence in both the process and the new recruit.

9.4.2 Automated tests

The dream of any CTO, engineer, or product owner is to have all the code covered by an automated test. An automated test is one where direct human interaction is not involved and that can be run as part of the build-and-release pipeline. An automated test can include unit tests, API endpoint testing, end user testing—anything that puts your code base through its paces without a human manually doing it.

Creating and maintaining automated tests is not easy because it can require creating specific scenarios and data inflections to properly execute a sequence of business logic. Say you have a test to delete a person's record. Part of the test is to delete the record and then confirm it was deleted. Easy? Yes, but now we need to create the person record in the first place to be able to delete it. Vicious cycle—welcome to testing.

From the field

Don't be seduced by quantity

Glen Martin, who served as Product Manager for the Java Enterprise specification back in its day, taught me a valuable lesson about the importance of quality over quantity in testing. He illustrated this by asking me whether I preferred to drive a car that had 10,000 tests run on it or the one that had only one test? Naturally, as a fresh-faced engineer, I answered the car with 10,000 tests, of course. Yet, I fell into the classic trap of assuming quantity equaled quality. He then noted that the car with 10,000 tests did not include one that turned on the engine, but the one test the other car underwent was turning on the engine. A simple and obvious example, but after nearly 25 years, it stayed with me.

Code coverage is an important metric to consider when evaluating the quality of tests. This is a measurement of how much underlying code was actually run as part of the test. Not all code is equal—there will be areas of code that are far more important than others, especially those that run the most often or provide a real crucial service.

Therefore, when evaluating code coverage metrics, you need to determine which modules are the most crucial. Those are the ones for which you need to have good coverage. Incidentally, it is nearly impossible to achieve 100% code coverage; if you are getting anywhere between 50%–70%, you are doing very well.

Automation takes the repetitive actions out of manual testing, helping to avoid testing fatigue where crucial steps are skipped. Developing an automation framework takes effort and continual maintenance. Every new feature added may break a test, which will then need to be updated.

When projects get tight on time, test development is usually the first thing to get lowered in priority. You may find yourself with a broken build process because an automated test is failing. In your heart you convince yourself the reason tests are failing is because of new business logic—a safe fail (a false negative). So, instead of fixing it, you decide to disable it, thus allowing the build to complete and for you to meet the deadline.

Days pass. Weeks pass. Before you know it, the tests are never reenabled or resolved. We've all been there—another example of technical debt being introduced to the system. Automated testing takes a lot of discipline, but it is worth the effort, and a well-maintained test suite will always pay dividends in the future.

9.5 CI/CD

Building and deploying software is a complicated business—don't let anyone tell you differently. Teams are also getting bigger (and more distributed), with more hands in the code base at a given time and members coming and going. So, with more complexity and team fluidity, how do you maintain control over code infrastructure in such a way that guarantees everyone can build to the exact same solution? Code pipelines, or CI/CD (continuous integration/continuous deployment), are the answer.

> **From the field**
>
> *Only Fred can update that service*
>
> If you rely on a single machine (or person) to compile, package, and deploy production code, then you have a dependency problem. It is very easy to get into this sort of situation, and what has worked for years doesn't seem too much of a problem or a priority to fix. I see it a lot in founder-led portfolio companies that rely on a single person to keep things updated. I had one situation where the person responsible had allowed the Windows machine to be updated to the latest .NET libraries, causing the build to fail. This caused widespread panic because the company now could not update its core product. To resolve that issue (in the short term), we set them up in a virtualized environment to make builds more accessible and predictable.

As CTO you are responsible for the long-term maintainability of the enterprise, which means being able to reliably build, update, and deploy code at any time without relying on a single person to be present. Unfortunately, many smaller organizations exist whose release ability is determined by whether or not a certain person is on vacation.

The philosophy behind CI/CD, as the name suggests, is that as soon as code has been reviewed, approved, and merged into a branch, it is automatically put through its paces of compiling and testing and then deployed to a given server environment. Any failure in any part of this process is flagged immediately for resolution. An example of a typical CI/CD pipeline is illustrated below.

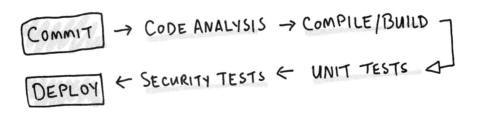

It starts automatically, when someone makes a commit to a given branch in a repository, typically the develop branch, after code has been merged from a pull request. This then kicks off the following series of events, or gates, through which the build process goes, that have to be completed successfully for it to be accepted and deployed:

- *Commit*—This is the event that triggers the start of the pipeline, usually a successful commit/merge of code to a given branch.
- *Code analysis*—The source code in the branch is run through a series of quality tests using a tool such as SonarQube.
- *Compile/build*—The code is then compiled (if applicable) and built into a deployable artifact that is ready for deployment.
- *Unit tests*—Once built, the code is put through unit tests that exist to make sure no bugs were introduced to the code base.
- *Security tests*—Any tests or checks specifically aimed at maintaining a high confidence of security are performed.
- *Deploy*—Finally, the code is deployed to a server environment, such as a development or testing server. Depending on the branch, it may even be the production environment.

Naturally, you can add as many steps, each doing something different, into the pipeline as makes sense for your environment. This is a powerful automation pipeline because it makes sure no step is left out and every piece or library is buildable in an environment away from the developer's desktop machine. That way, you never need to worry about that classic excuse: "Well, it works on my machine."

Getting such a CI/CD pipeline set up is nowhere near as daunting as it once was. Tools such as GitHub, Bitbucket, and CodeCommit all offer some form of CI/CD pipeline support, and if you really want or need to get sophisticated, you can employ an orchestration tool such as the popular open source Jenkins to manage the complete pipeline across multiple repositories and services.

As you evolve and get more comfortable with the pipeline, you will look to build in more checks. If this is all new, do not be too clever or overreach straight out of the gate—a simple *Commit > Build > Deploy* has served many an organization just fine.

When something does go wrong and a stage fails to pass, then you will know exactly who it was that introduced the problem, thanks to the audit trail from version control. This is not to point the finger of blame but to create an open environment, where no one is above reproach and everyone pulls together to create the best quality software.

A strong CI/CD pipeline will set up your department to quickly scale out resources, safe in the knowledge you have guard rails to keep people on the straight and narrow. Common issues that would stop a build can include the following:

- Compilation error
- Missing library dependency
- Code compliant/standard violation
- Test failure

- Security scan failure (leaving in passwords or hardcoded keys)
- Database misalignment

More tests, however small, all add up to greater confidence when your team releases code, and reduces dramatically the risk. Such a strong set of checks promotes the confidence for the "release small; release often" mentality. How many times you actually release is up to you, but why sit on a bug fix any longer than you have to, especially if you have a zero-downtime release infrastructure (such as a serverless environment)?

Some teams do a couple of releases a week, some once a day, or some even many times a day (one large Fortune 100 even performs thousands a day across their infrastructure). If you get your pipeline right, there is no limit, especially if you are using a cloud environment where the build environment is spun up on demand.

9.6 *Technical debt*

Imagine running a car but never getting it serviced (changing oil, filters, and tires). Sure, you are saving a little money in the short term, but each time you skip these maintenance tasks, you are incurring a little bit of "car debt." At some point, that debt will be greater than the value of the car, resulting one day with the engine locking up or tires blowing out on the highway, resulting in a much greater cost to rectify. It is, therefore, cheaper to keep up with the smaller items to avoid the large, unexpected outages or costs.

The same thing happens in the enterprise, but instead of a car, it is source code or systems. Every time a shortcut is taken (hardcoding a value, doing minimal checks on a function, or not applying a security or upgrade patch), you are incurring technical debt.

Technical debt occurs naturally throughout the course of running a fast-paced enterprise. This is okay— and encouraged to get the job done. Notwithstanding, think of it like using a credit card: it's okay to put the short-term cost on the card, but be sure to pay it off at the end of the month.

How much time should you spend on paying down technical debt? This largely depends on the type of organization you have, but a good rule of thumb is anywhere between 10% and 30% of your team's output should be devoted to getting rid of the debt.

Measuring the quantity of debt in source code can be quite easy with the right code-quality tools in your pipeline (SonarQube, again, is a good example). As part of the code review process, release, and upgrade, it's a good idea to flag the technical debt as you see it and add it to the backlog for later. For example, a piece of code may not be flagged by a code analysis tool, because syntactically it is perfectly legal, yet you know it was a short-term fix that needs to be redone to be a little more encompassing.

A good CTO knows the level of technical debt their group is carrying at any point in time. A good tip, especially if you work in sprints, is to consider a rest period between every two or three sprints to take the time to pay down the technical debt.

9.7   *Release*

As the old saying goes, you are nothing until you deliver. Releasing code or updating a living, breathing enterprise platform is something that can be a painless and trivial event, but it takes a lot of effort and work to make it look effortless.

In the old days, updating software was a project in and of itself—scheduling out-of-hours downtime, notifying customers, preparing a list of steps, and then executing, hoping nothing goes wrong, because rolling back was something no one ever wanted to even contemplate. Contrast that to the modern-day architecture where zero-down-time updates are expected and completed multiple times a day.

In this section, we are going to go over what makes for a good release strategy and the considerations and communications for creating an environment for success. "Release small; release often" isn't just a pithy saying—it is an achievable discipline.

9.7.1   *Outage release*

The first type of release is one that requires actual downtime: the system needs to come offline. This may be due to the components that need restarting, or data that needs a migration process to go from old to new. Planning this type of release requires more effort and up-front planning. This can include the following:

- Determine what needs to be taken offline: which servers, components.
- How will this look to end customers: will you need to put up a maintenance page?
- Calculate a time frame that includes the following:
  - Time to shutdown
  - Time to update software and hardware
  - Time for starting back up
  - Time for preuser testing
  - Time to enable users to go back in
- For each area, detail the precise steps required to achieve success.
- Allocate a resource to each step and the hand-off process to the next.
- Talk with the business to come up with the potential release dates, preferably at the lowest usage period.
- Determine the list of those needing progress reports and those to be notified when the release has been done.

Once you have this, it will be your release plan going forward. Build in time for things going wrong. For example, if the business can tolerate a weekend outage, yet you think you need only 2–4 hours, take the weekend. If you get it done earlier, great, but if something goes wrong, then you have time built in without having to ask for more.

When the release project begins, each step is executed and communicated to those identified. Do not shy away from communicating bad news—if things take longer, or start to go off plan, it is better than going radio silent and having your audience think there is no one at the helm.

Ideally, especially if you have to do this process often, you can find some time to practice. It is not always possible, depending on the type of system that requires updating. For example, if you are migrating a back-office system (such as email) from one system to another, then it will take considerable time, and a practice run at scale will not be feasible.

After the completion of the release, do a postmortem to celebrate what went well and learn from what went wrong or could be done better next time.

9.7.2 *Blue-green release*

Historically, when you think of updating, you think of replacing code on a server (physically replacing files on a server filesystem). This comes with a lot of risk and, of course, makes rolling back harder, because no matter what, something changed on the filesystem.

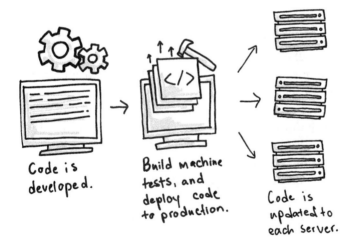

Code is developed.

Build machine tests, and deploy code to production.

Code is updated to each server.

The advent of virtualization, delivering the ability to spin up servers in minutes or seconds, opened up opportunities to radically rethink a lot of ways we dealt with the enterprise, with release being one of them. So, instead of updating servers, you create a completely new environment, loaded with new software, all configured and ready to go. Once stood up (and if using something like Docker, this can be scripted to perform quickly), you can test it while the "current" architecture continues to service current traffic.

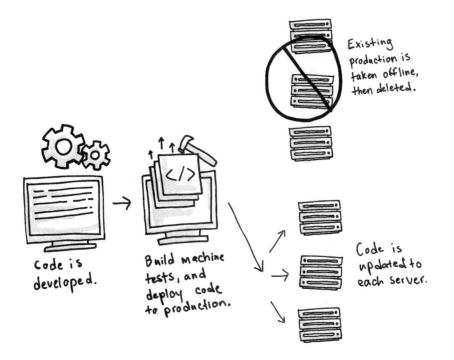

After confirming everything is good, you can start to direct traffic over to the new "release" environment, and when all traffic is there, you can tear down the old one and let the new one take all the load. If, on the other hand, things are not quite right, then tear down the new one and try again—no harm done to existing traffic.

This style of release is called blue-green, and if mastered, it can make for a painless and stress-free release cycle. It also has the added advantage of testing your infrastructure-creation scripts. The more complex your architecture, the harder this technique is to master, but not impossible. It is ideal for web-style applications.

One of the hardest things to manage in any release is database schema changes. The rule is simple: always add, never drop. Dropping makes it impossible to roll back without resorting to backups. You can drop tables, columns, and indexes much later in future releases, once you are confident the release was successful and never needs to go back.

Getting to a stage where releases are well practiced and painless takes a lot of the pressure and risk away from updates, making them nonevents. Irrespective of which release strategy you opt for, creating release notes—a document of everything that changed—is a good habit to get into. This can be a basic text file, a wiki, or even an Atlassian Confluence page. Some ticketing systems make it easy to tag various tickets or sprints for a given release and effectively produce the release notes automatically.

This is a very useful document, especially if the business has to communicate to the end client what was released. They may want to take this raw list and contextualize it into language that has more meaning to the end user.

9.8 Client requests

When running a large, successful enterprise, you will no doubt be fielding feature requests from all quarters. Larger clients will probably carry a lot of influence, and these are the ones that, if you don't manage, will become your worst nightmare. The business will be keen to keep their biggest customers happy and will, naturally, want to serve their wants for their continued business.

Yet if left unchecked, you could find yourself authorizing charges that are only for that specific client, creating unnecessary overhead and ultimately an anchor on the platform. You don't want to say "no" all the time, so what is a modern CTO to do? Continually putting up blocks isn't going to endear the business (or clients) to you. Instead, you have to treat each feature request in the context as if it were for all your clients. Things to consider follow:

- Is this something others would see value in? If so, then it should be on the road map anyway.
- Does it need extra definition or discussion to make it appealing to a wider audience?
- If it doesn't make sense for everyone else, is there another way to achieve what they wish?

Creating a way to export or import data affords the client an opportunity to build something external, maybe using your API if you have one available. For very customizable systems, build in a plugin pattern, so it allows the system to be extended without touching the core system. The situation you never want to find yourself in is the one we all have seen:

```
if (Client == XYZ) {
  // do something client specific
}
```

This is the surest and quickest way to create technical debt. It leads to a complicated code base, creating areas that are really hard to test, and saddles you with code that you may never get the opportunity to change because the client will be depending on its existence.

> **From the field**
>
> *The client is always right*
>
> I have seen many examples in portfolio companies of various ages and sizes of the "if client, then" style, and each one comes with a regret, because they are locked into that path, creating more complexity with each release. The other end of the extreme is when a complete repository is branched for a specific client. This is the most dangerous situation and sets you up for sure-fire failure. All that has happened is you have doubled your workload on all fronts. Any new feature enhancements or bugs have to be applied to all active branches and tested. If you find yourself ever uttering the phrase "It's just for this one client/feature," it's time to snap out of it! Your future self will thank you.

Summary

- Defining a project timeline is hard, due to external or unknown events that can occur.
- Breaking a project into smaller components, such as with the agile process, can make project timeline prediction easier.
- A well-managed and structured ticket system can give you and your team deep insight to the state of tasks.
- As your team grows, a strong project manager will be worth their weight in gold as they guide projects through their lifecycles.
- Laying down some simple and basic development standards makes code more readable and, hence, maintainable as the team grows and evolves.
- Version control is a powerful ally in your fight to control an ever-changing and dynamic environment.
- Getting the right branching strategy can create parallel develop streams without needing to wait or orchestrate complicated timing schedules.
- Recognizing technical debt is the first step to getting a handle on reducing it.
- Testing comes in different forms, be it manual or automated. Acknowledge that it is hard, but no matter what, something is better than nothing.
- Releasing need not be complicated or filled with risk; the secret is in the planning and practice, and then communication.
- With virtualization and the cloud, the risk of releasing can be dramatically reduced through the use of a blue-green strategy.
- Clients and users should be encouraged and welcomed to give feedback; yet, it needs to be managed in a way that your code base doesn't become a fractured mess.

Checklist

How many of the following items can you lay claim to having covered?

- Planning and managing the work of others (if you don't have a project manager)
- Have tracked all your team's work through some sort of ticket system
- Have a defined cadence on how projects are laid out and planned
- Clearly understood development standards to which your team adheres to
- Employed a strong version control culture, with everyone understanding the importance and role it plays
- Repeatable build and deployment process that is not reliant on a single person or machine
- Have a handle on the amount of technical debt being carried and a plan to pay it down
- Dedicated test environment that sits outside of the development team
- Release process that permits rolling back if need be
- No if-client type of constructs in your codebase

Contract management

This chapter covers
- Managing the contract for engaging third parties
- Detailing a statement of work
- Evaluating external vendors
- Software licensing and support contracts

Contracts, agreements, and licensing are definitely not the most glamorous side of being a CTO. We didn't sign up to manage legal documents—we're engineers! Unfortunately, though, they come with the territory of a growing technology team. Whether you need to engage third-party vendors, review service-level agreements, or examine software licenses, a high-level knowledge of how each of these play into your world will be advantageous.

In this chapter, we are going to go over the basic contracts that are likely to come over your desk at some point, the role they play, and how you can make them work. To be clear, these are legal documents, with all the usual legal language that comes with that. I strongly advocate that proper legal advice should always be sought before you agree to sign, or produce such a document. Too many times, a headstrong engineer has inadvertently signed something they shouldn't have, believing they understood everything contained within. Legal documents are not code—they don't have a logical structure or a single computational value. A good CTO knows this is not their area of expertise and allows their legal counsel to articulate the spirit of what they are looking to turn into "legalese."

A brief word on storage: typically the CFO keeps all paper (or hard) copies of the contracts, all signed and sealed. However, it is a good idea for you to keep a digital version of them in your usual file space (Google Drive, Dropbox, Office 365) for fast retrieval and reference.

With that, let's go through the contracts that are the typical vehicles for your "spirit of intent."

10.1 Service agreement

There will come a time, or maybe you are already there, where you will engage the services of a third-party company. Some reasons to do this follow:

- Staff augmentation
- Specific project
- Support
- System management

A successful engagement is one where both parties are clear on the responsibilities of each and the cost associated with rendering the service. That doesn't mean you need to get into pages of legal contracts, but at a minimum, a service agreement should lay out clearly what your expectations are.

Like a book, a service agreement should have a beginning, a middle, and an end. The beginning states the commencement date and any prerequisites that need to be completed and lays out the costs. If this is an engagement that produces something, then spell out clearly the assignment of ownership of the produced work, usually tied to the payment of each monthly invoice.

From the field

Read the fine print

Philosopher Eugene Lewis Fordsworthe is credited with crafting the phrase "assumption is the mother of all mistakes," and nothing can be truer when it comes to service agreements. I was involved in due diligence on behalf of a private equity company looking to purchase a software company. The company didn't have any of its own developers and had outsourced all its development to a third-party development company. It was assumed they owned all the work that was paid for. The problem: the agreement that was signed had no transfer of the IPR of the final product—it wasn't theirs to sell. Thinking it was just an oversight, and with their great multiyear relationship, this was not going to be a problem to resolve and get the legal side of things squared away. However, people do funny things when they see large dollar signs. Assignment wasn't forthcoming. It got a little ugly with more demands. Needless to say, the private equity firm walked away, all because someone never read the fine print of the service agreement.

The "middle" is the details of what it is you need from this relationship. This includes deliverables, responsibilities, reports, and availability, if applicable. It doesn't need to be too detailed or, conversely, too vague.

Finally, the "end"—this is how the service agreement will come to an end and how things will be handed over. Clauses in this section will include provisions for each party to terminate the relationship prior to completion, if applicable.

Termination need not be for negative reasons. It could be because the business is no longer going in the same direction. It is common that support contracts for legacy systems that are no longer being used are terminated—that is one of the reasons for upgrading or replacing them: to reduce the continued spend.

That said, sometimes the business relationship doesn't work out, either for not delivering, personality clash, or poor performance. The termination clause is required to allow you to terminate in a reasonable, timely, and professional manner. Typically, it includes some time period to allow the other party time to plan for an alternative, usually around the two- to eight-week mark, with a month being common for contracting resources.

The following are a couple of documents often associated with a service agreement:

- Statement of work
- Service-level agreement

10.1.1 Statement of work

Choosing your service vendor is not unlike hiring for a member of your team. The first thing you need is the list of items you expect from this engagement. This is the *statement of work* (SOW), or support contract. This is detailed enough that the companies tendering their bids know what they need to provide for the contract to be successful.

These documents are commonly negotiated under an NDA (nondisclosure agreement), which gives both parties the latitude to discuss the requirements at hand without fear of losing confidential information. That said, just because a party is under an NDA doesn't mean you should discuss everything—the conversation should still be restricted to as little information as possible and only to what is relevant for the contract at hand.

DEFINITION   A nondisclosure agreement (NDA) is a mini contract that exists between two parties for them to be able to exchange information confidentially to advance discussions without fear of loss or misuse of IPR (intellectual property rights). It is usually limited in scope and has an associated time span. Having an NDA established and validated by your company's lawyer is good for your arsenal so you have it when needed. Typically signed by your CFO or CEO, this document safeguards your trade secrets and processes, while letting you have limited conversations to advance your short-term goal. An example of an NDA can be found here: https://www.lawdepot.com/contracts/non -disclosure-agreement/.

Looking at a typical statement of work, you may have the following areas:

- Scope of work: areas that will be worked on, areas that won't be
- Definition of deliverables: source code, library, or service
- When the assignment of the IPR of the rendered work occurs
- Access required to fulfill the contract
- Flexibility/restrictions on personnel, or subcontracting the work
- Authorization steps for any out-of-scope work, additional licenses, or travel
- Warranty on any rendered work
- Time frame of contract
- Extension/renewal/termination procedures
- Limitations on solutions offered
- Payment terms

The granularity of this agreement is something that depends on the type of engagement required. For rapid, on-demand resources (such as developers), it is usually not that detailed in terms of the work being provided. It may say "Java development services, as dictated by the project manager," but it wouldn't detail the precise tasks. It would, however, have a minimum time frame associated with it and a clause to note the company can't directly recruit the person without prior approval for a period of, say, up to two years after termination.

For support contracts, the statement of work may limit the version of the software they are providing support for, how often they are going to be performing upgrades, and if they need to take it offline, how that is managed with the business.

A good statement of work is detailed enough for both parties to know exactly what is expected of them but still adaptable to a changing and evolving environment. Neither party should feel beholden to the other, so beware of any agreements with too long a commit period. For examples of an SOW see: https://www.projectmanager .com/blog/statement-work-definition-examples.

10.1.2 Service-level agreement

The *service-level agreement*, or SLA, is commonly used to define the minimum or maximum limits of a service or product. For example, if you run a service, what is your expected uptime, and if you fail to deliver that, what is the recourse for the user?

AWS, in their SLA for the Elastic Compute Cloud (EC2) service, states they will have a monthly uptime of 99.99%, and if they fail, there will be a credit in the bill of 10%. This equates to roughly anything more than six minutes of downtime a month; beyond that, Amazon owes you 10% of your EC2 bill (https://aws.amazon.com/compute/sla/).

The purpose of an SLA is to provide the confidence and faith that you can rely on a given service. Say, for example, Amazon didn't have an SLA, or, even worse, it had an uptime of only 50%. That means they could be down for up to two weeks in every month, with no recourse for the customer. Could your business tolerate such poor availability of service?

An SLA agreement is very common for cloud and X-as-a-Service types. For anything where you are relying on a third party to power some or all of your business, an SLA will allow you to determine how much uptime, at the very least, you can expect, which in turn informs your customers what their expectation can be of your service.

SLAs can come in different levels, with the more 9s (.999999) of reliability you need from a service, the more expensive it will be. Finding that balance will depend largely on your need and may not be the same for all. Some parts of your ecosystem will be able to tolerate more downtime than others.

An SLA can also define how long to expect between when a bug or issue is reported to when a successful resolution would be delivered. The more important a service is, the more you will want to demand from the SLA.

DEFINING AN SLA

Looking at it from the other side, if your product is one that delivers an X-as-a-Service product or API, then you should have your own SLA in place that you will aim to uphold. This is the level of service you expect to be able to deliver to your users and the compensation you are going to provide if you fail to do so.

If your users are external, then the compensation piece is something you will work on in conjunction with the business. Your primary responsibility is coming up with the SLA you feel is achievable within a reasonable budget.

The first thing to note is that an SLA with 100% availability is unattainable—too many variables are in play to make this truly achievable. So, as you come up with your uptime assurances, here are the things you need to factor in before delivering your number:

- Of all the third-part services you rely on, what has the worst SLA in that list? (You are only as strong as your weakest link.)
- How much downtime do you need to do releases or system upgrades?
- Are you able to offer an SLA for a full 24 hours each day or only during core business hours?
- What is the time for resolution on a given reported issue?
- Do you have the necessary support staff in place to cover support, especially during vacations?
- What has been the track record of your offering thus far?

- What is the weakest part, or single point of failure, in your offering that would affect uptime?

Whatever you do, do not simply pluck a number from thin air. It should be based on something real and deliverable and be defendable and achievable.

10.2   *Evaluating vendors*

Having identified an area where you want help from a third-party vendor, created the outline of the service agreement, and defined your requirements for an SLA, your effort now moves to vetting vendors. This process, or going out to tender, is to compile a list of potential providers and start evaluating them. It seems obvious to say but I will say it nonetheless: price is not the winning attribute. You should consider the following factors before making your final decision:

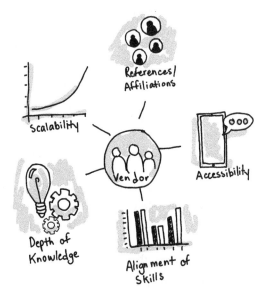

- *Alignment of skills*—Determine whether the skills of the vendor will align with your needs. You don't want the vendor you are outsourcing to to be learning on the contract. Their skills must compliment your needs from the moment they start the engagement. This may involve you interviewing the resources that will be working directly on your project for you to gain confidence.

- *Depth of knowledge*—Cursory knowledge of a subject isn't going to work for you. The purpose of engaging a vendor in the first place is because your team lacks the expertise. Testing the company with some exercises will give you the confidence they can handle any problem you throw at them.

- *Accessibility*—As you think of your requirements, will you need out-of-hours coverage (common for support contracts)? There may be specific times of the year you need the vendor to be more attentive than others. You should rate how they handle requests (both during and outside of regular hours), their response time, communication style, updates, and messaging.

- *Scalability*—As you grow, will they be able to grow and adapt to your needs? Be cautious if there is only one expert in the company. What happens if they go on vacation or, worse, leave? You are relying on them to share their knowledge with their team so you have continuity of service.

- *References/affiliations*—Ask for references from clients who have requirements similar to yours. If they are providing support for a given product, does that product have recommended service vendors or partner programs, and are they part of that?

Other considerations will include, of course, price and contract tenure—can they provide the necessary services to you and will they be able to scale with you as you grow? Weighing everything and rating them in various areas will allow the right vendor to rise to the top.

When you get to the actual fine print, this is when you should bring in your CFO or CEO (and legal counsel, if you have ready access to one). Negotiation, hammering out the fine print, a second pair of eyes who isn't as close to the deal will be a welcome addition, because they will challenge each point and translate the legalese of the various clauses to see how truly workable they are.

10.3 Software licensing

A software license is a way we pay for the use of a piece of software, whether it is downloadable, a service, or an operating system. The world has moved largely toward a pay-as-you-go model, including many popular desktop packages (which historically were a one-time cost). However you pay for the software, you need to keep track of its usage, for both budgetary and compliance reasons, but also as a check that you are complying with the terms of the license.

For example, are you using private or student licenses for commercial purposes? This situation comes up a number of times in audits—companies believe they are at least taking steps in the right direction, so their conscience is clear, but the eyes of the law don't see it like that.

Many software applications can help you keep on top of your licenses. If your organization isn't of the size to really benefit from such an extra expenditure, keep it simple to begin with and track all software licenses in a shareable spreadsheet. Capture the following details at a minimum:

- Date of acquisition
- Renewal date/cost
- Contact details
- Contact details they have for you, such as email/phone/address
- Notes on internal usage
- License keys/codes

This list should be reviewed at least every six months to make sure it's kept up to date as well as anytime a new purchase is made or renewal is done.

Often companies both underspend and overspend on licenses. Large software vendors (such as Microsoft, Oracle, IBM) have complicated licenses that change often. It was simple in the old days, when the software was basically for a given server. But with the advent of multicore processors and virtualization, it was no longer easy to just assume a single hardware server could be hosting 10 virtual servers. How does the license change? What if the server is run only for a given period of time, such as with a public cloud? The vendors naturally felt they were getting shortchanged and adapted accordingly.

Being out of license can happen quite easily and innocently as your enterprise evolves. It is, therefore, important to check the fine print as and when you make significant changes. Reach out to your account representative—who will be more than happy to take your call—and they'll be able to advise you accordingly.

Licensing operating systems and databases can become very expensive very quickly if you're not careful. Although the decision to use Microsoft's SQL Server is zero cost at development, as you move into production, you can be hit with a significant license cost—the equivalent of a salary in some cases.

Most vendors are happy to give you full access to their suite for development because that is their way to get you hooked or locked in. Choosing wisely and understanding the license considerations before green-lighting any technology decision can pay dividends in the future.

Public cloud vendors are bridging the gap here a little. Both Amazon and Azure offer virtualized commercial offerings, where the cost of the license is built into the price of the per-minute cost. Running a Windows Server EC2 instance, instead of a Linux one, will be a few cents more per minute to cover the cost of the license. This removes all worries of whether you are legal from a licensing viewpoint.

We have addressed previously the benefits of open source alternatives, such as Linux versus Windows, MySQL/Postgres versus SQL Server, and so on. But what if you want commercial support—a telephone number to call if something goes wrong? The good news is that all major open source software bodies have their own ecosystem to provide you a wide range of support. Prices and services differ, but finding one for your requirements should not be difficult.

10.4   *Support contracts*

A question that comes up time and time again is, when should you buy support? The question is a fair one, because the majority of software runs absolutely fine for the job they are doing. So, why spend the extra money if you don't have to?

It all depends on the level of skills and experience you have in house on your own team. A support contract makes sense to fill the gaps where your team either lacks the experience or it's time to keep patches updated. Another way to determine whether you need support is to do the exercise in the accompanying sidebar.

Identify all the major components of your enterprise

For the sake of this exercise, we will consider a major component to be a piece that is critical to customer service and continuity. Now let's assume something goes wrong with that component: who do you call for help?

If you have someone experienced and knowledgeable on your team, great. What if you don't? Or what happens if they can't resolve it (or are not available, say, on vacation)? You have now put the business at risk of not being able to service clients.

Don't necessarily go and buy support for everything—it can be very expensive. In addition, you probably don't need full coverage, especially if you have a strong internal team who knows what they are doing, and you are not relying on a single person. Buy support for the gaps, the areas where you are a bit thin.

A special word on hardware components, such as servers and networking equipment: if you find yourself managing significant hardware servers, this is one area you definitely want to make sure you have the support needed to cope with failures. Physical items break—even the ones that don't have moving parts. A good support contract will give you the peace of mind that components (e.g., hard disks) can be sourced and replaced quickly should the worst happen (though a good support partner will replace items before they are due to fail). That said, hardware support can be expensive (another reason to consider moving to the cloud), but, unfortunately, it is one you shouldn't go without.

From the field

Dumpster diving

As we know, time marches on without a care or thought of what is going on. Years seem to slip by without notice, and before you know it, the piece of hardware you thought was purchased only last year is actually 10 years old and is no longer supported. I have seen clients get stuck with legacy kits, ending up scouring second-hand sites, such as eBay, looking for spare parts that will work with their hardware. There is quite the subculture in trading old hardware as companies try to eke out as much life as possible from their hardware. If you find yourself in this situation, be sure to get the replacement on the road map.

Summary

- A statement of work (SOW) is an agreement that details the service that is going to be rendered.
- The SOW is there to protect both parties, so everyone is clear about what is expected.
- An SLA (service-level agreement) defines the level of service that can be expected.
- It also defines the consequences should the SLA limits not be met.
- After defining what it is you want, putting out for tender is a way to attract potential vendors.
- Evaluating each vendor is not dissimilar to interviewing candidates, complete with reference checks.
- A software license defines what you can and cannot do with a piece of software, hardware, or service.
- Support contracts are designed to be your safety net for when you need to maintain a system.

Checklist

How many of the following items can you lay claim to having covered?

- For any contracting resource you engage, the assignment of IPR is clearly stated upon payment or completion.
- You have an NDA available and ready for when you need to engage with a third party.
- You understand the SLA of any third-party service you rely on and what it means for your role in keeping your enterprise available.
- You have an SLA defined for your own enterprise, either for internal or external consumption.
- You have a defined and documented methodology for evaluating vendors.
- You have a handle on the licenses for all third-party software being used, including their restrictions.
- You have necessary support contracts for major components.

Documentation

This chapter covers

- Reasons why documentation is important
- Different types of documentation
- How powerful diagrams and drawings can be for communicating
- Strategies for weaving documentation into your current process

You know this chapter isn't going to tell you anything you don't already know— as technologists, documentation is the one area where we fail terribly. It is rare to encounter a company who has adequate documentation—they're all full of good intentions, but nothing is written down.

Documentation is like test cases: you can never have too much. Though, what is the right level? How do you know whether you have the right amount?

In this chapter, we are going to highlight the areas that need at least a cursory level of documentation and the areas that need more thorough detail, including those that are crucial to the smooth running and continuity of your team. Although this is not an exhaustive list by any stretch, it does serve to get you thinking

about the types of documentation that you should consider to support the systems powering your organization beyond the working lifetime of each member of your team.

Documentation is one of those things that if you keep updated as you go along, it somewhat takes care of itself. If left to languish, however, it quickly becomes a massive undertaking.

From the field

One of my best hires

In one of my engagements as CTO, I recognized that I needed the group to produce significant amounts of documents for both internal purposes and external communication/educational purposes. I hired an experienced technical writer for the team, with a background in software engineering. The role was not to document everything but to take the notes and create diagrams (literally on the back of an envelope at times), flesh out these notes into more of a structured document, organize them, and convert the diagrams into a common format. They also identified which ones needed reworking and kept an eye on the release notes to flag any areas that potentially needed updating. It truly was one of my best hires, and I advocate for a technical writer to be added to any engineering group of 20 or more people.

11.1   Why document?

Why bother? Your team knows how things work, like the ancient stories passed down from each passing generation to the next. Besides, your stack is so well designed and maintained, any competent person could understand it. If you believe that, then you probably believe your code has no bugs and consequently requires no testing! Absurd when you see it written down like that—yet many sincerely believe it.

Documentation is continuity. Documentation is scalability. Documentation is freedom. It is not a sign of weakness or an administrative chore that must be tolerated and put off until the very last minute.

No matter how modern your architecture or readable your code is, a level of rules and logic exists that is applicable only to your organization. This is the detail—the reasons behind the design decisions—that reading code will never thoroughly explain. Documentation is the operating manual for your enterprise, and without it, no one will be able to fully get the benefits from your enterprise.

Humans forget details. As the days roll into weeks, weeks into months, and months into years, the reason something was done the way it was gets lost. An eccentric business rule or obscure restriction that at the time drove the design/implementation down a given path (the right decision at the time) may not be as obvious sometime in the future. With the reasons lost in the mists of time, one of two things will happen:

- Someone new will look at it, think there is an easier way, change it, and subsequently break something in the process.
- People are scared to touch or ever think about redoing it. It takes on mythical properties that are seen as too complicated or crucial to risk any change.

Both scenarios introduce way too much risk, yet both of them could have been avoided completely by having a little documentation sprinkled around to explain what was going on. As a sage developer once noted, "[code] comments are little love notes to your future self."

11.1.1 Audience

Documentation is not a singular entity that can serve every reader's requirement. It is a series of documents, aimed at a given group of recipients, depending on how they interact with the system. To help you think through these different types, consider the following breakdown:

- *End user*—Users of the system who interact with the finished product
- *Support*—Frontline support who assists end users with their queries
- *IT/DevOps*—Backend team responsible for keeping systems up and functional
- *Developers*—The team who creates or fixes features

As systems grow and age, the specific requirements of each audience begin to expand. Smaller teams, at the start of their entrepreneurial journey, may have a lot of overlap, with roles being served by the same people with maybe no documentation at all for the end user.

As things grow, each audience will have their own process flow and responsibility that will require support and documentation from the tier below. Having a good source of information ensures each audience can onboard new people (from end user to developer) quickly and efficiently, allowing them to fully succeed in their role.

Contextualizing the documentation for each audience type, so it speaks to them in their own vocabulary and language style, makes the assistance more accessible. For example, explanations of algorithms will make little sense for the end user or support staff but will assist developers in maintaining and adapting the software. Likewise, detailed walk-throughs of a series of screenshots isn't going to help the IT/DevOps team, who don't really care what the app looks like. They just want to know how to manage things, say, the backups. Speak to the audience.

11.1.2 Format

When we think of documentation, we tend to lean toward the classic format of text: easily created, clear, storable, portable, referenceable, and searchable. Increasingly, though, videos are becoming more popular, especially ones that effectively record a desktop session, as if you are looking over the shoulder of someone showing how something is done. Given the broad accessibility of the tools to create and edit short videos, they can be quick to record and share or publish—a 5 minute video can be the equivalent of several pages of traditional descriptive text.

A successful documentation strategy should be accessible and available when it is needed. No matter how good a piece is, if it can't be found when needed, then it is next to useless.

Locking documentation away in PDF or DOC files, although great 20 years ago, is no longer the go-to method. A document, particularly one whose purpose is to describe or educate on the platform, is a living, breathing entity. It needs to be updated on every release or when a new discovery has been made. It has to be quick, easy, and effortless and not become a project in and of itself.

When Tim Berners-Lee first came up with the web, his goal was to share information easily. So, it makes sense that the web should be the focal point of a document store. Tools like wikis, Atlassian Confluence, Google Docs, and Office 365 are all great in-browser contenders. When evaluating documentation platform solutions, consider the following:

- *Linking directly to specific content*—Make sure you can send someone to a specific section without giving them a series of navigational steps to locate it.
- *Organizing related content*—It has to be easy to bring together related areas to make it simple for the reader to find deeper content. Ideally, this should be done automatically, through tags or semantic intelligence.
- *Easily augmented*—As new information comes to light, the content needs to be updated, particularly for support.
- *Versionable*—Most modern-day tools do this out of the box very well. The ability to go back to a previous version quickly will allow the docs to age and grow gracefully, while also giving the reader the ability to determine whether what they are consuming is relevant to the version they are working with.
- *Secure*—Not everything should be accessible by everyone, so you need the ability to protect various areas or sections for different groups.
- *Feedback*—Readers should be able to leave comments or small notes to augment the content.
- *Attachments*—How adaptable is the ability to add third-party files (images, video, PDF)? You want to keep this data close to the document it pertains to.

Good content doesn't have to look great—it just needs to be of help to the reader. Encouraging everyone to contribute to this emerging knowledge base is paramount to the success of its usefulness. The less friction to authoring and contributing, the better.

11.1.3 Validation

We are familiar with the need to test code before releasing it, whether that is automated or, more commonly, manual testing, to confirm the code is doing what it is supposed to. As we know, "assuming" that everything will be fine is not the way to run a modern technology platform. The same goes for any documentation that is produced. Before it is read and consumed by its constituent, it should be validated as being worthwhile to produce in the first place.

Each piece of documentation, especially in the early days of its inception, should be validated by someone other than the author to confirm its usefulness and make sure it hasn't made too many presumptions or omissions regarding the consumer and subject matter. It doesn't have to be a formal document review process, but it should include a second pair of eyes.

Take, for example, the build process for producing, validating, and releasing your platform. Instead of keeping it only in their head, the person who created the process documents it. How do you know whether it's thorough enough? It needs to be tested, have someone run through it (ideally someone who is not that familiar with the subject and won't subconsciously skip over the gaps). This would be a great litmus test of how well the content stands up.

Areas that are usually performed by a single person are the places you want to pay particular attention to—has everything they do been adequately captured so anyone can help backfill the role? Only by testing the documentation can you really answer that question with confidence.

11.2 Documentation types

In this section, we are going to go over the typical types of documents that, as an organization, you should consider having in your library. This is not an exhaustive list by any stretch, but a starting point, if you are wondering where to get started.

11.2.1 Meeting notes

Meetings are events that should be few and far between and can be a huge distraction and take up a lot of time. When you do decide you need a meeting, it should be as productive as possible.

A good meeting is one that has one or more objectives or agenda items with a goal-driven outcome. Meetings can be a great source of information exchange, with lots of ideas and suggestions. Yet they can be an area where little or no notes are taken, so much valuable information is lost—what a waste.

Meeting notes should be part of the main knowledge base, detailing the history of decisions to reach a given point. Some organizations maintain a separate "decision log," collated in a single place, detailing why certain big decisions were made.

For every meeting, designate someone to take the notes, and build into the meeting the time to put together the meeting notes. Some people will keep notes in a Google Doc in real time, noting down key moments and decisions. If a quick meeting has been called for a particular ticket, create a series of bullet points in the ticket comments capturing the meeting output.

Given the postpandemic world, a lot of meetings have gone online via video. This is a good time to record and keep a library of all key meetings, so crucial decisions are not missed.

Exchanges over chat (Slack, Microsoft Teams, etc.) can also contain gems of knowledge. Encourage your team to copy and paste some of these to be added to the main knowledge base or ticket. You can even find bots or plugins that make it quick to tag an exchange and send it to a remote repository.

11.2.2 *Walk-throughs demos*

Think about the number of times a product demo or walk-through is done. How many of these were recorded? No matter how many times they are performed, each iteration will yield something new, whether a new or different question from the audience or something unique that happened.

It is good to watch sales demos of the core product, as you get to see how the sales team pitch features and discover how the client/user perceives the feature and what they need from it. There can be quite the gap between the two different constituents.

Keeping these recordings helps the product group to understand what users need, helps the engineering group to understand what is important, and finally, helps new team members come to understand what it is they are involved in helping build.

These will build up over time; however, don't be scared of volume. It has a wonderful side effect of being a time capsule, for historical versions, for those coming into the company to consume to learn how the evolution has shaped the environment.

11.2.3 *Owner's manual*

Probably one of the most important areas of documentation is the one that explains how to keep the enterprise up and running—the owner's manual, if you will. This is not code deployment. Instead, this is all the pieces of the platform and how they function, how to monitor them, and what needs to be done to bring them online in the event of a power outage (or some other offline event).

The level of detail here has to be sufficient that anyone can step in and execute the procedure. Simply saying "Make sure to restart component XYZ" is not enough. How do you restart component XYZ, what commands need to be run and from where, what should you be looking for to determine success, and what are the steps required to remediate any issues that come up? Too much of this detail is often overlooked and forms part of someone's muscle memory.

For example, starting up a system may produce a lot of console output. The person not used to seeing these lines of log output may get overwhelmed at first, unsure of what is good, what is bad, and what to ignore. A simple screenshot of this output included as part of this documentation can ease so much anxiety and up the confidence level. As the old adage goes, a picture is worth a thousand words.

An owner's manual does not have to be verbose. You are not writing the next Harry Potter book. You are giving detailed steps on what needs to be completed. Keep it simple: a list of numbered steps, each one cogent enough that the reader has the clarity and confidence to know when the step has been completed successfully and can move on to the next one.

This area should also cover keeping an eye on running systems—what are the early signs you should be watching for that give a clue to an impending problem? This can be quite intimidating to create at first. A small tip is to ask the principal person who manages a particular system to pretend they are going on vacation and to write an email to the person taking care of it in their absence. An email is less formal, and people have a tendency to be more verbose in an email, than when faced with a blank wiki or Google Doc page. Take this email and add it to the knowledge base. This exercise works many times, resulting in a rich, deep library of how-to documents built up over time.

No one on your team should feel that the only reason they have a role on the team is their in-house knowledge of a particular system. This was a relatively common attitude 10–20 years ago, but it is something I rarely bump into today. People's values and job security are not what they know but what they contribute to the team.

Everyone loves working on the new and shiny thing—we're technologists. It's in our DNA to keep looking for the next best thing. It is important that the current systems are documented to a level that no one feels they are being left behind because they are the only one who knows a particular system.

11.2.4 Backing up and restoration

An area that is often underserved in the documentation department is the backing up and restoration of a system. This is more than just the database export/import path (though that needs to be detailed, too). This is about the enterprise as a whole, from hardware to operating system to software—everything.

What is required to breathe life back into a component? What parts of an operating system need to be available to allow a component to run? What seems obvious today may not make the same sense months or years later.

> **From the field**
>
> *It's the small things that will catch you*
>
> I ran into a situation years ago when someone trying to rebuild a new machine to perform thumbnail generation kept hitting a wall when running up the Java application. It turned out the Java app needed the popular open source ImageMagick library installed on the operating system for it to work. The Java app had a really poor log output, so this was not as obvious as it should have been. There was no documentation or clues as to where to look, and only after cracking open the code to figure out what was going on was the dependency discovered.

With the popularity of container computing (like with Docker), dependencies at the operating system level should and are caught during the build process. That doesn't negate the need for dependencies to be clearly listed, though. Even if everything is just a container, how the containers all fit together and run at a higher level needs to be detailed so anyone coming behind knows how to manage this. There should be enough notes and guidance that anyone technically competent should be able to rebuild every component of the enterprise from source control. If this is not achievable, then you are in document debt. Keeping this up to date naturally should be part of the release process, as new components are introduced and older legacy ones are replaced and removed.

As I have mentioned before, this is another area that needs to be practiced at least once a year, if not more often. If you are running in a cloud environment, it is trivial to manage without interfering or putting at risk any live environment. A good practice to get into is to have new hires execute this restoration process in a clean environment. This exercise serves as a neat way to get people familiar with the process, while learning how everything fits together and ensuring the documentation is relevant.

11.2.5 Deployment process

Releasing and updating the enterprise should be a path that is well trodden, predictable, and without risk. To make that happen, you need good tools and documentation to support that effort. Even if you rely on an automated orchestration tool (such as Jenkins), it still warrants a guide on how it has been configured for your environment.

All the steps required to prepare a build need to be laid out, with an explanation of what is going on, what the criteria for success are, and how to detect failure. Then, as these all fit together, in what order should they be executed and at what point can you cancel before making changes to the environment? If you have a different process for releasing a patch, hot fix, or full release, then these should also be detailed.

Successfully documenting these steps will keep everyone informed and ensure releases are never bottlenecked on one person. It's not uncommon to come across a company whose ability to update is dependent on their senior DevOps person—when they're not out on PTO.

11.2.6 Source/code comments

If you want to ignite a debate between developers that is on par with the legendary "tabs vs. spaces" conundrum (spaces, for the record), ask how many comments should be in code. The replies will range from, "My code doesn't need comments—it's readable as it is," right through to, "Yeah, that is quite the mess to untangle."

Two primary areas that require further explanation than what is gleaned from simply looking at the source code are "what" and "how." To a lesser degree the "why" should be captured as well, if it's not obvious.

"WHAT"

This is the level of detail designed to be read by other developers using that piece of code. Consider a library with public functions or methods that will be consumed by other developers for other systems. This can also include API endpoints that are consumed remotely.

Most modern-day languages have a convention or meta language that can interpret function-level comments as library documents. This allows developers who have imported the library to see this code help through their IDE's code-completion mechanism.

Java is a great example, with its Javadoc standard of class- and method-level documentation, which is used not only for code completion but also for producing a set of web pages with the code documentation. Another example is the Swagger library for documenting API endpoints in an HTML format, complete with a utility for remotely invoking the endpoint for testing and research.

The big advantage of this documentation is that it is kept in the same source file as the code, which makes it easy to keep updated as code goes through its evolution. This type of documentation is vital, particular for large teams or times when external parties will be consuming APIs.

"How"

The other type of documentation exists within the source code functions and methods and is designed to be read only by other developers maintaining the same code. For this level, do not advocate too much detail. Well-designed and -written code should be obvious to the reader. This is assuming sensible function names and variables that pertain to what they do—code should be written for readability, not performance. That said, if a block of code requires a little more explanation, then it should have a few lines of comments associated with it.

Ideally, leaving web links to the ticket number is great to give the future developer more depth as to why a component is doing something. That weird-looking `if` statement can be explained by a ticket number, instead of some future developers thinking they are doing everyone a favor by refactoring it away and potentially introducing more bugs than they are solving.

Make sure adequate source documentation is incorporated into code reviews. Once developers get into the habit, they will never look back.

"Why"

If something can't be conveyed in the "how" section, then it should be promoted to the "why" area, which usually details at a much higher business level what the function or area is attempting to do. Is there a business rule or a specific way a third party operates that has forced a design decision that isn't at first obvious?

11.2.7 Architectural diagrams

When you get a box of upmarket chocolates, what is the first thing you look for? The map, of course! This representation of the box's layout gives you a fighting chance of avoiding the hazelnut hiding within. True chocolate connoisseurs will use this map to plot their upcoming taste journey to maximize the flavor infusion. The map lets us navigate with more authority and confidence.

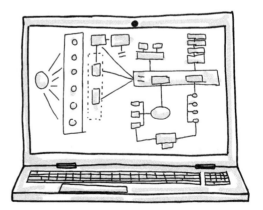

The enterprise should have the same "map," or architectural diagram. When you are introduced to a system, always ask for the map to be drawn on the whiteboard. If you still get blank, quizzing stares, just answer, "Draw some boxes with lines."

It need not be complicated or formal. These are not building blueprints that adhere to some surveyor's stringent protocols. They are simply guides that help frame the narrative that describes the platform.

They should include the major components of the enterprise, with lines joining the pieces that are connected. Do not get into too much detail on the logistics. It's enough at this level to know that the File Microservice is used by the module for the user's profile photos. The "how" doesn't matter at this level—it could be an API call, a queue, or even a shared directory. That detail is for another document. What you are describing here, to go back to the map analogy, is the state-level boundaries with the interstate highways marked to show how they are connected, with only major cities as the details.

Do not get overdetailed, because this makes the map busy and hard to comprehend. For each component (or state, in our map), you provide a separate map, exploring in more detail (exposing rural highways and towns).

The map analogy works particularly well for microservice- and API-driven architectures. Like the US states, cities and highways never change, but the local roads within each state and city are continually evolving.

When you think about your architectural maps carefully, you can find particular renderings still relevant, even years after code evolution. The top-level map should be something that can be used to communicate how things are set up to others outside your group without bogging people down in details or complicated terms. Don't be surprised if it finds its way to a board deck because a good diagram is a great way to sell your vision.

11.2.8 Process diagrams

Closely related to the architectural diagram is the process diagram. This is a representation on how data flows around the system, and what happens to it as and when it goes through a service or library. If the architectural diagram is the state or interstate highway map, then this is Google traffic flow overlaid, showing where the cars are.

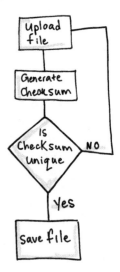

The process diagram is a good logical flow, detailing where data is stored, cached, or exchanged. Again, too much detail will bog down this area and create more complexity than is required.

The purpose of this type of diagram is to frame the data movement and show at a high level where and how data flows, paying attention to how data enters your world and how it leaves again.

11.2.9 Network diagrams

The network diagram isn't too different from the architectural diagram, except it is produced through the lens of the real networks and servers that make up the enterprise. Pertinent network addresses are encouraged, including any routes, firewalls, or gateways that connect pieces together.

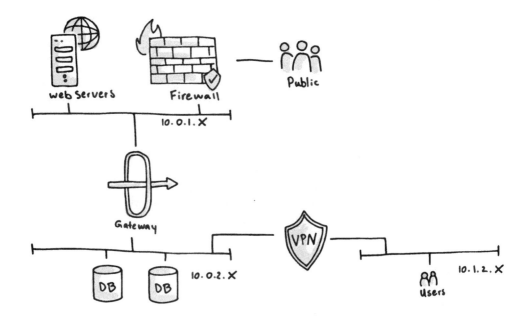

If you have physical servers, this diagram should show where physical machines are located (data center and rack, for example). Another document will detail the physical specification of each component, including purchase and expiration dates and configuration records.

11.2.10 *Data schemas*

Databases are at the heart of most company enterprises, holding precious data and relationships that keep your company alive. Yet, given the importance of this role, it is one of most undocumented areas, but it doesn't have to be.

The irony is that many tools are available (DB Schema, for instance) that can introspect a relational database and draw a schema overview, dissecting the foreign keys to produce the table relationships. Taking this as the foundation, you can easily augment and annotate this diagram to include the business knowledge to make sense of the data layout. Modern-day databases all support the ability to add comments directly to the tables and columns, in much the same way comments are part of source code files.

Other data stores may not support inline comments and, therefore, require manual external documentation. This is something that needs to be added to the release cycle, so if anything changes, there is a note to update the documentation.

As long as the layout and location of all data is documented to a level that lets those coming behind to find and use the knowledge, then you are in good shape.

11.2.11 Compliance documentation

You may find yourself in an industry where you are required to keep a level of documentation, which includes process steps, audit reports, and summary reports. Health care and financial industries are common examples with a heightened need for documentation. Certain government and military projects will also demand a level of shown process (ISO standard is an example).

The specific details of HIPAA, PCI, ISO, and so on is beyond this book's scope. For companies that have to achieve a given certification, it is advisable you work with a third-party expert who can take you through the process. Large accountancy firms have departments dedicated to such initiatives, for example. Although the process can seem quite daunting, it need not be, if treated with the right mindset.

No matter the standard or level of compliance you are aiming to achieve, treat it as a set of commonsense protocols to keep all parties operating honestly. Organizations with no documentation, process, and flows struggle the most. Everything has to be created from scratch, and it feels like such a long endeavor. Those with good documentation and standards find it nowhere near as painful. Yes, there will be areas that need addressing, parts that require tightening up, but it is all going in the right direction.

Compliance is, of course, more than just documentation—you need to walk the talk. This may require code or architectural charges, so see these things as opportunities to fine-tune and tighten up.

The majority of the big compliance requirements offer great insights into security and data management. If you think your organization is going to be falling within the compliance radar, start doing some preliminary reading on what needs to be done, get ahead of it, and start introducing the practices into your team's DNA. Treat it as a badge of honor. You are responsible for the safeguarding of your organization's systems and data. Take all the guidance and help you can get.

11.2.12 License and audit tracking

One area that is easy to leave behind, but at some point will be required, is the need to look up licensing and software assets. Create a place in your knowledge base to keep a record of all your external reliance on software, both purchased and open source. Encourage everyone to keep this updated, no matter how small or big. Every time a

Java developer adds a new library to their Maven project, or a JavaScript developer imports a new npm module, make it part of the process to update the documentation, including source and licensing terms.

A list of software is a standard part of due diligence, and as of writing, I have not come upon a team that has this information at their fingertips. This list is needed for other conversations also, such as renewal and upgrade times and, for those not in the cloud but looking to go, figuring out whether their license is compatible.

11.3 Whitepapers

Although not strictly part of the core documentation, it is worth calling out the vehicle that is known as a whitepaper. A whitepaper is a published document designed to be read by an external audience. It details a given philosophy or process for a specific area.

Whitepapers are very handy when your organization has to educate your client base before they can truly take advantage of your offering. Often used as part of the sales cycle, it is a great opportunity to show the professionalism and depth of knowledge that has gone into something.

A whitepaper doesn't give away any trade secrets or detailed engineering methods. It is designed to bring an external party into your line of thinking so it's easier for them to interact with your product. Examples of white papers include these:

- API security principals
- Data usage recommendations
- Best practices for API integrations
- Data state transformations

11.4 Best practices

Documentation may not be the most glamorous part of the role, but it is one of the crucial ones that make scaling and growing your engineering group smooth. Here are some best practices and tips to get you into the rhythm:

- Choose your knowledge base tool carefully to deliver as many of the core documentation features as possible in one tool.
- Create templates so your team can quickly add to pages. It's much easier to edit something than create something fresh.
- Start small and build slowly. This is a marathon, not a sprint.
- Encourage everyone to augment content with emails and chat messages.
- Video and screencasts are quick ways to fill out content.
- Describe what source code does as part of the code-review process.
- Practice all the process details when it comes to managing systems.

Summary

- Document early while the knowledge is still fresh.
- Choosing the right tool makes it easier for everyone to contribute.

- Keep it simple—this will encourage those less prose orientated to not feel intimidated.
- Videos, voice notes, and diagrams are rich vehicles for capturing details.
- Validation of anything that details the running and management of a system is important.
- Even simple notes or bullet points are better than nothing.

Checklist

How many of the following items can you lay claim to having covered?

- Provided a collaboration tool for your team to contribute knowledge
- Created a document that explains how to build and maintain your enterprise
- Listed components, including version/license details, within your enterprise
- Designed an easy-to-understand diagram of how your technology is laid out
- Listed detailed steps on creating and restoring backups
- Encouraged a culture of openness and sharing of knowledge

12

Security

Security is one of those areas that, if done properly, looks effortless and easy. If done poorly, however, like doing the minimum to tick a box, it gets in the way. Some organizations, on the face of it, have great security, but scratch the surface, and you'll discover that they have left the key under the mat, digitally speaking. Security is a seductive force—the longer you go without any sort of incident, the more you can convince yourself into believing you run a secure environment, not unlike thinking your house is fireproof because it hasn't suffered a fire.

There is no doubt that layering in security at the end creates a lot of work and takes a concentrated effort to get right, with much disruption. That said, you can do a lot to secure an existing platform even if you have made no real effort to build it in from the start. In this chapter, we will go over some of the steps you can take to make significant progress to create a secure environment.

> **From the field**
> In my role mentoring CTOs and helping them grow into their role, I see those who see security as a one-time exercise that needs to be done before moving on to the next thing. They don't see it as something that is ongoing and always a moving target. Good security is more than installing a firewall or having strong passwords. It is a continual process: evaluating the threat surface, monitoring systems for attacks or breaches, and trying to keep one step ahead of the attackers.

One common assumption is that you don't have data valuable enough to steal. This attitude is then used as an excuse to not implement any sort of defense. Although your data or systems may not be a destination, they could be a gateway to a greater prize. If they can crack open your systems and, say, get credentials to a third-party service, then what damage could a determined hacker do, using your brand for their nefarious purposes? We all have a responsibility to make things as secure as possible from internal and external attacks.

This chapter is not an exhaustive look at everything you need to do to make your enterprise secure—that would be a separate book. This chapter is an overview of the high-level efforts you need to be at least thinking about to take the steps for creating a secure-centric environment that lets you be good stewards of your clients' data.

12.1 Patching

Software is never bug free, no matter who develops it. Bugs are never intentionally introduced or created but arise from something being used in a way that was never thought of or tested for. Issues can be harmless—something not quite rendering right—or potentially fatal (depending on the environment). Once a bug has been identified, you can be assured someone will think of a way to exploit it for some sort of advantage, nefarious act, gain, or simply for the bragging rights.

Therefore, most security issues originate from one of the following scenarios:

- Poorly developed/tested code
- A well-intentioned feature that had an unforeseen side effect (e.g., Apache Log4j logging library in late 2021, which will be detailed later)

In today's modern computing landscape, most organizations are very reactive in putting out fixes or patches when a bug or security hole has been discovered either by an internal team or reported externally. No one wants the finger of blame to be wiggling in their general direction when it comes to issues relating to security.

The key is keeping your enterprise up to date with patches and not letting yourself fall too far behind. For this to be effective you need a two-pronged strategy:

- Identify patches and files
- Scheduling the update

12.1.1 Identify patches

The first thing you need to know is the list of all the software (including libraries) and versions you are running in your enterprise. We covered the need and logistics of this list in the documentation chapter because it serves many different needs. Failure to keep an updated list puts you at risk of missing out on a critical patch—you might easily dismiss it, thinking it doesn't apply to you.

The first place to look for updates is the vendor's site. All major software vendors have a web page or mailing list that you can keep an eye on. Open source projects have release notes and forums you can easily subscribe to. For security alerts, the best source is the well-known CVE registry.

> **From the field**
>
> *Common Vulnerabilities and Exposures (CVE)* https://www.cve.org/
>
> CVE, an online database for tracking all known security flaws, has been tracking issues since 1999, with approximately 5,000 flaws registered each quarter. A CVE number is assigned to each one that details precisely the flaw, the versions affected, and links to resolutions, if applicable. This resource can be thought of as the "Wikipedia" of security breaches, and often, when you read about an issue in the public press, it comes with a CVE number pointing you back to this site for the technical details. A good sister site is https://www.opencve.io/, which lets you filter and subscribe for notifications.

You can easily get a setup where updates will come to you without you having to continually check. A word of caution: periodically confirm you are subscribed to the right outlet. Mailing lists and notification URLs can change.

Although this is a responsibility you can designate to your Chief Information Security Officer (CISO), it is something you can encourage your team to keep a lookout for as well. Like the beacons of Gondor (from *Lord of the Rings*), it takes only one person to see the fire so action can be taken.

12.1.2 Scheduling

Knowing what to update is possibly the easy bit. Now you have to figure out when to apply it. The temptation is to dismiss certain updates as not being applicable. Big mistake. Get into a cadence of at least monthly updates, small and frequent, which will allow impact in the short term but keep you protected for the long term. Ideally, you have a setup where you have more of a blue-green (see chapter 9) deployment so it is easy to test the patch/update before committing it.

The vast majority of updates, particularly from reputable sources, will work flawlessly 99% of the time. However good those odds are, you can't assume they will always cover you. Test, test, test. Use your development or staging environment to test the patch, or at the very least, roll it into your periodic updates. That way, your test team can catch any oddities as part of the process.

For systems that don't have an environmental setup, you have to effectively play with live ammo—update production. Back-office systems (such as email and file servers) fall into this category. In these situations, out-of-hours updates are always preferable—Saturday, ideally, so if anything really goes wrong, there is a spare day built in (Sunday) to resolve the issue.

12.1.3 *Special considerations*

Hardware, such as printers, scanners, and TVs—don't usually fall under the CTO's umbrella, yet these are systems that need continual monitoring for security updates, too. Modern hardware (e.g., Google with its Chromecast/Nest products) will routinely update automatically. Not all manufacturers are as stringent, though. Routers and network switches will need extra attention, and sometimes it is not as obvious when they are available.

Some devices require someone to manually log in to their administration console and check. It is a step that is worthwhile and should be part of your IT management duties. Get into the habit of logging the latest check in the global or asset management log. Any device that has a network connection needs to be treated like a production system, with their security and password management, however benign, needing your attention. Hacks can come in from any device on your network. Assume that if it's got an IP address, it is a potential threat.

> **NOTE** This is why it is good practice to keep your production environment in a completely separate, isolated network. Sharing the network with the back office and your production network is opening up your attack surface to unknown devices coming on and off the network.

12.2 *Penetration testing*

Penetration testing is, as the name suggests, when an external entity attempts to penetrate your system from the outside, looking for holes or cracks they can exploit to gain entry or cause disruption. Of all the security testing that goes on, this process has one of the biggest placebo issues: too often, companies feel at ease with their penetration certificate only to discover it is more than six months old.

As soon as your penetration test is completed, it is already out of date. Hacks are continually evolving, and you should never assume you are impregnable just because you passed a test. Another note to remember is that the next time you perform a software release, all historical penetrative tests are rendered null and void. Why? Because you don't know whether this release has exposed a new flaw or hole in the defenses. Therefore, penetration testing should not be a one-time or periodic event. It should be a continually ongoing, integral part of your continuous deployment.

A good penetration test will probe within layers. For example, the most obvious test is from the public. But what access or naughtiness can one of your employees who has elevated rights get into? These are the next levels of security testing that are often overlooked.

You can add many open source penetration tests to your security arsenal, but don't rely exclusively on one, particularly one that doesn't get updates. Employ a third-party service (if you can justify the extra budgetary overhead), especially if you are tasked with managing sensitive data, such as financial or health care data.

12.3 Social engineering

Most will have heard of social engineering—the ability to convince someone inside a company to do something that will enable the attacker to gain entry, all while the poor victim believes they are doing nothing wrong, and possibly even getting personal satisfaction from helping someone in a perceived time of need.

A good example of this exploit is calling up a support line, convincing the support person you are someone you are not, and, therefore, gaining access to sensitive data. It can be something as innocent as someone trying to gain entry to an office building, bypassing buzzing in with a security key, by walking closely behind someone, with the person more likely than not holding the door open. A confident person can go a long way by acting as if they belong there.

Although it is easy to highlight cases such as these that are obvious when written down, it is a completely different matter in the real world, when guards are down and the natural human instinct to please and be accommodating kicks in.

From the field

It can happen to anyone

An engineer of mine fell afoul of this simple form of social engineering; fortunately, though, it was innocent. Two people turned up at the office, whom he assumed to be the landlords, asking if they could see the cupboard behind the door because there was some work being done on the office next door. Being a small office, this cupboard was the drop point for Verizon and had a number of networking devices in it. Our engineer, normally very vigilant online, not only didn't ask them to confirm their identity but held open the cupboard door while they looked and poked around. After this, he was suitably embarrassed and realized he completely failed every check by allowing two complete strangers access to the office backbone. I did confirm it was indeed the landlords and all was well, but the lesson was made nonetheless—anyone can be caught off guard.

We have all been tricked at some point, and, in most cases, it has been harmless. Yet we can't secure an environment on the basis of "hope"—hope we won't be tricked into something nefarious.

Although everyone in your group is a potential target, the most likely targets are those who interface with external people—support, naturally, but also account managers and anyone helping sales land accounts. Take them through training on a regular basis.

If you really want to test your group readiness, do a "mystery shopper"-style exercise. For example, if you have a visitor who is unknown to your team but who you trust come for a meeting, ask them to try to get to your office without signing in. It's a simple and harmless thing but can highlight weaknesses in an environment that you can do something about. Their mark is to try to get seated in your office before you are there, in true Hollywood/TV theatrical style. Do not underestimate the human desire to please and the lengths people will go to exploit that.

12.4 Data leakage

Just like a cracked pipe or rusted faucet leaks water, your enterprise can also leak data, in small packets, that on the face of it seems harmless but if unchecked can create a major area for a security attack.

Detecting data leaks is a lot harder than noticing the dripping faucet creating a puddle of water; you can't listen for the drip or splash. Data leaks require concentrated effort and constant vigilance. Balancing accessibility and security is a difficult act to get right. Think carefully about what is important to your organization, and build safeguards around those areas. Data leakage can appear in the oddest of places. Let's take a look at a few areas that are common sources of leaks to get you thinking where in your enterprise you might have a data puddle evolving.

12.4.1 Logging

Assuming you are actively logging information (and why wouldn't you be?), your logs are a treasure trove of useful debugging and profiling information. All good. But wait, just what are your developers tossing into those log statements?

If you are logging API requests and responses—again, very common—what about any sensitive data that is coming over that API call? You go to great lengths to store and encrypt, say, Social Security numbers or driver license information, only for this data to end up on a log repository because they appeared in an API payload.

From the field

I once worked with a client who proudly demonstrated they never stored the end user's password. Instead, it was salted and hashed. Brilliant. However, their logging infrastructure had all the passwords in clear text, easily searched because they captured all incoming POST API requests. Oops.

Logs can be quite the treasure trove of data, and generally they are not as secure as their database counterparts. Be deliberate about what you log, and put in the safeguards to mask sensitive data prior to committing it to your log environment. Don't use security as an excuse not to be verbose with log statements—just be mindful of the data inside the messages.

12.4.2 Application errors

Have you ever visited a web page and, instead of getting the desired page, you receive an error page, sometimes filled with lots of debugging data to help the developer diagnose the issue? However, you are not the developer; you are just a member of the public browsing.

Such "helpful" logs can contain a lot of sensitive data pertaining to database connections and other environmental data. Crashing a website can yield huge clues for would-be hackers.

In the old days, websites powered by the likes of JSP, CFML, and PHP would dump complete stack traces and everything in the server memory on a failed page. This information was never designed to go into production, but somewhere along the line, that switch was never turned off as it moved outside of the development/testing environment. Although this situation is rare, error logs, if unchecked, can leak a lot of data.

12.4.3 Data exports

Your enterprise might permit users to export data or run their own queries or analytics through an interface, or even an API. Is there too much data being made available to the end user?

Too often the business intelligence tool or reporting can leak data innocently enough if the data is not locked down properly. What is being rendered on the screen may be only a subset of the data that is actually returned, and a quick inspection of the browser's developer consoles yields much more (and possibly more valuable) data.

12.4.4 Version control

Code is the heart of many organizations, but it can be a real source, literally, of sensitive data. Credentials (such as usernames/passwords for services) that are committed can end up in a variety of unintended places, for instance, code-quality tools that do inspection and make their own copy for performance and analysis reasons. Some of the commercial or open source versioning tools (such as GitHub) will perform a rudimentary check and send alerts detailing what they found.

12.5 *Password rotation*

Passwords are still the authenticator of choice for most of the systems we have to interact with. Passwords are not inherently bad. Where they get a bad reputation is in their generation and management. A password that is never charged and hardcoded is no longer serving any security role—it's merely an additional configuration attribute.

A good password strategy should be one where the password itself is of sufficient length and complexity (a mix of characters and symbols) and can be easily changed without too much consequence. Passwords that have to be hardcoded or placed into files to be used are going to cause issues. If a password is in a file, then it can be read easily by anyone who has access to the filesystem where the file resides.

It is not uncommon, particularly for some older systems, to have database credentials in an XML file that, if changed, requires the server to be restarted. A lot of application servers suffer from this failing. In those situations, changing a password becomes quite the logistical nightmare of updating files, restarting servers, and bringing things back online in a scheduled manner. It's no wonder passwords are rarely charged.

Passwords should be living entities and be able to be changed and updated frequently if need be. Software that requires a password should be able to ask for it in real time from a password or security manager. The cloud providers all provide such services that form the basis of a strong cloud-native app (neither the local or remote credentials are known until a connection is initiated).

Chances are, though, you need to live in a hybrid world, manually maintaining passwords in a static file (even if the file is generated securely via a script). Subsequently, you need to identify all the areas that require a username/password combination and, for each area, detail the change policy procedure—what needs changed and restarted.

A simple spreadsheet, stored alongside your inventory of systems, to track all systems that need access to credentials can manage this, as shown in this table.

Area	Software	Format	Restart	Target
Web	Tomcat	web.xml	Yes	Database

12.5.1 *System credentials tracking*

Consider rotating credentials when

- An employee leaves the organization
- A suspected security breach occurs
- Software is updated
- It's time for periodical updates (every month, for example)

Getting your team disciplined and practicing password rotation will take the fear and uncertainty out of the process. A general piece of advice: if you are doing a rotation, do it across the whole board. If you suspect one or two credentials have been compromised, assume all are at risk. Resist the urge to only do selected items.

12.6 Secure environment

Security is not a feature, something you add or a thing you buy. Instead, security is a philosophy and a set of principles you live and work by, and an area you keep a constant eye on. Creating a secure environment centers around these three basic actions: identify, protect, and monitor.

12.6.1 Identify

You need to know the areas you have to protect before putting up the right "fence." This is called the "attack surface," and it defines all the possible avenues where a potential attack or leak could occur. As CTO, your job is to reduce the attack surface as much as possible and, when you can't, to make it as secure as possible. Examples of an attack surface in your organization, with some ways to reduce it, include the following:

- Production servers running in the same network space as the development servers. Too many people have access to it. Reduce the attack surface by putting the production into an isolated network.
- Shared credentials to a database creates no accountability or ability to exclude a given individual. Reduce the attack surface by giving only those who need access their own username and password.

These are examples, seen in the wild, that don't require huge, sweeping changes to make a significant impact. Finding all your attack surfaces is not a one-time exercise. Every time a new release is deployed, or a new service introduced, your attack surface changes, and you must reevaluate whether your current defenses are sufficient.

12.6.2 Protect

Having identified all the areas where you are potentially at risk, the next logical step is to protect them. This is the trickiest part of the process. Each protection layer comes at a cost—financially and with potential user friction. Consider the following scenario for access to a database (or any authenticated) system:

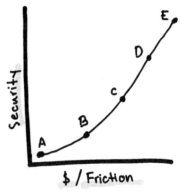

- No username or password
- Shared username or password
- Individual username or password
- VPN access to get at database
- MFA (multifactor authentication) and VPN and individual username and password

As each layer is introduced, more cost is associated with managing the process, in time and additional features and licenses. Yet, each layer is adding more friction or hoops for the user to contend with.

This is the trade-off you face when protecting systems. The most secure database, for example, is one not connected to the network and with no one having any access to it. As appealing as that is from a security lens, it is completely impractical in a business. Data needs to be accessible to provide value and intelligence for the business. Finding the balance between security and accessibility will be different for each system and requires consideration and then consultation with the business, so everyone buys into the processes and policies.

As the old saying regarding the number of times one can part a cat from its skin goes, the same is true of security. Protection comes in many layers, and the biggest mistake (or assumption) you can make is to assume a single layer means you are secure.

Instead, think of many layers, each one protecting different areas. This is often known as the Swiss cheese model. The big advantage of this model is not relying on the defense of one mechanism. An example of this in action would be a firewall blocking all but a handful of ports, which only lets users into a network subnet that serves as a bastion network for further access deeper in. Hardware protections along with software like this can be a formidable force.

From the field

F5 Big-IP Spring 2022

I have noted security isn't something you can outsource and forget. Investing in large enterprise protections, such as the product F5 BIG-IP, is a logical step (the "IBM" of security). Yet, even a company that is purely focused on providing security, with all its checks and balances, still managed to ship a product that permitted unrestricted root privileges to be executed from a simple HTTP POST request. CVE-2022-1388 has a 9.8–10 rating and is one of the most severe security alerts in modern history. Security is hard, no matter who you are, which is why you should never rely on a single solution, but instead use a variety of solutions that all augment one another to provide the best defense at the time.

The point is, relying on a single line of defense is putting all your eggs in one basket with the hope that the basket is never dropped, smashing all your eggs!

12.6.3 Monitor

Having identified and taken steps to protect, the next and final stage is to continually monitor for attacks and breaches, should someone manage to get through the defenses. This has a twofold goal: first, to have the confidence that the current defenses are still intact and working. Nothing is worse than realizing after a reboot that the firewall software didn't properly come back up again. Second is to spot potential weak areas that could do with tightening up. Attackers are always evolving their techniques, and your objective is to make sure your team and defenses are at least one step ahead of them.

The common source for this monitoring is the logs from the output of each of the protection layers. That is easier said than done. In reality, each layer or type will have its own console or log files. It's completely impractical to have someone log in to each system to check. Human fatigue will eventually kick in, and things may start to get missed.

What is required is a way to bring together all the different logs into a single aggregator so they can be monitored at a holistic level. This overview lets you see what may on the surface seem unrelated but in reality forms part of a coordinated attack.

The sophistication of this "dashboard" depends largely on the budget and value of what is being protected. For example, a tool such as Elasticsearch or Splunk, the well-known log aggregates, is a great start. Some very advanced tools, using artificial intelligence, continually analyze the logs being ingested.

Whatever way you go—and it is an evolution—make sure you instill discipline to keep a continual eye on things. Do not rely on or assume any protections put in place are all you need to do. It is an ongoing and core part of your team's duties.

It is worth noting that this aggregation forms part of your auditing process. An area that is sometimes overlooked is the recording and logging of logins (successful and failed attempts). Adding in this level of detail permits you to observe any unused activity—for example, an employee account being used late at night or access to a recently closed account being attempted. The level of detail will depend on your organization and the type of data under your stewardship.

12.7 Developing with security

For organizations that develop and deploy code, the following two areas need specific security considerations:

- Security measures within the developed code
- Security in the build and deployment pipeline

12.7.1 Creating secure code

Developing secure code is hard. If it were easy, we wouldn't need to keep patching and updating software. Code becomes vulnerable for two primary reasons:

- Poor coding or a bug that creates an opportunity for nefarious exploitation
- Well-intentioned features that have created unintended holes through their complexity

Different languages have their own ways in which poor coding can have an impact. Languages that require the developer to self-manage memory present more risk for memory overrun attacks than those for which the memory is managed automatically. Another example is the infamous "SQL injection," whereby a single database statement can be made into multiple statements by cleverly choosing the value for the first one.

SQL INJECTION: AN EXPLANATION

Consider a website that provides a lookup feature by allowing the user to type in a name to look up. Maybe the code touching the database could look like the following:

```
stmt = "SELECT id, email FROM table X WHERE name='" + inputFromUser + "'";
```

Innocent enough, yes? Except, on closer inspection, the developer has created a huge security hole here that may permit the whole database to be compromised or even deleted. How?

What if instead of typing in `noah` on the frontend search box, they typed `'2';` `TRUNC X;'` and sent that request to the API? This would effectively create two separate SQL statements that would be run one after another (assuming the driver permitted it, which most do). The first SQL statement would look for a name that equaled 2; that one isn't going to cause any problems. The second one, however, `'TRUNC X'`, will empty all the rows from the X table. After some trial and error, an attacker can wreak havoc on the database.

Think about this security hole: the hacker doesn't even need to gain any special network access or elevated database access—they are merely using all the paths that have been laid down by the company, including a new UI to accept the compromised SQL statement.

In the early days of websites, such attacks were common, and many went undetected. Although such holes are now rare, developers are still creating poorly structured code, especially those who have not been properly coached or trained in how to code securely and to basically trust nothing the user gives them. This is just one example. Developing secure and bug-free code is a whole discipline in itself, and many books exist to help address this area.

You can mitigate the risk by keeping your coding team trained and having coding standards and extensive code reviews. Code-quality tools (such as SonarQube) can catch some of the standard issues and are always evolving but will never replace the experienced human eye.

From the field

Log4j hack, late 2021

The other area, which has become extremely popular in our evermore always-connected world, is when features from different systems unintentionally create problems through no ill intent of the developer, and nothing highlights this better than the popular logging library, Log4j. The security firm Tenable cited it as "the single biggest, most critical vulnerability of the last decade." It allowed remote code to be run on vulnerable machines by simply having the end user put some special code in logging messages; a system that logged users' searches, input, or chat messages were all open. The feature was designed that way in the first place, but it was never thought someone would configure it the way they had—unintended consequences from altruistic motives.

An area ripe for unintended consequences is any system that enables extension via third-party plugins. The web browser is a good example of where plugins or extensions provide a richer experience for the user. Yet, there is a continual tug of war between plugin flexibility and security, because each plugin permutation figures out a clever way to circumvent restrictions.

12.7.2 Securing the build process

An area that does usually hold the same level of security afforded to the production environment is the development environment. On the face of it, you can understand why it is a little looser—you have developers cutting and experimenting with code and software, and security, for all its greatness and benefits, can get in the way.

That said, a lot of teams use the very same environment for building their software ready for deployment as for production. What measures are being taken to ensure that a rogue library or malicious piece of code has not been added in without anyone noticing?

If your build pipeline is not secure, it will be easy for someone to make a small modification. Likewise, if your version control is not locked down or your library manager (Maven npm, for example, where the library version is not locked down) is not secure, you run the risk of deploying code and may not know what is really in it.

This is how the infamous SolarWinds attack happened, which had a huge impact across all manner of industry because the software was used by large organizations to help manage their IT infrastructure. The hackers found the perfect Trojan horse: they didn't need to hack each target, just the one common piece of software they all shared. Then, as part of the normal software update process, malicious code would be distributed, deep inside networks, with no alarm bells going off.

The safest mindset is to assume every area in your organization is a potential target and take the necessary steps to build in as many protections as possible, which includes putting your build process in a separate environment, locking down specific version numbers of third-party libraries (upgrading only when you decide and have validated them), and taking note of any sudden changes in file size that are not attributable to major code changes (e.g., a deployment being twice the size it usually is should set off an alarm bell).

12.8   *"We are under attack"*

One of your worst nightmares is the moment you realize you are under attack. The other one, closely related, is not knowing you are under attack. That hopefully will not happen as much, assuming you have taken all steps necessary to be monitoring in real time. An attack may come in a number of different ways:

- Denial of service attack
- Data being exported
- Data being deleted or encrypted
- Someone actively moving around your systems without notice

It can be an extremely stressful situation in which to find oneself, but the important, though obvious, thing to do is not panic. Others will be looking to you for a reasoned and responsible plan. The first thing you need to try to get a handle on is the area of attack and how you can limit further damage—much easier said than done.

12.8.1   *Kill switch*

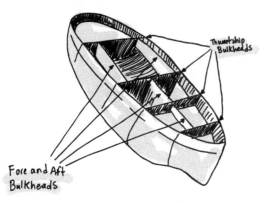

Instead of waiting for an attack before deciding on what action to take, you need to look at your enterprise and come up with a series of responses, or *kill switches*. These are the digital versions of bulkheads in a ship that are designed not only for rigidity but also to seal and isolate a hull breach so a hole doesn't sink the whole ship. (If the bulkheads aren't designed correctly, they can cause more problems than they solve, as was the case with *RMS Titanic*—and while we are on the subject, in the movie, *Titanic*, two people could definitely have fitted on that board!)

The idea of a kill switch is not to solve or eradicate the problem but to buy time to resolve the issue at its core. Two examples of a digital kill switch follow:

- Disable network access to the machine or subnet.
- Power-off (or suspend, if virtual).

> **From the field**
>
> *Leaking data like a fire hose*
>
> One client we worked with integrated with a third-party payment provider. Part of the integration was our API being notified, letting us know when a payment was successfully cleared. Because of our monitoring, we noticed bizarre behavior on our

receiving API; not only was it getting more volume than normal, but it was causing a lot of unknown payee errors. On closer inspection, it turned out our API was receiving lots of sensitive details on payments being made across their entire platform. We instantly reported this to the provider, who at first didn't believe us (they lacked the proper logging), and when they did acknowledge it, it still took them nearly a day before they turned it off (they lacked a kill switch). Had they had the proper logging, or even a kill switch, they could have gotten ahead of the problem and stopped the leak while investigating the problem. We were later told it was a poor query that was missing a WHERE statement, which meant we got everyone's payments, not just ours. They clearly lacked code review and testing, too—a whole host of issues at play with this incident—and this from a public company (even the "big boys" can get it spectacularly wrong).

Limiting the damage while an attack is ongoing is paramount. It doesn't necessarily mean you take down the whole enterprise to the detriment of the company. Maybe you can isolate the area by designing your kill switches properly, but if that is not possible, then it is safer to go dark for a period of time, especially if you suspect sensitive user data is being compromised.

12.8.2 Communication

Communication is important. Keeping your executive team in the loop throughout a situation will give you the support and space to work out the problem. It will feel like a distraction, but as noted earlier, the periodic no-update-update keeps people in the know and your team focused on the problem.

Once you have isolated the problem, the focus shifts to determining the damage, so you can then start to figure out how to resolve and prevent the problem from arising again. Damage can extend from misuse of resources (as in a denial of service) to removal or deletion of data, right through to encryption for a ransomware attack. Determining the damage is one thing, but you also have to make sure the attackers are no longer in a position to continue or restart their attack after you think you have resolved it.

Depending on your team's experience, no one is going to look at you funny if you engage the services of a specialized security firm. They will have the expertise not only to help eradicate the problem but also to help make sure it doesn't happen again.

Identifying how the hackers gained access and closing that down gives you the confidence that, once restored, you won't be right back at square one again. There is nothing worse than playing "whack-a-mole," thinking you have resolved it, but as soon as you shut down, up again they pop.

Sanitizing an environment will take effort, time, and expertise, and no matter how clean you think you have it, there will always be a small doubt that you have caught everything. If you find yourself in this situation, I definitely highly recommend hiring the expertise of a third-party service. Although modern architectures, with all their interconnectivity, can pose greater security risks, they can also make it easier to restore an enterprise, especially if you are using containers in a virtualized environment—just destroy and respawn the container fresh and clean (assuming you haven't let in a rogue library in the build process).

12.8.3 *Managing a security breach*

Another area you may find yourself having to manage is the aftermath of a security breach or data theft. This is the situation where you have to determine what was stolen. Unlike when physical assets are removed—it is obvious because they are no longer there—digital assets can be transparently copied, leaving no trace. Hopefully, your logging is sufficient that there will be some trace; otherwise, how would you know of the theft in the first place? This is often called *digital forensics*.

The safest thing you can do is to assume the attackers took everything that was accessible to them. Once you have determined the list of things, you need to figure out the following:

- Who needs to be notified?
- What steps can you take to neutralize the value of data?
- What safeguards can you put in place to prevent further thefts?
- Are there any legal ramifications from the theft?

My best advice is to not try to do this on your own. Involve your executive team, consult legal counsel, and get the services of a specialized company.

We all have received the "do not be alarmed, but" emails from CEOs/CTOs of large firms after a data hack. They are a result of their investigation that your account or data was potentially compromised. They are alerting you, as good stewards of your data, so you can be on alert for anything suspicious.

Steps we have all seen include a forced reset of everyone's password or a one-time reset of an account that requires a confirmation code via email or SMS. However small, it is an effort to neutralize the usefulness of the data. For certain data theft, however, such as name, address, or Social Security numbers, very little can be done, which is what makes data theft such a serious act. Your clients, who entrusted you to look after and take care of their precious data, have been let down in the most egregious of manners.

Depending on the type of data, you may have to file publicly about the breach. Typically, any data involving financial or health care falls under this umbrella, but seek the advice of your legal team before doing anything.

Getting to the bottom of any sort of attack or breach can take time. What will inevitably happen is that you will discover that the breach is in an area where there is a lack or absence of logging. This is to be expected, and is easily remedied.

Be thorough with your investigation, and present it in a way that is easily digestible by those not necessarily technically savvy. Consider the following simple four-step framework to structure the incident report—issue, identify, impact, remedy (IIIR):

- *Issue*—Define what happened, including how it occurred
- *Identify*—Illustrate how the issue was brought to your attention
- *Impact*—Review the result of the issue
- *Remedy*—Detail the steps to resolve and address the incident

An example IIIR statement looks like this:

- *Issue*—The web form used to update users' address details allowed anyone with an account to see any other address, by simply incrementing the ID to the API call via the browser's developer console.
- *Identify*—An increase in usage of API calls alerted the Ops team to look further, and they found suspicious address API calls from the same IP address.
- *Impact*—A single IP address, thought to be one user, viewed approximately 1,000 addresses before the Ops team shut down their access. The user could not be identified because IP logs are not stored with recent user logins.
- *Remedy*—The API endpoint has been updated and deployed to return only the address of the logged-in user. All other APIs are undergoing a similar audit and update. IP logs are being stored as part of the user's session tracing. A list of all accounts whose addresses were viewed has been created.

These IIIRs can be lengthy, depending on the incident. They are intended for internal purposes only, giving enough detail that would serve as the source to draw on, should a public announcement be deemed appropriate. This should be a statement of fact, not a plan to determine what to do next—that is the responsibility of you all as an executive team.

12.9 Chief Information Security Officer (CISO)

You will eventually reach a given size where the role of maintaining security and monitoring and tracking compliance will be too much and too important to distribute among the engineering team. A dedicated officer to manage this, and potentially grow a team, will be the best way forward. Typically, we call this person the Chief Information Security Officer (CISO). Some companies refer to the role simply as the Chief Security Officer.

Up to this point, more than likely, all responsibility for maintaining and monitoring security has been yours and your team's. For a CISO to properly stretch their arms and get ahold of the security, they must sit outside your group.

Andy Wu, CEO of CodeArcs, loves the well-known Latin phrase, "*Quis custodiet ipsos custodes*," which roughly translates to "Who will guard the guards?" also known by the variant, "Who watches the watchers?" when it comes to describing security oversight. In this world, it means the CISO should not be under your leadership as CTO. The CISO can't be in a position where it is easy to overrule or dampen their impact. They need to work alongside your group while, at the same time, holding your group to account.

Although this may feel like a loss of power or yielding ground, it is quite the opposite. It is an acknowledgment of the growth and maturity of the platform powering the business. How do you know if you are ready for the office of the CISO?

- Your company needs to adhere to various security-related certifications, including compliance.
- The type of data being handled requires specific procedures and audit trials.
- The security-auditing environment becomes large enough to be a full-time job.

A good CISO will be able to dedicate the time and depth to keep your company and data secure, working in partnership with all groups involved in handling or producing data.

Summary

- Patching is more than updating software; it requires testing and scheduling.
- Penetration tests, if not done after each release, are no more than a placebo.
- Employees are the weakest link in the chain, due to socially engineered attacks.
- Passwords that can't be changed easily are no longer performing any security function.
- Securing an environment requires constant vigilance and work.
- Developing code requires education and review to make sure no breaches are introduced.
- The building's environment can be a source of security holes.
- Creating digital bulkheads, or kill switches, will enable the containment of a breach.
- Managing a security breach requires level-headedness and good internal communication.
- You will grow to a point where a dedicated resource is needed to manage security.

Checklist

How many of the following items can you lay claim to having covered?

- Use third-party software and libraries on a regular patch schedule
- Have a penetration test report that is as recent as your last release
- Carry out ongoing education process to remind or update employees of socially engineered hacks
- Can quickly rotate all passwords without the need to restart components
- Possess sufficient logs and alerts to know when something has been breached
- Implemented a number of kill switches to limit an attack or breach
- Institute an education and review process for developers to not introduce security holes
- Create a build environment that is as secure as the production environment

Housekeeping

This chapter covers

- Maintaining hardware
- Monitoring the health of your platform
- Backup and restoration techniques
- Adhering to your budget

Managing the health and ongoing maintenance of the enterprise or platform is something we take for granted. We spend all this effort in the design, build, and deployment, but sometimes we forget what it takes to keep the lights on, head off any potential problems, and create an environment where, should something go off the rails, recovery is available.

In this chapter, we are going to touch on some of the higher-level areas that have caught out many CTOs. They will most likely be obvious procedural items, but sometimes, even the obvious things are overlooked. For example, many of us believe we are fully backing up our platforms, but when was the last time you actually tried to restore a system? How sure are you that the backup has covered everything you need?

As we touched on technical debt being produced when developing code, technical debt can also occur if you are not keeping an eye on the enterprise or platform as a whole. Keeping the platform serviced so no surprises pop up is an often-overlooked role.

13.1 Managing hardware

If you find yourself with physical servers or network equipment in your platform, you need to create a management plan for them. Hardware is a living entity that requires nurturing and continual maintenance, particularly those items that have moving parts, and we include cooling fans in that mix. Anything that has a moving part will eventually stop moving, causing untold consequences. The goal is to ensure you get ahead of failure, plan for it, expect it, and ultimately not be concerned when it happens.

As stated before, maintaining a reliable and up-to-date inventory is crucial to your hardware health. This includes such details as the following:

- Manufacturer
- Type/model
- Purchase date/install date/next service date
- Support details
- Maintenance log
- Location/login details

A simple spreadsheet will suffice, but specialty inventory software exists to aid you with this. Hardware servicing is like servicing your car—yes, you can skip changing the oil and save some coin, but at some point the engine will blow up, costing you even more money as well as inconvenience and downtime. While there is no oil to change in the tech hardware world, you do have hard disks (including SSD drives) and fans that should be replaced. Each component has a MTTF (mean time to failure), which is basically an expected lifetime. Components can last longer, but they can also die sooner. It is important to source components early and keep replacements in stock, if possible.

Hardware becomes troublesome when it reaches an age where sourcing components becomes hard or nearly impossible. It is not unusual for companies to resort to eBay auctions, seeking secondhand units. Plan to get well ahead of that stage because if you're not careful, it can sneak up on you.

13.2 Support contracts

Support contracts have gotten a bad name over the years, being seen as an overpriced option, where you end up paying more over time than the license itself. Some of the well-known database vendors were renowned for this.

Support contracts should be thought of as insurance policies—when things go wrong, they are there you help to get back up and running. That said, as with insurance policies, not all support contracts are the same, and they may not provide the sort of help or support you really need. Therefore, before signing up for a lengthy contract, make sure it is giving you the level of support you need to keep your enterprise up. Common types of support follow:

- Fast, minor upgrades or security updates
- Guaranteed response time to a query (this does not mean resolution, just an acknowledgment of your question)
- Scheduled backups (if online)
- Disaster recovery/failover
- Parts/components replacement on failure

Depending on your organization's in-house expertise and ability, you may not need the same level of support that others would benefit from. Determining whether you need support (and if you, at what level) comes from doing a risk analysis on each of your components, asking questions such as the following:

- If the component fails, how does this impact end user delivery?
- How much knowledge or training exists in-house to resolve an issue?
- How often have you experienced issues?
- Is it a single point of failure?

Sometimes a support contract is nothing more than a priority weighting. For example, take a problem with the internet line coming into your building. Of course the provider will resolve it at some point, but chances are, they will prioritize clients with a support contract over clients with none.

The same thing happens with software. The cloud providers offer a basic level of support for free but can take days to answer or restore systems versus hours for those with a support contract. Think of a support contract as a lifeline—that number you call when all other avenues have been exhausted. For older systems that have not yet been modernized or updated, you should definitely have a support contract to bridge that gap until such time as you plan to address the underlying component.

Open source libraries or software that you rely on are also support candidates. Many of the larger open source projects (Mongo, Postgres, MySQL, Elasticsearch) have their "commercial" version that can be purchased, which is usually just a support contract with the same open source software underneath. Some offer a commercial version, which, for a small price, is a few revisions behind (sometimes with extra enterprise-only features) so you don't have to tolerate release "teething" issues that sometimes come with rapid-release software. They also make sure you are kept informed of important security updates in a timely fashion without relying on someone in your team checking online resources.

Hardware support contracts can range dramatically in cost and service. Top-end contracts will have your hardware monitored remotely, with an engineer being dispatched automatically to replace a part before you ever realize it has failed. This type of contract is common for large SAN (storage area network) servers as hard disks come to the end of their life. The lower-end contracts will determine the issue, via phone or email, and send out a replacement for your team to install themselves. As the old saying goes, you get what you pay for. Not everyone needs the full top-line service, but that is for you to decide.

13.2.1   *Providing support*

While we are on the subject of support, it is worth considering the other side of the table: for the systems you are providing to your clients, what support levels are you offering for when they get into difficulty? In larger organizations it is common for the frontline support group to be under the COO or CIO. These people directly interface with the end client, trying to diagnose and resolve issues. If they need assistance, it is escalated to the engineering group. So, although you are not involved in end user support directly, you still have to have a process to define a timely response to your support team. This is often known as an SLA (service-level agreement), which outlines the level of service the end user can expect to receive (see chapter 10). This type of agreement usually includes such things as the following:

- Up time for a period of time; for example, 99.999% over a year means you will not have downtime for more than 8.7 hours.
- Time to acknowledge an inquiry, detailing business and out-of-hours response times.
- Remote monitoring you may have.
- Software patches, including bug fixes and security updates.
- Maximum time spent on an individual issue or overall.
- Billing for any "not-at-fault" issues.

You should not come up with this list in isolation. It will be in partnership with your sales team, product manager, CEO, and CFO. It is a result of what the client wants, what the sales team can sell, and, ultimately, what you can deliver. So, if it's decided that out-of-hours support will be provided, then you will need to staff this (remote teams in different time zones, a rotation of employees with a pager, or around-the-clock staff) and put it in the budget to pay for it.

   Never be in a position of offering 24/7 support with no real plan to deliver it. There will be a need to deliver on it just as Thanksgiving or Christmas dinner is laid out. Relying on your team's years of goodwill, or hoping it will never happen, is not a support strategy. Provide the level of support you would demand from a vendor.

13.3   *Monitoring*

There is nothing more unprofessional, and frankly, embarrassing, than having a client report to you when something is down or unavailable, yet, at some point in our careers, we have all been at the wrong end of this. Building a monitoring culture takes a little thought but, once completed, gives you and the executive team a level of comfort.

13.3.1 *Outside looking in*

If your primary user or client is external, you have to monitor as if you were in their shoes. As obvious as it sounds, that means any monitoring software needs to reside away from your existing network. For example, if you are hosted on AWS, consider a solution that uses Azure or Google, or, at the very least, a completely separate AWS account in a different geographic region.

External monitoring entails periodically accessing your infrastructure in a way that would emulate a real client interaction. It can be as rudimentary as simply detecting the availability of a given service, right through to measuring latency and response times. When designing such a remote monitor, be sure to design it so that should something alert, it gives your team clues as to where the problem really lies.

For example, you could simply monitor the availability of the web page used for logging in. Although this is a good first step, it doesn't confirm the API for authenticating clients is available. Continuing down this path, if you have a test account you can log in to, that would confirm authentication; however, is that touching the primary services? Can you hit another API that would run a query (low overhead) against the main database? By adding a few extra steps, look at how much more is being validated: network, API, and database. Do this every 5 to 30 minutes (depending on what makes sense), and you will know when things start to go south very quickly.

When something starts to alert, where should those alerts go? The logical answer is to generate an email, but which one? If you manage email on the same network as that being monitored, you run the risk of the email not arriving because the same problem stopping client access could be preventing email from getting through. This is another good reason to outsource your email needs to Google or Microsoft—no matter what is happening on your own network, the mail will always be available. If you do host and manage your own email server, look to use a free email address (Gmail, Yahoo, etc.) that will then forward the email to the relevant people, choosing emails not on your primary domain.

If you do outsource your email, use the same process: create an "alert" alias, which then forwards to everyone who needs to see it. It's much easier to administer an email list than to try to maintain individual emails.

Another good thing to consider is a public status page with indicators on the up time of each public component. You will have seen these from the likes of Amazon and Azure. Plenty of open source initiatives make creating one of these trivial. Again, make sure the status page is outside of the organization's main network.

From the field

Manual status page

One portfolio I worked with had to interface with a public company via an API. This particular vendor had a terrible up-time record, yet every time you would visit their status page, it was always green across the board. As it turned out, their status page

(continued)

was manually updated only after a meeting was held and it was agreed that a public notification was warranted. They didn't want to show how poor their API up time was. Such political games are counterproductive, especially with the popularity of public validation sites such as Downdetector and IsItDownRightNow. All that was achieved was confirmation of how untrustworthy this organization was. Hiding things in the technical world does not work, especially in the long run.

13.3.2 Inside looking in

Although looking from outside in is valuable, you have much greater access and granularity from monitoring internally, heading off potential problems before they impact clients—for instance, keeping an eye on disk usage and freeing up space before the server stops working. These examples are rudimentary but effective. The basics such as CPU, memory, and disk, though not glamorous, do catch a lot of things before they become bigger issues.

Determining the "normal" operational usage will help spot spikes or abnormal usage for further investigation. If a sudden drop in memory occurs, that could signal a process that has died, or one that is flapping (going up and down). You are looking for unexplained charges—spikes in usage that are not attributable to increased traffic or client uptake.

Depending on your setup, you will be looking for triggers to inform the increase or upgrading of services (more web or database services) or the removal of resources no longer required. These basic metrics are vital to the health of your resources. Another level of monitoring is the application logs—the messages logged as part of normal execution. Every application generates logs somewhere from individual files on a disk to the Windows Event service or in Amazon CloudWatch. Those are lot of places to keep an eye on.

The modern way is to transfer or pipe all logs to a central service (such as Elasticsearch) and use that to compare, contrast, monitor, and alert. Not only is this a single place to analyze logs, it offers an opportunity to easily detect links between systems, so if one starts to exhibit issues, it may be a symptom of another, more serious problem. Classic examples here run from increased SQL errors from the web application points to a database server having issues, maybe due to a long-running statement that has locked-up tables. Such unintended consequences are very hard to spot, so you'll need to go and check various subsystems.

Ideally you want all logs to end up in a central location. This includes logs from operating systems, routers, firewalls, applications, the VPN, and networks. Include when users, clients, and processes authenticate. It's amazing how much intel can be gleaned—for example, you might discover that every time a given entity logs in, a set of behaviors is observed. You can never log too much.

> **From the field**
>
> *Centralized time*
>
> This isn't so much of an issue with today's modern operating systems, but it is a good idea to make sure all systems are kept in sync and to a common time zone, usually UTC (Universal Time Coordinated). All operating systems offer a time-synchronization utility that realigns periodically. The advantage of doing this is that is makes forensic analysis of log tracing much easier to read, because you can spot cause-and-effect patterns by following the timeline.

Creating dashboards to provide a snapshot of the overall health of your enterprise will take trial and error and will evolve over time as you home in on the areas that are contextual to your environment. Your goal is simple: get as much lead time as possible before problems become an operational issue so you can take the necessary corrective action. Never be in a position where the only monitoring you have is your clients calling in. This inspires no confidence in you or your company.

13.4 Backup and restoration

Almost everyone claims they have backups, at least of the crucial components, but as Ryan Burch, director of IT at New Harbor Capital laments, "It may seem obvious, but a backup strategy that has never been restored is not a backup, but merely a storage utilization strategy—something to make you feel safe, like a safety net that is not tethered to anything."

Creating backups is hard, and until you have gone through a full restore to another system, you will never know whether you really have backed up everything.

The first question you have to answer is, what are you backing up? Is it data only, configuration and data, or application, configuration, and data? Answering the question depends on the goal of the backup in the first place. Some reasons to create a backup strategy follow:

- Continuity of service in event of a failure
- Periodic record for compliance
- Testing/development purposes

The vast majority of backups are made for continuity events, and in these cases, time matters. Each minute you are down costs both financially and the reputation/trust of your brand. Creating a strategy, and rehearsing it, will give you not only the peace of mind should the worst happen but a defined plan and time expectation for when a service will be operational again.

Depending on your setup, it is advisable to keep your backup files encrypted on a separate network or cloud account. More often than not, particularly for smaller organizations, it is common to have the backups sitting on the same machine, and not even on a separate network. Always work on the assumption of not *if* but *when* failure will happen.

Backups should involve third-party services, too—not just the services you maintain directly. For example, source code sitting on GitHub or Bitbucket should be regularly backed up to a secure, managed location. Another area often overlooked is Salesforce, particularly if you are using this more like a database in the cloud. If you use Google Drive, Office 365, Dropbox—anywhere you have data—ask yourself, what is the consequence if that is no longer available or you get locked out of the account?

Getting a good strategy in place takes effort, as well as the initial extraction or copying. But after that, it should be on autopilot, with reports being logged to your central logging environment, so you create alerts for when a backup fails or hasn't even run.

Practice your restoration. Build a plan that is clearly available so anyone with the necessary administrative rights can easily build and restore. Have fire drills, once a year at the very least (or more frequently), to confirm that everything is being backed up as expected.

13.4.1 *Frequency/retention*

A question that is asked regularly is how often backups should be made and how long they should be kept. Let's look at each of those issues in turn.

The biggest factor in how often you should back up comes down to how frequently your data changes. If it changes only once a week, then a daily backup isn't going to yield much difference between archives. Backing up too often may generate too much overhead, both in performance and in disk usage. If you need a high resolution of recovery, you should be looking at building that into the storage from the ground up, for example, multiregion data replication in near-real time.

The time to retain backups used to be a factor of available storage space. With the advent of pay-as-you-go cloud storage, that practical limit is no longer there. Now the question shifts more to what is useful for a recovery scenario.

In the old days, the recommendation was to keep the last three backups, to cover any loss or failure of a backup. That isn't the issue it used to be, with big storage and sophisticated checksums and encryption. As long as you have at least one backup archive, that will suffice for most incidents. However, if you think you will be looking to reach into the backup for a partial recovery, that means holding on to archives for longer than normal.

Say you discover a given set of data was accidentally deleted, but it took a few days or weeks to discover—a not-uncommon situation when handling multitenant client data. Being able to reach back and do a partial extraction for a given point in time may be better than nothing. Therefore, keeping data for months can be justified.

NOTE This doesn't mean you need to keep six months' worth of daily data. You can start aging it out: after, say, seven days, you only keep a weekly archive; then after four weeks, keep only monthly archives. This grandfathering technique keeps storage costs down.

13.4.2 Archive security

Before we leave this topic, a word of caution on the security of the resulting archive: it is very easy to expose sensitive data through poor security and access to the resulting archive. You don't want all your security efforts maintaining multilayer access to be null and void by making the zip or backup file accessible by anyone with DevOps control.

The person charged with running and validating the backups doesn't need to be able to see the data in the archive. By controlling access to the encryption keys, you can maintain the integrity and visibility of the backup archives.

Treat your backup files with the same level of attention as the environment they are related to. Don't let your backups leak data.

13.5 Budget oversight

As we went over in earlier chapters, creating a budget will give you and the business a benchmark for delivering what you need. That is only part of budget oversight—the second part of the challenge is keeping to it. This means tracking expenditure and costs as they happen and not being caught off guard by any surprises.

Good news: if you are in the cloud, this information is very easy to get at through daily alerts, should certain thresholds be surpassed. It is very easy for cloud costs to spiral, especially if developers create new services (maybe too large for their needs) and then forget to terminate them.

A good habit to get into is having, at least once a month, a cloud expenditure review to go over the current resources that are currently running and determine whether they are necessary. Use the tags liberally that cloud providers give to track various services, maybe at a project or department level. It is all too easy for servers to be spun up, then their real need is forgotten about, and over time, they become sacred. People fear untold damage if they terminate them, so it's just easier to keep them running (spending money). Before you know it, the cloud bill is running out of control.

The other reason a cloud bill can go up is through increased usage. A strong and well-architected cloud-native project will autoscale up and down, based on traffic levels. As the product grows, the sales team lands some new big clients, so the usage will increase, as will the expenditure. This is good and natural. However, you need to be able to identify the reason for the increased cloud bill, so when the CFO asks, you can celebrate the reason with them.

Either way, continual review and monitoring will head off any surprises, and if you need to make adjustments to your original budget, then so be it—it was only ever an estimate, and as time goes on, you are firming it up with what is really going on.

If you find yourself off the cloud, then your expenditure will come in large one-off amounts, as you look to add servers or more memory or disk space. The same rules apply here as for the cloud: review current usage of services, making sure they are being used as efficiently as possible. Storage is an area that can be never ending. If you see an increase, then consider offloading your long-term storage requirements to the cloud—pay for what you need, with no hardware renewals to worry about.

Software licenses and support costs are a little easier to predict and budget for, yet they can and do increase from year to year. License costs for commercial databases tend to run high, so as you need to grow, step back and determine whether alternatives (cheaper or free) are available.

Although it is recommended to get support when first getting a new software application, when it comes time for renewal, ask whether that money is being well spent and whether you really need the software. This is one of the reasons many software companies have moved away from support contracts to a more subscription-based model, forcing you to pay as long as you continue to use the product. Again, as CTO, you are responsible for the costs of your department, and you should fight for the best value for your allocated budget.

Summary

- Keep an inventory of hardware under your control to better schedule preventive maintenance.
- Determining component lifetimes will guide your purchasing requirements ahead of time.
- Support contracts are like insurance policies, but make sure you are covered for what you need.
- Monitoring from a client's perspective will give you the necessary insight to any issues before they need to alert you.
- Internal monitoring of systems can give insights into performance to let your team get ahead of potential problems before they become real problems.
- The frequency of your backups depends largely on how frequently your data changes and how far back you need to go for recovery.
- Restoration needs to be practiced on a periodic basis, to validate the backup coverage.
- Keeping an eye on the budget, on a weekly or monthly basis, will head off any surprises.

Checklist

How many of the following items can you lay claim to having covered?

- Created inventory of all hardware complete with maintenance log
- Listed spare parts of hardware available to replace components that are out of warranty and may break soon
- Developed a support contract for the crucial parts of your enterprise
- Monitored solutions, looking from the outside in
- Monitored solutions, keeping an eye on the internal metrics
- Set up automated backup with secure offsite archives
- Periodically confirmed backup through restoration
- Reviewed budgetary spend, at least on a monthly basis

Company growth

14

This chapter covers

- Different ways a company can be acquired or grow through acquisition
- Being prepared to put your best forward with no notice
- Performing due diligence and getting to what really matters
- Taking over from a CTO, or handing over—how to do it properly

At some point in the growth of the company, a number of the following events, or transactions, may occur:

- Be acquired by another firm
- Be acquired by a private equity or investment group
- Purchase a smaller company
- Merge with another

Each of these occurrences comes with its own challenges and strategies for success—which we will dive into in this chapter—but they all share a common threat of being a huge distraction and time sink if not properly handled.

14.1 Investment groups

The executive team, which you are part of as CTO, is always looking for ways to create value for customers, employees, and investors alike. A well-executed transaction serves all constituents. Whether you are being acquired or doing the acquiring, it is a huge validation that something in your organization is being done right.

What does this mean for you, as the leader and visionary of your organization's technology? It means you are responsible for positioning all the work done to date and all future plans in the best possible light without misrepresentation or lying.

As soon as an investment group, such as a private equity (PE) company, shows interest, a new level of oversight is placed on the company as a whole. Contrary to popular belief, investment groups are not just rich old men with money. The vast majority of these groups are pension funds, university endowments, and family trusts. Think of it like this: your success will be helping fund people's retirements and help put students through higher education.

Hopefully, the reason for the extra oversight is obvious: when putting other people's money to work, you want an extra level of care and attention. Private equity firms are managers and stewards of other people's money—they have been charged with taking a lump sum, investing it somewhere relatively "safe," and within three to five years, typically returning the investment, all being well, larger than what they started with. An investment group, therefore, makes its money or returns when a transaction happens—when they sell their share. Contrast this with venture capital, which is more about investing in an idea and building a company around that, than investing in an existing, successful, operational company.

Different groups have different investment philosophies. Some will want to be the only investor and have controlling interest; others will want to coinvest with another group. Some will hold their investment for longer than the typical three to five years; some will be very hands off, leaving the running of the company to the executive team. Increasingly, investment groups look to get more involved, offering their expertise and network to help the company grow. This is where they can bring a huge value to the company as they open up access to people who have been there and done that, in a safe, controlled environment. In PE parlance, operating partners are those who will roll up their sleeves and help assist. A word of advice: should you find yourself working with an operating partner, embrace it.

Do not feel threatened—they don't want your job. They want to lift you up and prepare you for success. Conversely, if they think you are not qualified for the role, they can replace you. That is a worst-case scenario, but it would be remiss of me to pretend it doesn't happen. By the time it gets to that stage, you've managed to ignore all the advice and guidance that has been given to you, and it still isn't working out. Fortunately, you have this book to fill in any gaps you may have had.

14.2 *Impromptu pitch*

As the Boy Scouts' motto goes, "Be prepared." You never know when a group of "suits" will be touring and you will be asked to give a review of where things are now and, more importantly, where your plans or vision will take the company in the future. We went in depth about the importance of having your vision at hand in chapter 3—this is one of the moments when you need an answer.

> **From the field**
>
> *Be ready*
>
> Frequently, particularly in the early phases, such meetings will be made discreetly, with not a lot of time for preparation. I have been put in a position where my CEO at the time asked at 5 p.m. if I could join a dinner—a couple of PE partners had stopped by and wanted to get to know us. No presentations, no deck, just good, old-fashioned discussions over a dinner table (with way too much cutlery for a simple engineer to grasp).

Do not underestimate the impact and lasting impressions these types of encounters have—they can make the difference between moving forward or killing the deal there and then. Your greatest contribution is to instill confidence (not arrogance) that the technology, while maybe not perfect, has a future and a plan to take the company on its next phase of growth.

14.3 *Investment cadence*

Understanding how your investors prioritize and make their money will factor into how you plan and execute your vision. As noted, most make the bulk of their money on a transaction, which typically happens around three to five years after initial injection. This could be selling to another investment group or to a strategic investor (a company who acquires for product, client, or talent).

If you think of selling a company like selling a house, then you know you prefer to present the house in the best possible light. The last thing you want is to be in the middle of replacing the kitchen as you tour prospective buyers through a construction site. They will look at it and make the logical conclusion they may end up finishing the kitchen themselves. It would have been better to not have started it in the first place and leave the new buyers complete creative freedom to reimagine it as they would like. How do kitchens relate to the office of the CTO?

The same principle should be applied before embarking on any large projects, particularly ones that could last a year or more. Given when you believe a new transaction is likely, you should determine whether you could get the project completed in time. For this type of long-term planning, always seek the counsel of your CEO, who may have a better sense of the future.

If you have a relationship with an operating partner of the current investment group, you should definitely consult them. They are in the best position to help you weigh the pros and cons of the project, and whether completion can be done in time and make it easier to position the company on the market.

Classic projects that fall under this careful consideration are modernization ones, where replacing an outdated technology with something more manageable helps everyone. A new investor would prefer such projects be completed while all the in-house knowledge is still present and no one is feeling nervous or distracted by new owners.

Even if you know the project won't be wrapped up in time, you may be given the green light to start. If this happens, carefully consider the milestones. You may have to adjust your project plan so that, by the time the transaction happens, there is value with a clear path to the finishing line. Going back to our kitchen refit analogy, you would want to get all the plumbing and electrical completed, at least, so the kitchen could be semi-usable.

When faced with such project planning, involve as many of the stakeholders as possible. Consult them for their input, and do not overpromise. Build in a lot of contingency time, because if a transaction is looming, then you and some of your team may be involved: documents, presentations, and due diligence are prepared—this is time away from delivering the project.

14.4 Preparing for integration

A common practice in the investment world is that of the "tuck-in" acquisition. That is when a smaller company is purchased to augment a larger company. The smaller company doesn't have the complexity or overhead a larger transaction would have—maybe only 1–10 employees with a particular niche. These are attractive prospects, because it is a very quick way to grow and scale a larger entity in the portfolio company. These are not mergers in the classic sense, where both parties have nearly equal footing. Think of a tuck-in as more like purchasing a fully formed, self-running department.

That said, successful tuck-ins are ones that do not remain as independent departments but are integrated fully, pulling in the same direction. This takes effort and careful planning in the execution. The last thing you want is a completely different tech stack, with different skills, making it hard for you to move resources around.

This doesn't mean that every tuck-in has to be rewritten; rather, it means that the technology should be able to use a lot of the "housekeeping" facilities, such as logging, security, platform, and monitoring. For example, say you have all your infrastructure in AWS and the tuck-in company has Azure as their cloud. An argument could be made to port them into AWS.

Depending on your size, you may find yourself being the tucker, or the one welcoming a tuck-in. Regardless of the side, some basics are the same and should factor into your long-term vision.

The success of a tuck-in transaction is predicated on the speed of integration and how quickly the acquired business can start adding value to the organization. Integration time is a consideration for investment groups when evaluating targets. Therefore, you want to make sure your technology stack can quickly absorb or be absorbed by another. Modern micro architecture or API environments are great foundations to build upon. An API buys time for evaluating whether the backend should be rewritten or ported to something more standard to the host's infrastructure. Things like version control and build processes are areas that should be targets for consolidation. We will address the issue of onboarding the team later in this chapter.

From the field

IT

Areas such as email and file storage typically lay outside of a CTO's realm, yet depending on the size of your organization, they may show up on your radar. These should be one of the first things to be done—nothing makes a new team feel more welcome and at home than using the same email and chat system.

14.5   *Due diligence*

The words *due diligence* can strike fear into the hearts of even the most seasoned CTOs, believing it will be a full-on interrogation, complete with judgment and condemnation. Anyone who has seen the classic movie, *Office Space* (1999), is familiar with the scene with the two Bobs, where they are interviewing everyone, looking to make cuts. The famous line that resonates so eerily and sums up what many believe due diligence embodies is, "What would you say you do here?"

Due diligence is an opportunity for a party to get to know what it is they are going to be buying, warts and all. Going back to the home-buying analogy, due diligence is akin to the home inspection report, a document created by professionals who will know what to look for, so you, the buyer, have no surprises after purchase (like a leaky roof or an A/C unit that needs replacing).

Even the due diligence performed by the big accountant firms frankly can lack a lot of detail and context. What many people who are conducting due diligence process miss is the "why." Due diligence is not running down a list of prepared, standard questions in a spreadsheet. That then becomes an interrogation, a Q&A, with no feeling or opportunity to celebrate what is being discovered.

When someone is buying something—a TV, car, house or company—they are doing it for one reason: to solve a problem. If you want a TV to simply use for your Xbox, then you do not care about any smart apps or the number of channels it can receive. You are interested only in resolution and refresh rate. A different buyer may be looking to watch local news and Netflix, and their due diligence is going to look a lot different than that of the gamer. This is the "fit for purpose" question, or the "why."

Before any due diligence can begin, you must determine the reason or plan for what the purchase will yield. This will let both parties focus on the areas that actually matter and are relevant. Due diligence is, therefore, a conversation and not a scene from the TV show *Chicago PD*, questioning suspects handcuffed to the table under intense circumstances.

By the time a potential transaction gets to the stage of due diligence, it is fairly advanced in the process, with the "why" being well understood. The goal of the overall exercise is simple: can the technology do what we need, and if it can't, how much money and effort will it take to do so?

We are going to look at this process from each of the two sides. You may find yourself needing to perform due diligence or being the focus of one. We will start by performing one, because this will give greater appreciation and context to being on the other side.

14.5.1 *Performing due diligence*

The chances are, given where you are in your career, you have conducted at least one or two due diligence processes. You probably didn't call them that; you more likely referred to them as an evaluation. It probably wasn't related to a company but more to do with a piece of software, language, framework, or service. You researched as much as you could in advance, formulated your own thoughts, and came up with some questions.

By the time you were talking to an expert (other users, or even the technical sales engineers), your questions were extremely relevant to the problem for which you were looking to deploy this solution. You probably didn't have a spreadsheet of generic questions that, if answered, wouldn't have moved you a single inch closer to an informed decision. What you did have, though, was a list of notes focused more on the operational aspects that, if addressed, could inform you whether this was still going in the right direction. The difference: you have the "why," looking to see if a given entity is indeed fit for purpose.

The same mentality is applied when evaluating the technology of a complete company—just a little more involved, but no more complicated. You are a technologist, in the business of solving problems. Most things you will come across will either be Coca-Cola or Pepsi (in other words, not wrong—just different) or small enough they are easily resolved. That is why you, and not an associate in an accountancy firm, are best placed to perform this. You can spot these issues quickly, allowing the time to focus on the areas that could become a problem.

We are going to go over the big areas that require deeper exploration. As you perform your analysis, keep in mind that any problems or issues unearthed will become yours to address if the transaction goes through successfully. Hopefully, though, there will be things that will assist your team that can be used postevent. Maybe they have solved a problem your team has been wrestling with or are doing something with a little more efficiency. There is always something to glean.

TECHNOLOGY STACK

How different is the tech stack from yours? Does your team have enough knowledge to be able to consume it? If the stack is outdated, what would it take to continue to support it, including any challenges to recruit engineers or maintain the hardware (if relevant) or operating system? Are there things being done that can be more efficient or streamlined using modern techniques? If a rewrite was to be done, how much of an effort, cost, or disruption would it be?

INTELLECTUAL PROPERTY RIGHTS (IPR)

How much of the technology is unique to the business? Is their IPR (or secret sauce) the algorithms or code, or is it more the application of the tool? Are there any patents relating to the technology, and if there are, who owns them—an individual, a company, or a third party? As strange as it seems, who actually owns the source code? It's not always obvious, especially if the company has outsourced its principal development.

DATA

How is data stored and used? How much is kept and available for analysis? Who are the main producers and consumers? Who owns the data, and what, if any, restrictions are on its usage? What jurisdictions does the data fall within (is GDPR relevant?), and is there any sensitive data that comes under compliance (such as PII, PCI, or HIPAA)?

> ### From the field
> *It's my data—I will do with it what I want*
> I have often come across companies who think just because they have an email address stored in their database it's theirs to do with as they please. This is not the case. How was the data collected? If the user didn't consent to their data being used (or sold), then its perceived value is worthless. I have seen the blood drain from many a face when they realize they don't have as much value in the data as they thought.

TEAM

What is the structure of the current technical team? What is the average tenure and skill set? Often in smaller organizations you find people who have been with the company from the start, with everything they know learned on the job. If that is the case, who did those people learn from?

Of all the engineering team, which individuals are crucial and the most knowledgeable? The best way to determine this is by asking, "Which person is missed the most when they go on vacation?" Most teams will answer this quickly, without giving it a moment's thought. Small companies rely too much on the loyalty and support of a single individual. Sometimes they are the one who designed the systems, and they're likely the very person who is answering all your questions as part of the due diligence.

Are there any contractors or outsourced firms used for support or development? What are their areas of responsibility and contract length? You want to see if there are any contractual considerations that may cause problems in the future (such as ownership or termination).

SUPPORT

What issues typically are reported by the users or clients of the systems being maintained? How much time is spent on support versus new feature development?

Depending on the organization, how much effort or time is typically spent with onboarding new clients? Is this something that is ever done by the technical group? What major outages or issues have occurred in the last 12 months? What was the impact on clients, and what has been done since to avoid reoccurrence? What is the one thing that keeps the current leadership up at night, or, if they had a magic wand, what would they like to be addressed instantly?

SECURITY

What is the general attitude toward security? When was the last time core passwords were rotated? How much visibility does a developer have? Is there a separate production environment, away from the development one?

If credentials for users are stored, how are passwords stored in the database (plain text versus salted)? You will be surprised at how many still store passwords in clear text!

What tests have been run, either SQL injection or penetrative tests on the production environments? Security is something a company either builds in from the start or layers on at a later date—the latter is not what you want to see, ideally.

SOURCE CODE

If the target produces source code, it is vital you take a deep dive to get a general feel for overall quality and design philosophy. It is neither practical nor fair to pore over every single line of code. For one thing, you don't have time, and secondly, you are not going to be able to appreciate the years of production, review, tweets, and fixes from a multitude of developers in just a few hours. It is better to focus on a selected few areas to gauge an overall metric.

We all have code in our past we would not wish to be judged against, so pick some code that has recently been committed. Find this from the version commit history or the ticket system, and follow its journey from reporting right through to fixing to release.

Other areas to look at are around security. See how configuration, usernames, and passwords are handled in code. If the infrastructure is heavily powered by APIs, look at how they are constructed—is there consistency? How are errors and exceptions handled? Is there too much assumption that things don't fail, or is there plenty of checking being made throughout?

Another area that will tell you a lot about code maturity is the overall structure. Is it clumped together, functional, or is the code laid out in objects, with strong code reuse? On code reuse, what (if any) open source libraries have been used to help with a lot of common tasks? Of those open source libraries, are the licenses compatible with the business and being legally honored?

Finally, look at the logging that has been employed throughout the code. Logging, as we have gone over in an earlier chapter, is something that helps us quickly monitor and diagnose a live production system. Is there consistency with logging, making it easy to filter out exceptions or errors from purely informational or sanity-check entries?

If the organization manages the production of code, it is worthwhile to explore the overall management, including code reviews, version control, test, build, and release management. It is common for small teams to be very informal—rudimentary, if you will. The important thing is not to judge—these are merely data points in the journey. No matter what they are doing, good or bad in your view, they are doing something right overall, or you wouldn't even be thinking of acquiring them.

PRODUCTION SYSTEM

The last area that is relevant is how they deliver and monitor their production environment. One question that is good to ask, complete with dramatic pause for effect is, "At this moment, this very moment, how do you know all is well?" The answers to this simple question, including the most honest shrug noting they had no real idea, can yield a lot of data on how they manage production.

You want to get a feel for what it takes to keep their lights on. Remember, if this transaction is successful, this will become your responsibility. So, get an understanding of what daily checks are made, what logs are looked at, what the early signs are that something might be afoot.

Dive into their fault-tolerance plans. How do things fall over in the event of something going wrong? Discuss areas of weakness and single points of failure, and how they are being addressed. Backups and recovery are related to this area, including identifying any documentation or read-me files someone could follow to restore the environment.

As part of this area, confirm who is responsible for paying and renewing services. It is not uncommon (particularly in smaller companies) to have common services such as AWS, GitHub, or GoDaddy accounts being "owned" by the original developer simply by virtue of their credit card being debited each month, which is then reimbursed with an expense form.

From the field

Google forgot to pay their domain bill

Production systems go dark for the silliest of reasons, and today, in our modern, connected world, if you don't pay your domain or SSL certificate, then the service will stop. One of the big boys, Google, with their Blogger service, got caught out when someone didn't pay for the blogger.in domain and lost control of it for a period of time. See https://www.androidpolice.com/2020/07/16/someone-at-google-forgot-to-renew-a-blogspot-domain-still-offline-a-week-later.

Most of these are problems to resolve, as we have gone over in this book, but the legality of such core accounts when it comes to ownership needs to be identified and resolved before any transaction is completed.

14.5.2 Conducting due diligence

The previously discussed areas are merely the big areas you should consider to give you the necessary thinking points to start contextualizing how the company will be relevant for your target. The question then becomes one of "how." This is not an interrogation or a list of predefined questions. Asking each one in turn will neither set the right tone nor yield the level of detail you require. Instead come at it with the conservational mindset—two technologists sharing and getting to know one another. Make the other party feel excited, comfortable to share information without feeling they need a lawyer present!

Go at each interview with a celebratory attitude, lifting the other party, praising them for getting to where they got. Again, the very fact they are even being considered for purchase means more things are going right than wrong.

You are not there to pass judgment or to determine what is right or wrong. Chances are, you'll find plenty of things that can be done better, but now is not the time. You learn about what pressures or circumstances led them to where they are. Maybe it was a lack of funding from management or simply not knowing an alternative existed.

You are there to create a bond, a connection. If things go to plan, then this person you are talking with will be part of your engineering team. You want them to feel like they could be a valuable member of your team.

Through conversion, with plenty of whiteboarding and diving into code, much information will be imparted naturally, without feeling forced. A common technique I use, which gets everyone in the right mindset, is for them to go through two role-play scenarios. The first one is to pretend to be a new customer and have them take you through the onboarding process, including any demos and training. This is a wonderful exercise that puts everyone at ease because they get to show off and be proud of their product. It serves multiple purposes for you, including the following:

- Discovery of the language or terms they use to talk with clients. This allows you to formulate questions using their language, thus reducing any intimidating questions you may ask by choosing the wrong phrase or word.
- Understand the real features that matter most to clients. Typically, things like "We can do this, but no one uses it," will kill off a whole realm of questioning that isn't necessary while learning a data point that may contradict a management proposition.
- Enable a way to probe for more detail as and when an area is touched on, which gets you closer to some of your goals. For example, say a chat portal is being demoed and they can upload a file. You can ask, "Where does that file actually go?" and then ask whether and where it's backed up.

Once the client portion is done, it is a good natural break for lunch or coffee. Take that opportunity to praise and thank them. Be genuine—be real. Let people break and take a small rest before the second role-play session.

Depending on the type of engineering department you're dealing with, this process changes slightly. The goal is to get as much information as possible without it feeling like a lot is being shared.

The second role play is to pretend you are a new developer, engineer, or team member to their department, and you are then onboarded to be in a position to start contributing. Armed from your client onboarding, you now have the company vocabulary at hand, so you can relate and ask more relevant and pointed questions, in pursuit of being a well-formed, newly minted team member.

This gives them the license and opportunity to go deeper, but in a way that is probably familiar to them, especially if they have recently hired someone. By going through this exercise, you will be introduced to their processes, the way they communicate, how tasks are managed, how code is developed and released, as well as the major components that power the system.

Once this task is completed, you will have hopefully built up a good rapport and open atmosphere. You will have shared some of your experiences, maybe helped solve some low-hanging fruit along the way, and sympathized with their hard problems. From here, you can then easily fill in any discovery gaps.

Keep a high-level "bingo" card of topics you need to cover. Every time you get what you need, mark that box. There is no specific order, no set of canned questions. But it gives you a cue card to know whether, throughout all the conversations, you have indeed covered everything. Successful due diligence should be educational, enlightening, and fun for all parties.

14.5.3 Presenting your findings

Now that you have done all your interviews and sessions and got all your notes, you need to distill this down to a format that can be digested and acted on, mostly by nontechnical people. Executives, bankers, lawyers, investors, operating partners, and accountants are all likely consumers of your findings. You have to refer not to the technical reasons but to the consequences of each finding, and then the level of effort required to resolve it.

Let's go back to our house analogy. Assume it was discovered that the electrical breaker for the hot water tank was not working. There's too much detail up front to explain this; instead, you would note there is no functioning hot water and it will take three weeks and an approximate cost of $2,000 to resolve. Now the buyer can do so much more with that detail. They know they need to find an extra $2,000 (either additional investment or a discount from the purchase price), and they won't be able to shower for at least three weeks.

Technology is the same. As technologists, we list something technical (e.g., the main database has no active standby and is configured in a standalone mode with a public IP address), and we believe everything is clear as day. What we often overlook is the "so what?" or consequences of what we just stated.

For our database example, we could say, "In the event of a failure (including power loss), the company will no longer function and may take days to restore. This will require an investment of $X to determine and implement an acceptable solution to maintain business continuity." You provide the technical reasons and sources that led you to that statement as part of the appendixes or supporting documentation. A typical due diligence report should be as follows:

1 Overview of target
2 Methodology: when was it conducted, who was present, what materials were provided, what was not available
3 Summary findings
4 Supporting materials

The summary findings should be a list, ordered by severity of the consequences of what was found. In a separate list, you can detail all the good things that were found that are cause for celebration.

Write this document in a manner that anyone of whatever technical level can understand. You want to represent a truthful picture, never misrepresenting anything. If the target chose X over Y, but Y is your preferred choice, it makes no difference and should not be highlighted as an area of concern.

If you have time, take the extra step of having the very people you have spoken to review the document prior to presenting it. This serves two very important goals. First is accuracy. Maybe you misheard something, or got it mixed up. This gives an opportunity for such mistakes to be cleared up. This is not something that would offend—this is not opinion, but facts. The second purpose is to create a bond and trust with the very people who could be working on your team. They can see the issues that matter to you and a path to resolution. They will also see how open and honest you are, that you are someone with integrity. End every session noting that they will get to review the report for accuracy and there will be nothing in it that will be a surprise and that you haven't already talked about. No one needs that level of stress or mistrust.

From the field

Traffic lights for issues

I have many times conducted due diligence over the years, both for the acquiring company and for private equity firms. I developed a scoring scale that makes it easy for the reader to focus on the "red" areas, keep an eye on "amber," and be glad to see the "green" areas as they relate to the goal of the purchase.

14.5.4 Answering due diligence

So far we have discussed the execution of due diligence, but what happens if you are the target, the one being interviewed? Now that you know how to conduct this process, you have a greater appreciation for what is being asked. The one thing to bear in mind is you are not being judged—if you feel you are, that is the fault of the other person.

You may come across many "experts" who have completely blundered the process by sounding condescending or arrogant. Sadly, there is little you can do in this situation but smile through it. Contrary to popular belief, the highest bidder doesn't always win—most of the time, the decision comes down to who is the best cultural fit. Due diligence is a data point involved in that decision.

Preparation is key to a successful session. Some will come with their prepared set of questions, and after the first 20 minutes, you will be bored senseless. If you spot this, then politely say if it would be quicker if they just emailed you the list of questions to be answered.

You don't need to create pages of documents, but you should be able to produce the following without too much issue:

- High-level diagrams of architecture/network
- List of all technologies (including versions)
- Licenses, renewal dates, and costs
- Organizational chart with everyone listed
- New employee onboarding document
- Recent support issues
- Future development priorities

The more astute reader will recognize this list: they are the very things this book has been highlighting that should be continually maintained as part of being CTO.

You want to impart as much detail as possible, without giving away the core secrets, that will help the buyer make an informed decision. There will be areas that you may not wish to disclose. This could be for a variety of reasons, but whatever they are, you discuss them with your CEO (and HR, if need be) so there is a consensus on what you are able to divulge.

What you should never do is lie or misrepresent—this will only end in tears. You can politely refer a question to the CEO if it truly has gone to an area you are not comfortable with. This rarely happens, especially at the size of the company you are most likely representing.

That said, when it comes to trade secrets, this is an area you need to discuss clearly with your CEO. At some point, you will need to address it, but early on, you won't hit up against it.

It is okay, and encouraged, to allow access to source code if asked. You can either do this via a simple zip file logged to the data room, or you can create a read-only account to the version control. Access to databases, however, should be restricted to a screen share at best, with no direct control permitted. This is your clients' data, and it should be safeguarded. You can run counts, show sample records, but take care to protect your data.

Infrastructure is the same. If you have a cloud environment, then reviewing this will be on the agenda. Take steps for someone to create a specific read-only account that gives enough visibility to look around without fear of changing anything.

From the field

Saying no

A reputable professional conducting due diligence will never ask for any sort of access that could compromise or change a system. They do not want the responsibility of being the cause of something going wrong. Keep your systems secure, no matter who you think they are. You ultimately have the power to say "no" and ask why they believe they need to see it. Maybe there is another way to achieve the same result. Make a note of it, refer it to your CEO, and move on.

Even if something does not necessarily put you in a favorable light, be open and honest. Who knows—these may be the very people who can help you solve it. Above all else, attempt to enjoy it, learn something from it, and no matter how well prepared you think you are, you will find something you can improve on.

A word of caution: if you are in the process of being sold, you could be doing this a number of times, with different suitors over a short period of time. Do not forget to run your department. Clients still need to be serviced and the team to be led. Either delegate or build in enough time to allow you to step away. The same can be said if you are performing due diligence; it takes more time than you may allocate up front, so be prepared to make plans in your absence.

14.6   Handing over the reins

At some point in your career, you will find yourself handing over responsibilities to someone new. The reasons for this could be many, such as outgrowing the role, or the role no longer aligned with what you want to do. Another reason, relating to this chapter, is being acquired and there isn't room for two CTOs. Like the classic '80s *Highlander* movie, there can only be one.

Either way, how you hand over power will define your time and legacy with the company. You want the incoming, new CTO to be successful. Even if they redo everything you have done, so be it—it's not your concern. You can be held responsible only for the moment, not the future in your absence.

Every decision you have made was made with the best information you had at the time. Seldom, with the benefit of hindsight, would we make the same decision. This isn't meant as an excuse for any poor or questionable decisions but as retrospect for the constraints you were

dealing with. These constraints are what should be communicated and shared with the new CTO. These reasons are valuable business knowledge that even the smartest CTO will not know.

As you know, a department is only as strong as its people. Going through each of the members of the team, highlighting their strengths and weaknesses for the new CTO, is valuable. This, however, should never descend to a personality evaluation. A good place to begin this conservation is to go over the last review process, highlighting improvements (or backward steps) since. This gives you a good lexicon to keep the conversation focused on the areas that will help the new CTO understand their team from day one.

It is important to outline your vision for where you were going. It may seem pointless, given you won't be there to see it through or the new CTO may go off in a different direction. However, your vision is steeped in years of in-depth business knowledge and experience of the client issues that keep occurring. This insight is crucial for the incoming CTO, who, again, will not have any of that context.

Outside of the normal technical knowledge transfer that would happen in most senior roles, it is important to give the CTO taking over a full 360-degree view of the issues that you have dealt with. Some advise to go through 24 hours, as if it's a day in the life. This does not give enough context to the role you played. Instead, open up your calendar, and go through the last 30 days. Talk a little on your recurring meetings, but focus on the meetings with those outside of your department. This will allow the new CTO to see how and who will interact with them. By going over the content (and outcome) of each meeting, you are giving them a head start with ongoing initiatives or issues.

No matter the circumstance that is having you step off, there will be sadness. This is completely natural. Embrace that feeling, and augment it with pride that you did your best and got the group to where it is to date. Evolution tells us that each change should be better, and a change or handover of leadership is the same (though not always—remember, even Apple eventually had to bring back Steve Jobs).

Never leave under a cloud, even if one was put there. Think of the team you are leaving behind, hoping they will be well taken care of and will have the opportunity to learn. You are setting them up to succeed by preparing the new CTO.

14.7 *Taking the reins*

Having discussed handing over the reins to an incoming CTO, let me address the other side: when you are the one stepping in or being promoted. Let's assume you have been taken through some sort of handover as discussed. So now you are on your own, with a group looking at you for leadership and an executive team relying on you for continuity and growth. What now? Easy—do nothing.

You have much to learn about the company, so take your time to familiarize yourself with the company, the product, the clients, and the employees. No one is really expecting anything from you in the first 30 days, and you have 90 days before any sort of vision starts to materialize.

Resist the urge to change for the sake of change. By all accounts, make small improvements if they are warranted. Sit in on as many meetings as possible, and just listen and observe the interactions between all the attendees. As noted in chapter 1, like Maverick sat and watched the poker players for the first hour before playing, you are doing the same technique here—observing your new team.

Have as many one-on-ones as possible within your group. I like to ask this question as an opener for discussion: "If you were king/queen for the day, what would you change/fix?" This will yield a wide range of responses, all from the individual's viewpoint. Most will have some actionable item, however small, but it will give you an insight on the issues being raised on the ground.

Offer no solutions or assurances. There may be good reasons things are the way they are, and you will hopefully discover them. You are there to listen, absorb, and build a picture of the landscape.

Charles Moon, who has served as CTO/Head of R&D in many organizations, puts it best: "Be thoughtful regarding the internal politics since you may be surrounded by those who supported the previous technology roadmap. Most changes should be handled as positive enhancements due to technology/market advancements."

As discussed in some of the earlier chapters, get to know other peer executives. You have this wonderful "honeymoon" period when you are not expected to know all the company, and you can ask the most basic of questions without anyone raising an eyebrow. Use it.

Summary

- Being acquired can be a huge distraction if not managed properly.
- Buying a smaller company can yield huge, nearly instant benefits if you can integrate or use their offering as quickly as possible.
- Building an architecture that makes it easy to integrate opens up your company for more strategic conversations.
- Due diligence is not an interrogation but a conversation designed around a specific goal.
- Contextualizing the results into a language that nontechnical people can process will allow high-level strategic decisions to be made.
- Taking over from an existing CTO is more about listening and learning their struggles and challenges instead of changing everything.
- When handing the reins to another CTO, it's important to set up everyone, including your team, for success.

Checklist

How many of the following items can you lay claim to having covered?

- Able to present a realistic but optimistic view of your enterprise with no notice
- Knowing the chances of you being part of a transactional event

- Are prepared to go through at least minimal due diligence
- Understand the strengths of the architecture but are not ignorant of its areas that need more work
- Can take a new CTO through the processes that led to some of the decisions

15

You, Inc.

This chapter covers

- Identifying and reviewing your progress to date
- Trying to keep up to date and avoiding imposter syndrome
- Making yourself irrelevant while at the same time more valuable
- Planning for the future to ensure you don't waste time in a role you don't enjoy

One of the great honors and rewards of the role you are in is helping others achieve success and growth in their careers. Building, fostering, and mentoring teams to do great things is something that brings a huge smile to my face. There is only so much you can do by yourself—two hands and 24 hours in each day are the constraints we all have to deal with.

Yet, while you are doing all this great team building, who is looking after you? Who is keeping you focused on what you are looking for from your professional life?

We are going to go through some things in this chapter that will hopefully help keep you happy and focused. The last thing anyone wants is to suddenly realize 5 or

10 years have slipped by and you really haven't advanced as far as you dreamed. That sounds like a long time, but it can whip by very quickly, especially if you are head-down, making great changes.

15.1   *Reviewing yourself*

As CTO you will (or should) put your team through annual reviews, tracking progress and ensuring there are no surprises for you or them, as they grow in their career. Yet, depending on your organization, you may be missing out on your own annual review. You can address this in a couple of ways.

First, talk to your CEO and ask them to review you. Detail the sorts of things you are interested in working on, and from their vantage point, they can ascertain whether you are making the mark. Areas can include the following:

- *Communication*—Are you keeping the business adequately informed of projects, directions, and issues?
- *Level of detail*—Is the level of detail being communicated—too little or too much?
- *Business intelligence*—What is your contribution to the overall business intelligence? Are trends or industry shifts being properly tracked and talked about internally?
- *Initiative/vision*—Is confidence high that the technology is tracking to cope with projected future growth and opportunities?

Your immediate boss, most likely the CEO, wants you to succeed because your success is their success. It is common for organizations to have a formal review process, yet skip the executive team. Do not use that as an excuse. Run toward feedback and set up a small structure so you can get formal input on your progress. You should be meeting with your CEO regularly on all matters related to the execution of the business. Take one of these meetings, ask them how you are doing, and ask point blank what else you can do to be (more) successful.

This gives an opportunity for feedback in a way that doesn't make it awkward for either party. If no critique can be had, then invite your CEO to set some goals for you, or define areas in which they would like to see more from you. All good CEOs are interested in developing their executive team and will be forthcoming with their feedback. If yours is not, help them get there with a little nudge and guidance in the right direction.

From the field

The Office

Whether you are a fan of the UK or the US version of the classic sitcom, *The Office*, it highlights perfectly how an out-of-touch boss appears to his team. In their heads, David Brent/Michael Scott are super popular, loved, and count their team as friends. We know, from the side looks and horrific expressions, that that is far from the truth.

It is easy to recognize this on the screen but much harder to see it in real life. The series is extremely popular because it plays on this disparity for comic pleasure, and it hits home more often than not—we've all had a *The Office* situation in our careers at one point.

The other direction in which to look for feedback is from your own team. This can be tricky to navigate initially, because subordinates may feel uncomfortable, or lack confidence or faith, that their feedback won't come back to haunt them at a later date. This speaks a lot to your management style. If people feel they cannot talk openly and honestly to you, then that is feedback in and of itself that you can do something with. You don't want to rule with an iron fist through fear and intimidation. You want to lead with confidence, compassion, firmness, and fairness. If your tone is right, your direct reports should have no problems in preparing a small review for you to act on.

Reviews are not character assassinations. They are there to help the person be better by understanding how their actions and communications are being received. In our heads, we always assume we are clear and articulate. We may be blind to the fact we are just shy of detail that would make a huge difference for the listener. Court their feedback. It is hard to read the label of the bottle from the inside. You need those around you to give you honest feedback.

The other person you can look to for feedback is yourself. A good leader has the self-introspection to be honest with themselves and know when something could have been done better or differently. Do not be too harsh on yourself or beat yourself up too much—just be self-aware and make corrections accordingly.

From the field

Common language separated by the Atlantic

When I first started working in the United States, being from the United Kingdom, I noticed some of my phrases and language, while innocent at home, were not landing the same on the other side of the Atlantic. I got to know HR very well, because they had many a word with me to explain how certain phrases would offend instead of offer support or mirth (the *Urban Dictionary* was my friend to prove there was no malice). Therefore, I had to learn to read faces and body language at a whole different level and check the way I phrased things before I vocalized them.

15.2   *Mentor*

A mentor is someone who has your best interests at heart but does not have a direct influence over your career. For instance, a mentor is typically not your boss. A boss can be a guiding influence and someone you learn from, but they are not a mentor in the purest form.

A mentor is someone in whom you can confide, seek counsel on matters you may be dealing with, and learn an outside perspective and advice without having a vested interest in the outcome. Mentors can come from all walks of life, but they are someone who knows you, both good and bad. Sometimes the mentor doesn't even need to know they are serving you in a "mentor" role—they offer advice and input without formal titles.

From the field

I have had two mentors so far in my career: one right at the beginning, who helped me navigate the business world as I was finding my feet after university, and the second helped, and continues to do so, on bigger issues that have presented themselves to me, both professionally and personally.

We all need a little help from time to time, someone to push us a little harder, or to offer some well-placed words to pick us up when feeling down. How do you get yourself a mentor? That is kind of like asking, "How do you get a life partner?" They emerge from personal connections and interactions. It is not uncommon to use your parents, relatives, or a family friend. If you find yourself in this situation, be conscious of their sphere of expertise. If the person is not familiar with your environment, they may not be able to properly appreciate the area you are seeking assistance or input on. It is perfectly acceptable (and encouraged) to have a number of mentors and advisors, each influencing a different area of your life.

How often you should be hitting them up for input is a good question. A mentor is not your new best friend (they can be, but when not in a mentoring capacity). They are not there to help in each decision but to help with the big life-changing events. For example, you would seek the input of your automotive mentor (if such a thing exists) only when you are looking to purchase a new car, not when you need to fill it up with gas. Even then, your automotive mentor isn't going to tell you what model to purchase. They will listen to your requirements, offer you other things to maybe consider, and help you think through your process. They may offer one or two solutions to think about.

They are not there to give you answers—you make all your own decisions. They help you with perspective and ask you the sorts of questions that will help you see with clarity. In the absence of a mentor, while you seek one, plenty of self-help books and articles can bridge the gap in the meantime. Just be mindful of the advice, because they don't know you or your situation personally.

15.3   *Keeping pace*

One of the most exciting things about our industry is its changing landscape, how it seems to reinvent itself every five years. One of the hardest things about our industry is its changing landscape, how it seems to reinvent itself every five years!

Yes, our greatest blessing is also our greatest curse. We are always in a state of learning, keeping up, wrestling new buzzwords, and frantically staying relevant. It is exhausting. It is stressful, especially as people look to you for future decisions so the company is not left behind.

This is the area where *imposter syndrome* rears its ugly head and eats away at self-esteem and confidence. What is imposter syndrome? It is that feeling you are somewhere you shouldn't be—a place you do not belong. You live in constant fear that at some point you will be discovered and asked to leave. Some mix-up in HR hired the wrong person, and you have been winging it in their place.

The good news is that at some point in their career, most people feel this, including well-known celebrities. We all have bouts of insecurity and feeling like we are in over our heads.

When this feeling comes along, the secret to managing it is to recognize it. Remind yourself of your achievements, your journey so far. Breath. Dig deep, and whatever problem or challenge you are facing, draw strength from your experience, because something within will guide you and reaffirm why you are the right person, in the right place, to move forward.

Remember, help is always at hand. Never feel you are an island. We live in one of the most connected times of human civilization—somewhere, someone will be able to help.

A small tip is to keep your résumé updated every six months. It serves as a very slow journal, letting you catalog major milestones. Two benefits from this follow:

- A reminder of your accomplishments.
- Your résumé is ready for any opportunity that may come along at a moment's notice.

In the heat of a self-doubt moment, you can forget all the good things. Keep your résumé updated, and keep it accessible. All the greats (and those heading for greatness) have moments of self-doubt and reflection. It is natural.

15.4 Monitoring change

Let's be honest: keeping up to date is hard and takes considerable effort. Nothing stays the same—versions keep going up, new frameworks pop up, and, if that is not enough, every so often, we go through major seismic shifts that make us feel we are falling ever further behind. Software, hardware, networks, operating systems—it's a wonder anyone keeps up!

How many of the big shifts did you actively track from their inception (see table 15.1), versus the ones you were forced to look at, and, finally, which ones did you miss so completely you still don't know what they really mean?

Table 15.1 Shifts in technology

Web	Web 2.0	Metaverse
Virtualization	Cloud	Serverless
Big data	Data lakes	Business intelligence
Machine learning	Artificial intelligence	Block chain
Digital currency	Encryption	Multifactor authentication

Table 15.1 Shifts in technology *(continued)*

Digital signatures	3G/4G/5G	Internet of Things
Virtual reality	Gaming	Mobile apps
Desktop	SQL/NoSQL	Warehouse
Messaging	Open source	Low/no code
Fog computing	API	Monolithic
Macroservices	Microservices	...

We could go on, and this before we look at the languages and both emerging and new features. For example, Java today looks nothing like the Java from 25 years ago. Then there are all the design patterns emerging, as we figure new and better ways of using technologies. If you think back 10 years, much of the list in table 15.1 was still an academic/R&D project yet to break into the mainstream. Certain items now have become so ingrained in our modern enterprise, it's hard to remember how we coped earlier. So how can you keep abreast of everything?

Let me ease your stress here and now and offer you an answer—you can't. Period. You have to focus on the areas that are relevant to your own personal interests and also to your enterprise. Choose at least three sources of industry news that fall within your area. Sign up to their email newsletter or feed—a way for information to come to you. Then just wait, and let it come in organically. Read, digest, and continue on. Over time, common themes will start to emerge. When you start seeing something popping up repeatedly, from different sources, you want to give that a little more attention. Maybe task someone in your team to explore it a little further, to see if it's something you should be focused on.

You don't need to be on the bleeding edge of technology, just the leading edge. The bleeding edge is too early—it is called *bleeding* because it is sharp and can hurt if it goes wrong. There is no need for you to take unnecessary risks and bets on technology that may not make it in the long run.

You can also keep an eye on your competitors and how they are positioning their products. They may be guilty of riding the hype wave (note how many block chain solutions are being touted?), but it will give you a reason to explore an area a little deeper, so you have an answer if asked.

Another great source of upcoming trends, if your organization can afford it, is to subscribe to the output of an analyst or research firm. Gartner and Forrester are two highly respected sources, and you probably have seen the infamous Gartner quadrant graph from many proud vendors who managed to show up on it. Their rates can be a few thousand a year, but it gives you insight into research and product comparison reports, as well as discounted conferences. They keep a finger on the pulse so you don't have to.

Finally, empower and encourage your team to keep an eye on various verticals, be it a framework or language. Have them present a proposal for research time to explore the opportunity for your organization.

Learning is fun, but it can feel like you don't have time to keep updated. You can't afford not to; however, you can share the burden and let it bubble up naturally.

15.5 Succession planning

At some point, you are going to look to move on; maybe your wants or needs change or the role has evolved into something where you no longer get the same satisfaction out of it. Whatever the reason, someone will need to take over from you.

As your organization grows, your hands-on work will decrease. As you focus more on management, you will have others pick up the areas you used to manage directly. This natural evolution, of you rotating out of day-to-day chores, is a form of succession.

The next level is to find who could step into your position in your place. This takes a lot of confidence on your part, because we always want to feel special and needed. To actively prepare, mentor, and train someone to take over is not a small undertaking or one to be done lightly.

For a start, you probably won't have much control over who is actually hired in your place. If you leave the right way, then your input, guidance, and wisdom will be welcomed and sought.

What you can do is give the person you believe can succeed the best chance to step up and be considered. You can be preparing someone, over a period of years, slowly, working at a pace that is comfortable for them. They don't even need to be aware of your overall plan; they will just see it as—which it is—your continued trust and confidence in them as you expand their field of responsibility.

15.6 Career success

What is your dream role? What gets you up in the morning, excited to get at it?

Career planning is not determining the salary you want to achieve at a given age. Planning your future is a concentrated effort of identifying your wants and desires and making the appropriate plan to achieve them. One thing is for sure: sitting doing nothing, waiting for the phone to ring, doesn't work.

As the old joke goes, "Oh God, why do I never win the lottery?" to

which God answers, "Meet me halfway and at least buy a lottery ticket!" Have a conversation with any focused successful person, and they will tell you it's all part of their plan. Hard work, with preparation and planning, will help you not only recognize opportunities but act on them.

You are reading this book because you are either looking to step up to becoming a CTO or have recently taken on the role and want some insight. Why now? What steps have led you to this stage? For the role you are in now, what does success look like? Knowing what success is will make it easier to rate your happiness and satisfaction and track your progress. As life moves forward, new experiences will be banked, and your outlook and ultimate plan will change or adapt accordingly.

> **From the field**
>
> When I stepped out from university as a fresh-faced graduate, I had no idea the role of CTO even existed. My only goal was to learn as much as possible and be the best at what I do. What that thing was, was not defined, but within my first few years in industry, I had a much greater view of the landscape and could focus my vision and plan for my career. Since then, as I have achieved each goal, I have been opened up to a new world, where I have adopted and refocused my next set of goals. For my own part, being a CTO has been the most rewarding (professionally speaking) thing I have ever done. To build, grow, and change lives is truly an honor and one I do not take lightly.

There is only one person responsible for your success, and that is you. Achieving the exciting position of CTO is the result of one goal—but now what? What are you going to do to make this a success and open up new horizons for you to run toward?

Take stock of your own career. Celebrate your journey so far, and think hard about all the major decisions you have had to make to get there. Success is making the right decision at the right time for the right reason. Make the most out of this wonderful opportunity, but keep an eye on "You, Inc.," and keep that business plan updated and measured.

15.7   *Stepping up*

One of the many questions you may have as you look forward is, "How do I become a CTO?" It is a fair question, and for organizations where there is a firmly entrenched CTO above you, how do you even try to take their place? Outside of waiting for them to move on or retire, you can't. So, you have to look elsewhere when you are feeling you are ready to take that next step.

The first thing you should do is to start looking at job openings. You will most likely be put off with some of the requirements, particularly experience. This is the classic chicken-and-egg situation: how do you get experience if you don't get a chance to earn it?

Look at the role as a whole, and determine whether the experience requirement is a soft or hard limit. Sometimes an organization is looking to firm up their technology leadership, and therefore, they are recruiting their first CTO. If you have experience in leading teams that is relevant to the job, throw your hat in the ring. Don't bluff your way into the role—be up front and note that although you have never had the CTO title formally bestowed on you, you have the relevant experience to take the step up.

When hiring for a CTO position, a company is looking for a reliable, steady hand to take on the responsibility of the office (with all the things outlined in this book).

They need to know you are capable and ready for the challenge. Hiring a CTO is not like hiring a senior developer—you will be judged on your soft skills and how you are going to manage a team to provide successful outcomes. This is where you need to focus your strengths when it comes to the interview stage.

The number of CTO roles is small in comparison to managerial or senior roles. Therefore, there will be a lot of competition from folks like you—those looking to take the next natural step. When applying for a CTO role, although your résumé is important, your cover letter is extremely valuable. This is your opportunity to lay out how you could operate at this level and why you are a good fit for this company. Your résumé should be focused more on your management skills than your technical skills.

Before you start applying, look around, and get a feel for the language of each job description. Get a feel for how they are positioning the need for a CTO, especially companies for whom this is their first CTO hire. As noted earlier, know your own worth, know your own wants, and do not compromise.

Summary

- Seeking input from your boss helps identify areas you can work to improve on.
- Take regular pulse checks from your team to make sure you are delivering what they need.
- Finding a mentor will help you think through some of the larger life decisions that come your way.
- Recognizing your achievements by keeping a journal or résumé will help you fight imposter syndrome.
- Don't stress about keeping up to date with everything—you can't. But you can take steps so you don't miss big moves.
- While you are lifting and building up others, keep an eye on who could potentially step in for you as you look to explore opportunities.
- Define what it is you want from your career. That way, you can recognize the success and achievements when they come.

Checklist

How many of the following items can you lay claim to having covered?

- Instituted a regular review process with your boss
- Put a mechanism in place for your team to funnel feedback about your leadership
- Found a mentor who you can turn to for handling a specific life event
- Gained knowledge of the latest emerging technology that is now commonplace in your industry
- Signed up to a number of sources that keep you informed of new trends
- Identified a successor who, if need be, can be a candidate for your role
- Developed a career plan with goals

index